Model Driven Architecture™
Applying MDA™ to Enterprise Computing

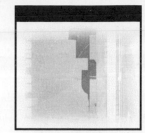

Model Driven Architecture™

Applying MDA™ to Enterprise Computing

David S. Frankel

Wiley Publishing, Inc.

Publisher: Joe Wikert
Editor: Theresa Hudson
Assistant Development Editor: James H. Russell
Editorial Manager: Kathryn A. Malm
Associate Managing Editor: Angela Smith
Text Design & Composition: Wiley Composition Services

This book is printed on acid-free paper. ∞

Published by Wiley Publishing, Inc., Indianapolis, Indiana
Published simultaneously in Canada

For general information on our other products and services please contact our Customer Care Department within the United States at (800) 762-2974, outside the United States at (317) 572-3993 or fax (317) 572-4002.

Wiley also publishes its books in a variety of electronic formats. Some content that appears in print may not be available in electronic books.

Library of Congress Cataloging-in-Publication Data:

ISBN: 0-471-31920-1

Printed in the United States of America

10 9 8 7 6 5 4 3 2 1

To my mother and my late father,
who taught me to value learning and truth.

To my wife Janice, my loving partner during
all the ups and downs of life.

To my children, Rafi and Ari, my connection to the future.

Contents

Preface

The computer industry is always looking for ways to improve software development productivity as well as the quality and longevity of the software that it creates. Object-orientation, component-based development, patterns, and distributed computing infrastructures are examples of new approaches that have aided in this quest.

Model Driven Architecture (MDA) can make an important contribution as well. It does not eclipse the other approaches. Rather, it works with them synergistically to further improve the way we develop software.

What Is Model Driven Architecture?

MDA is about using modeling languages as programming languages rather than merely as design languages. Programming with modeling languages can improve the productivity, quality, and longevity outlook. This book explains why this is so, and introduces the technologies that underlie MDA.

Who Is Using MDA?

MDA has been used for years to generate real-time and embedded systems, even though the term MDA was coined later. Now IBM, Oracle, Unisys, IONA, and other vendors are weaving MDA-based technology into their enterprise software offerings.

A Long-Term Transition

In the early days of distributed object computing, one of the fathers of CORBA, Mike Guttman, was asked to give a talk to an industry gathering to share his vision of where the technology was headed. He showed a slide projecting that there would be a point in the future when distributed object infrastructures and libraries of components that ran on those infrastructures would be mainstream.

An audience member asked him when he thought that would happen. He said that he thought it could easily take 10 to 15 years. He hastened to add that substantial business value would be gained at each stage of the transition, but that did not seem to stick in the minds of the sponsors, who were somewhat chagrined. They took the remark to mean that he was suggesting that nobody should invest in such technology for another decade.

I take a similar risk in presenting this book on MDA. To be sure, MDA principles can be put to good use now. There are specific technologies already in place based on MDA and a number of others are emerging as I write these words. Tools that automate some aspect of software development using models constitute at least a $500 million industry. Nevertheless, I stress that MDA is a budding technology that has years of work ahead before it can realize its full potential.

MDA and the Object Management Group (OMG)

Early in 2002 the OMG announced Model Driven Architecture as its strategic direction. The OMG is in the early stages of defining this course, and I have been deeply involved in the effort. I hope that this book will help guide this initiative, but I don't guarantee that my ideas entirely coincide with the OMG's.

As the steward of several modeling language standards, the OMG is positioned to play a pivotal role supporting the growth of this new industry. But other standards bodies such as the Java Community Process, ebXML, and RosettaNet are producing specifications that apply MDA principles to various technologies and application domains. As the industry gains experience, standards bodies will issue additional MDA-based standards. This book suggests some directions that these standards should take as they evolve. It also points out some deficiencies of the standardized modeling languages that must be rectified in order to fully realize the vision of MDA.

Goals of This Book

Despite MDA's successes in the real time and embedded systems world, until recently few had applied it comprehensively to the development and integration of enterprise systems that manage things like customers, accounts receivable, and supply chains and business-to-business integration.

This book focuses on MDA in the context of enterprise systems. I want the builders of enterprise systems to understand MDA accomplishments to date and the potential that MDA offers for improving software development. I also want tool builders to understand what they can do to tap the potential. I want both audiences to be aware of the kinds of issues they will face in trying to scale MDA up to where it can consistently support the development and integration of enterprise systems.

Non-Goals of This Book

In order for MDA to become a mature technology, one of the tasks that must be completed is the definition of a comprehensive conceptual framework for MDA. In this book I do not undertake to define such a framework, which would tie in conceptual advances in such areas as Aspect-Oriented Programming and Intentional Programming.

Furthermore, although the book explains what the general shape of a comprehensive MDA-based enterprise architecture would be, it does not actually define such an architecture.

In concentrating on the base MDA technologies, I don't intend to imply that the kind of comprehensive treatment this book does not supply is not important. I hope that others will find this basic work helps them to tackle these more ambitious tasks.

Organization of the Book

This book is organized into parts, each of which consists of a number of chapters.

Part One: Introducing MDA establishes the motivation for MDA and provides an overview of the subject.

Part Two: The Base MDA Technologies is a hands-on tour through the technologies that constitute MDA's foundation. This is the heart of the book, containing a large majority of the material.

Part Three: Advanced Topics outlines some of MDA's more ambitious medium- to long-range possibilities.

Epilogue is a reality check about the future of MDA.

A reader looking for an executive overview of MDA should read this Preface, Part One, and the Epilogue. More technically oriented readers should also read Parts Two and Three.

Acknowledgments

Most of the content of this book synthesizes work done by others. In particular I wish to thank Mike Guttman, my mentor and friend for over 30 years, who helped me edit the final manuscript, provided important suggestions and feedback, and of course wrote the Foreword.

I also recognize the contributions of Jack Greenfield, a pioneer in this field from whom I have learned a great deal.

Special thanks go to Scott Ambler, Grady Booch, Steve Brodsky, Steve Cook, Philippe Kruchten, Scott Markel, David Mellor, Steve Mellor, Mike Rosen, Bran Selic, Oliver Sims, and Jos Warmer for their reviews of the manuscript.

I would also like to acknowledge some other people who helped me develop my ideas on MDA. These include Don Baisely, Conrad Bock, Cory Casanave, Desmond D'Souza, Simon Johnston, Sridhar Iyengar, Haim Kilov, Cris Kobryn, Wojtek Kozaczynski, Jason Matthews, Guus Ramackers, Jim Rumbaugh, Ed Seidewitz, and Richard Soley.

About the Author

DAVID S. FRANKEL has held senior positions at QuarterSoft, Inc., IONA Technologies, and Genesis Development Corporation. He is a renowned expert in the architecture and development of complex, large-scale distributed computing systems. He has served several terms on the OMG Architecture Board.

David Frankel's contact information:
Email: df@davidfrankelconsulting.com (or dfrankel@quartersoft.com)
Tel: +1 530 893-1100

Foreword

On June 14, 1951—shortly after I was born—the U.S. Census Bureau bought the very first UNIVAC computer. This was arguably Sale #1 for the now-behemoth commercial computing industry. That UNIVAC, the first mainframe, was about the size of a one-car garage, and required a 125-kilowatt power supply to both heat and cool its 5200 vacuum tubes.

For the UNIVAC's million-dollar price tag (worth about seven times that at this writing), the Bureau's programmers got a whopping 1000 words of program memory to play with. Nonetheless, compared to any then-available alternative, this was powerful enough to drive the sales of no less than forty-five more UNIVACs over the next five years. It also spawned a slew of competitors. One of these, IBM, became the largest corporation on earth, largely on the back of its computer mainframe business.

In any event, the first programmers had their work cut out for them. Obviously, starting with just 1000 words of memory, they focused largely on optimizing the use of memory and the speed of calculations for a specific machine. For many years, software engineering was driven almost entirely by the requirements—and limitations—of the available hardware. This strongly influenced both the types of computing problems that were selected, and the specific way in which software was developed.

Amazingly—and despite Moore's much-vaunted law governing the exponential growth of hardware power—many aspects of this kind of platform-centric thinking about software have persisted up to the present. In 1970, I was cramming bytes into an IBM 360 MVS partition. In 1980, I was juggling to keep my programs within 64K on an HP 2100MX minicomputer. In 1990, I was still worrying about whether my code would compile into a DLL small enough to load efficiently on a PC, and whether I was using up too many Windows "handles." In 1995, when I worked on the CORBA Internet Interoperability (IIOP) standard, I found myself yet again twiddling bits to minimize the size of messages going out over the wire.

Nevertheless, there is a really big qualitative difference between 1951 and today. Today a steadily increasing percentage of the typical IT department's software development process revolves around issues related to modeling the business problems to be solved, rather than the details of writing code. This is true not because individual developers necessarily really want to move in this direction, but simply because the increasing complexity of the business problems that need to be solved demands such a requirements-driven approach. Perhaps reluctantly, some developers are now spending almost as much time fumbling with modeling languages like UML as they are fiddling with traditional programming languages like Java and XML.

This approach was presaged as early as 1960, when COBOL, the first platform-neutral business-oriented programming language, was introduced. The COBOL programming paradigm explicitly separated the software from the hardware, allowing programmers to think a lot more about business logic and a lot less about machine-level bit-twiddling. COBOL also introduced a significant amount of structure into software development, forcing its users to at least separate program flow logic from data descriptions and environment specifications.

Over the next twenty years, COBOL's increasing hegemony in the mainframe software market helped to foster an immense amount of de facto standardization of architecture and design across the entire computing industry. This was the first "Golden Age" of software development, and many of the systems created during that period remain the data processing workhorses of major corporations today. Remarkably, they still tower like Gothic cathedrals over the tenements of software bubble-gum and baling wire that characterize so many subsequent systems.

Ironically, it was the introduction of the PC—a great boon to computing in most respects—that brought the end of this Golden Age. The PC unintentionally ushered in a new period of chaos for software development. By historical accident, the structured, platform-neutral languages like COBOL were slow to move over to the PC, and a Babel of other programming languages and development tools emerged to fill the vacuum. To accommodate the new blend of hobbyist-programmer that gravitated to the early PCs, these languages tolerated—and even encouraged—low-level, platform-specific bit-twiddling.

So, in one sense, the PC era, which started in the 1980s and exploded in the 1990s, was a second great renaissance for computing, pushing software into areas—and in front of users—where it had never been before. At the same time, however, the resulting tidal wave of polyglot software pretty much overwhelmed the traditional IT software development community and, in many ways, actually pushed back the clock in terms of systematic software architecture and design. A similar discombobulating tsunami struck again with the commercialization of the Internet.

Of course, all during the PC and Internet eras, many industry pundits have continued to advise developers to "design before you code" and more recently— "to architect before you design." In fact, there have been many positive innovations in this direction over the last twenty years. But, for the mass of developers who grew up during code-centric PC era, old habits and attitudes die hard. To these developers, abstracting design (much less architecture) from programming can seem an innately uncomfortable experience that simply "delays coding." Because of this discomfort, they frequently (if unwittingly) sabotage whatever design process is attempted, thereby "proving once again"—at least to themselves—that they would have been much better off to have simply started coding as early as possible.

As a result, it has taken almost twenty years to reach the point where we can start recreating a level of rigor in IT software development that approaches that of the previous Golden Age of software. In the last decade or so, the idea that implementation-independent design and architecture have real intrinsic value to the development process quietly seems to be making a comeback. Sometimes this voice of reason can barely be heard above the incessant drumbeat of vendor hype and techno-babble that characterizes much of the software industry. Nonetheless, a new approach seems to be gaining critical mass in the developer and vendor community, reconstructing the best practices of the first Golden Age, while still incorporating the innovations in software engineering that came about during the PC and Internet revolutions.

Model Driven Architecture (MDA), which this book describes, is a major step in this direction. What makes MDA different from any of the myriad other TLAs (three letter acronyms) that constantly flood the software community? Well, first of all, the development of MDA is being driven by the OMG, the largest software industry consortium. OMG has an enviable track record for promulgating and maintaining some of the industry's most successful standards, such as CORBA and UML.

In addition, within OMG, MDA has enjoyed unusually strong backing from the systems and software vendor community. Usually initiatives of this kind take years to develop this level of consensus and support. However, even diehard rivals such as IBM, Sun, and Microsoft are already strongly behind MDA and actively support the major standards —UML, XMI, MOF, CWM, JMI, and so on—that MDA encompasses. They will no doubt argue incessantly about the details, but they are solidly behind the approach. This means that the supporting mainstream tools and platforms MDA needs to grow and prosper are certainly well on the way.

Finally, MDA does not purport to wholesale replace previous computing paradigms, languages, or tools. Instead, it attempts to harmonize them, allowing everyone to migrate gracefully to the MDA vision at their own pace, and in response to their real need to do so. MDA is also specifically designed to be flexible enough to adapt to the inevitable—new software technologies that, like the PC and the Internet, will soon emerge to upend all our previous assumptions about computing.

As a result, I believe that MDA actually stands a pretty good chance of revitalizing the practice of software architecture and helping to usher in another Golden Age of software development. This is none too soon, because, as the book suggests, the rising complexity of business problems to be computerized is currently testing the limits of the last generation of development paradigms.

As this book cogently argues, to deal with this complexity, design and architecture standards like MDA are needed now to supplant earlier approaches as the focal point in the overall enterprise software development process. This clearly hearkens back to thirty years ago when COBOL and 3GL languages were sorely needed to replace machine code and assembly language as the principal programming tools for business applications.

Nonetheless, some developers will undoubtedly try to ignore developments like MDA, and shoulder on as before, milking their existing code-centric development skills for as long as they can. In the near future, however, the most successful and productive developers will certainly be those who are willing to move aggressively to embrace the kind of design- and architecture-centric paradigms that MDA represents.

That's why this book is so important. As the first comprehensive book on MDA, it has the opportunity to set the standard for how MDA is received by the overall software development community. Fortunately, the author, David Frankel, is not just a good technical writer, but also a recognized authority on MDA and one of the driving forces behind the strategic and technical development of MDA at OMG.

Just as importantly, I can tell you from personal experience that David is an accomplished developer and development manager who understands what it means to get real systems out the door. As a result, while this is not a cookbook, it is peppered with examples that show how MDA can be applied to real problems faced by real developers today.

In short, I can think of no better person to clearly explain both the concepts and details behind MDA to software technicians and industry technologists alike. So, if you are new to MDA, or having any trouble understanding it, my advice is simple—start by reading this book. It will give you exactly the foundation you need to start mastering MDA and immediately applying its concepts directly and effectively to your own environment and problems.

—*Michael Guttman*

PART One

Introducing MDA

MDA is not a radical departure in the way we have gone about improving software development over the years. Rather, it is an evolutionary step that consolidates a number of trends that have gradually improved the way we produce software. This part of the book positions MDA on that evolutionary path.

Pressure and Progress: How We Arrived at This Point

This chapter begins by analyzing some of the problems facing the software industry. It then briefly chronicles certain aspects of the industry's history. Much of this history will already be familiar to many readers, but I present it here in order to identify advances that MDA builds upon.

Challenges Facing the Software Industry

It's common knowledge that difficult challenges confront the IT managers and entrepreneurs who develop the software that is increasingly critical to the functioning of the modern enterprise. Producing these systems involves painstaking, detailed work by highly skilled programmers. The recent contraction of the high-tech economy hasn't changed the fact that skilled software developers are expensive resources, making it a very costly proposition to staff enterprise software development projects.

Furthermore, many software development investments yield disappointing results. Some ambitious projects result in failure.[1] Others go so far over budget that management eventually kills them, which is another form of failure. Some systems that initially succeed prove to be unstable or inflexible over time.

---

[1] "85% of IT departments in the U.S. fail to meet their organizations' strategic business needs." [CW 1999]

The booming economy of the 1990s covered up many of the ramifications of frequent failure. Corporate earnings were so high that investors often ignored the schedule delays, cost overruns, and disappointing quality of business software systems built by high-tech startups and Global 1000 companies.

A frequent comment from investment analysts who were surprised by the steepness of the NASDAQ's decline is that they never expected such a drastic shutdown of technology spending. In a tighter economic environment, enterprise software development must prove its business merit. Corporate managers are unlikely to expend precious capital on projects and products that don't demonstrate compelling value.

This kind of pressure is not new. The computer industry has gone through repeated cycles of pressure followed by advances that relieve the pressure and open up new possibilities, whereupon pressure starts building again.

The Viability Variables

Our industry's economic viability is determined by the extent to which we can *produce systems whose quality and longevity are in line with their cost of production.* Building high-quality, long-lasting business software is expensive. As a result, sometimes we are forced to make unacceptable trade-offs among quality, longevity, and the cost of production, which I define as the software development *viability variables* (see Figure 1.1).

It's difficult to increase viability by addressing just one of the variables in the equation without considering the impact on the others. To promote economic viability, we must reduce the cost of production without sacrificing the quality or longevity of the software.

Interestingly, we can view the history of the software industry as a series of improvements that rebalanced the viability equation at junctures where growing demands pushed the limits of current approaches to development. New approaches arose each time to replace or augment current ones, slowly at first, then with increasing momentum, helping to align quality and longevity with the cost of production.

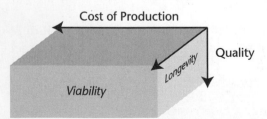

Figure 1.1   The viability variables.

Machine-Centric Computing

Early programmers literally coded instructions to the computer in 1s and 0s, laboriously writing out the bit patterns that corresponded to the native CPU instructions. That seems strangely inefficient today, but for some applications the rapid calculations that the computer could perform made this kind of coding economically sound. It also allowed programmers to optimize available memory and processor speed. However, the high costs inherent in labor-intensive 1s and 0s coding, coupled with high hardware costs, sharply limited the number of tasks amenable to computerization.

An important software innovation—assembly language—extended the serviceable lifetime of machine-centric computing. Assembly language allowed programmers to use simple mnemonics to represent the native instructions that the computer understands. The programmer could write MOV AX, DX to move data from the D register to the A register, instead of writing out the binary code for the move instruction. The programmer could also give a memory location a name and then address the location by that name instead of always having to refer to it by its binary address. The mnemonics and names were abstractions of the binary instructions and memory locations. An assembler translated the mnemonics and names into the 1s and 0s that constitute the binary representations of the native processor instructions and memory locations.

Many programmers in the industry today have only used assembly language in their college courses. But, in their day, assemblers significantly changed the economic viability equation. Writing a program became much less time-consuming, thus lowering production costs.

Furthermore, it turned out that programmers were less prone to error when using mnemonics than when tediously hand-coding 1s and 0s. Therefore, the level of quality rose.

Finally, programs coded with assembly language were less sensitive to incremental changes made to the patterns of 1s and 0s that constituted each of the native instructions. For instance, if a change in the 1s and 0s pattern for MOV instructions occurred from one version of the processor to another, a revised assembler could assemble the programmer's MOV instruction into the different bit pattern. The old assembly language program source code gracefully survived the change to new patterns of 1s and 0s. Therefore, the longevity of programs tended to increase.

Thus, raising the abstraction level above 1s and 0s favorably changed all three variables in the viability equation. Assemblers made it practical for large companies and government institutions to computerize certain aspects of their operations, such as payroll and billing, which consisted of relatively simple, repetitive tasks. See Figure 1.2.

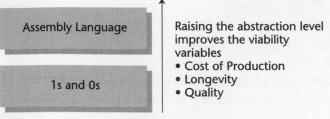

Figure 1.2   Raising the level of abstraction.

Application-Centric Computing

The success of assemblers pointed the way toward an application-centric world, where more complex applications solve a wider range of business problems that entail multiple steps, richer data structures, and human interfaces. Order entry applications are a prime example of such applications. However, the demand for more complex computing strained the economic viability of machine-centric computing.

From Assembly to 3GLs

Assembly language programmers, although freed from the tedium of 1s and 0s, still programmed directly in terms of the native instruction set of the processor. The native instruction set is a very low-level set of concepts. A routine to simply read an employee's monthly salary from a table, read a few tax percentages from another table, and calculate the amount of the check to be issued could require hundreds of instructions, each a separate line in a hand-coded assembly language program.

The advent of third-generation languages (3GLs) enabled a big productivity jump. Even the earliest 3GLs, such as FORTRAN and COBOL, raised the abstraction level far above the concepts of the processor instruction set. The developer now programmed with much higher-level constructs. A simple PRINT instruction in FORTRAN replaced tens or even hundreds of lines of assembly code. Language compilers translated the higher-level instructions into native processor instructions, which were now informally called *machine code*. The ability to program a piece of logic by writing a few instructions instead of dozens dramatically increased programmer productivity, and thus drove down production costs. It also allowed "mere mortals," such as certain classes of business analysts, to migrate into programming.

Initially some programmers legitimately complained that, when the compiler translated 3GL constructs into machine code, the result was less optimal than the machine code they could write by hand. In addition, early compilers occasionally introduced errors when translating 3GL code into machine code. Over time, though, the productivity improvement more than offset these problems. Machine cycles were becoming cheaper. Programmer labor was, if anything, becoming more expensive. The use of 3GLs to produce somewhat less optimal programs essentially offloaded some of the computing burden from expensive programmers to inexpensive machine resources. Improvements in compiler technology also gradually made it possible to generate more reliable and more optimal machine code.

New structured 3GLs, such as C and Pascal, introduced even more powerful programming models. System vendors began to use 3GLs instead of assembly language even to define operating system services. Source-level debuggers were particularly important in promoting the transition to 3GLs because they made it possible for programmers to think entirely in terms of the programming models defined by the 3GLs. Gradually, programmers let go of their reliance on assembly language.

The big reduction in the number of lines of handwritten code required to automate business functions also improved the quality of computer programs. They became more intellectually manageable. The opportunity for subtle error is greater when you have to write dozens of instructions for some purpose, as opposed to just a few.

3GLs also increased program longevity. The instructions used in 3GL programs were far removed from the minutiae of the native processor instruction set. If a change in hardware brought in a new processor with a different instruction set, a new compiler could process an unchanged (or minimally changed), preexisting 3GL program and generate machine code targeted to the new hardware. Changes in processor architecture no longer made programs obsolete. The ability to retarget 3GL programs to different processors became known as *portability*. At first portability, while nice in theory, was shaky in practice. However, over time, 3GL standards and tools matured and portability became a practical—if somewhat imperfect—reality.

Once again, all three of the viability variables changed in the right direction. A large reservoir of pent-up demand for application development was tapped. Whole new classes of applications became economically viable. It was possible to write more ambitious programs that would have been prohibitively massive in assembly language. Companies below the top tier could now computerize some of their operations, a trend that was reinforced by plunging hardware costs. Well before the end of the twentieth century, most, if not all, medium and large businesses had software applications managing at least some of their basic business operations and providing management decision support. Many small businesses were computerized as well. See Figure 1.3.

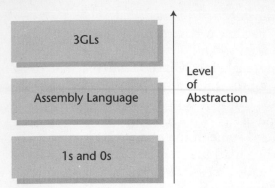

Figure 1.3   3GLs further raised the level of abstraction.

Operating Systems and the Abstraction Gap

Whereas 3GLs raised the level of abstraction of the programming environment, operating systems raised the level of abstraction of the computing platform. If a 3GL compiler has to produce detailed machine code for routine functions such as disk and display manipulation, its job is harder than if it can simply generate machine code that invokes operating system disk and display services.

Thus, by raising the level of abstraction of the computing platform, operating systems reduced the abstraction gap between 3GLs and the platform, as Figure 1.4 depicts.

Object-Oriented Languages and Virtual Machines

Inevitably, as demand for complex features and quick time to market increased, viability problems began to surface with application-centric computing, spurring efforts to improve development methods. The result was several important incremental improvements that extended the lifetime of application-centric computing.

Structured 3GLs evolved into object-oriented 3GLs, including Smalltalk and C++. These new languages make it easier to reuse parts of programs in different contexts.

Some object-oriented languages introduce an interpreter called a *virtual machine* that executes intermediate code generated by the language compiler. Smalltalk, Java, and C# are the prime examples of such languages. The intermediate code is processor- and operating-system-independent. Thus, implementing the virtual machine over different processors and operating systems makes it possible to port even the compiled form of applications to different computing environments. The greater portability improves application longevity.

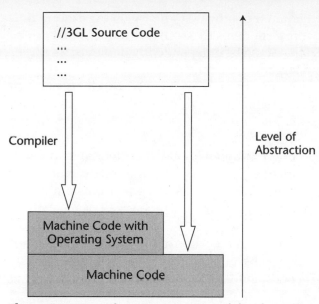

Figure 1.4 Operating systems narrowed the abstraction gap.

Enterprise-Centric Computing

Over time the expectations of the degree of automation that computing could achieve continued to increase. It was no longer enough to have islands of automation within the enterprise. The various islands had overlapping functionality that duplicated information and applied scarce resources to solve similar problems multiple times. It became necessary to integrate the islands across the enterprise.

Component-Based Development

Component-Based Development (CBD) draws on lessons learned from industrial production processes, promoting a world where applications are assembled from interchangeable components.

Componentization moves the production process away from reinventing the same solution in different applications, thus improving productivity and decreasing the cost of production. Componentization also tends to improve quality because it isolates functionality, allowing a team to debug and upgrade the functionality in one place.

There isn't complete agreement in the software industry on the exact definition of *component*, but usually the term refers to a software module that can be packaged in compiled form so that it can be independently deployed as part of applications or assembled into larger components.

In manufacturing industries, manufacturers of finished products produce required components or purchase them from a third party. The ability to use standardized components in different products was one of the prime drivers of the industrial revolution.

CBD, which is still maturing, presages another kind of industrial revolution, one that applies to the production of software. Large companies can afford to build some components themselves while purchasing some from component vendors, while smaller companies are more apt to purchase all or most of the components they use.

A detailed discussion of CBD is beyond the scope of this book. An important book by Peter Herzum and Oliver Sims, entitled *Business Component Factory*,[2] defines many important CBD concepts that I leverage in this book. I refer to their approach as *Herzum-Sims*.

Design Patterns

The concept of design patterns, which is also a key element of industrial production processes, has made an important contribution to improving software development productivity and quality. Programmers can reuse common design patterns that others have thought through and validated.

Generic reusable patterns have been published[3] as well as patterns specific to certain platforms such as Java 2 Platform Enterprise Edition (J2EE).[4]

For example, the J2EE BluePrints Value Object pattern[5] supports efficient information exchange with distributed components. Imagine a distributed component that has multiple attributes including the customer ID, first name, last name, address, Social Security number, and so on. Because remote invocation over a network is expensive, it's inefficient to simply provide remote get and set operations for each property. The Value Object pattern uses a *Value Object* that contains get and set operations for each attribute and a *façade object* that provides a remote operation to get a Value Object, thus making it possible to retrieve the values of all of the properties with one remote call. The façade object also provides a remote operation to set—that is, to pass in—a Value Object, thus making it possible to set the values of all of the properties with one remote call (see Figure 1.5).

---

[2] [HS 2000]
[3] [GHJV 1995]
[4] [ACM 2001]
[5] [JVO]

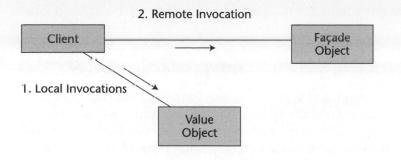

1. Client sets attribute values on value object via local invocations
2. Client passes value object to façade object via remote invocation

Figure 1.5   Using the Value Object design pattern to set attributes.

Distributed Computing

The earliest computers could run only a single job at a time, with any given job single-handedly controlling all of the resources of the computer. Soon multitasking operating systems were invented that allowed multiple jobs to run concurrently, each job running in a separate partition. These partitions evolved to provide each job with the illusion that it controlled a whole logical computer, a precursor to the virtual machine notion described earlier. This allowed many programs to time-share expensive hardware resources cost-effectively, without generating direct conflicts. A related approach, multiuser computing, allowed the computer to simultaneously control many input-output devices, and to manage the interaction of such devices with the time-sharing programs.

Initially, the management of multitasking and multiuser configurations, no matter how complex or physically distributed, was under the total control of a single operating system on a central computer—the *master*—while all other processing nodes acted as *slaves*. However, over time it became clear that much of this processing could be off-loaded to satellite processors closer to the user, allowing for a more efficient use of computing resources and communication bandwidth. This approach, generally called *distributed computing*, became even more attractive with the advent of the personal computer, which brought cheap processing power right to the desktop of the user.

A particular form of distributed computing called *client-server computing* allowed the central computer to act as a server to a PC client. Most early client-server systems perpetuated the master-slave relationship, with the server acting as master, and the PC as a very smart slave terminal. Over time, client-server computing has gradually been evolving towards a more peer-to-peer paradigm, allowing any node to act as either a client or server, depending on the context.

Middleware: Raising the Platform Abstraction Level

Initially, distributed computing of all kinds was mostly handled on a proprietary or custom basis, using private messaging systems to communicate between processors over low-level network protocols. Gradually, many of these proprietary systems were replaced by general-purpose systems generally known as *middleware*, so named because it sat in the middle, transparently connecting a variety of different platforms and operating systems.

Initially, middleware was viewed as just a way to generalize communications at a logical level a bit above low-level network protocols, a system totally subservient to the operating systems and applications running on the platforms it connected. However, it soon became clear that middleware could also take over many of the functions of coordinating the activities among processors that previously had to be handled ad hoc by each application. As distributed computing has become more important, especially with the advent of the Internet, middleware has gradually been assuming the role of a distributed operating system that controls many of the activities of the computers it connects. As such, it now provides a computing abstraction level well above that of traditional operating systems.

CORBA, J2EE, .NET, and message-oriented middleware (MOM) are important examples of middleware platforms that provide services more powerful than those of any particular computer's operating system. Middleware makes it possible for application programmers to concentrate more on business logic and less on the details of how to provide capabilities such as messaging, transaction control, security, and so on.

Two important ways that applications leverage middleware are:

Invoking services directly via middleware APIs. For example, the Java Authentication and Authorization Service provides services that applications can invoke to authenticate a user.

Using code generators that middleware platforms provide. For example, CORBA products generate code from declarations of object interfaces expressed in Interface Definition Language (IDL). The generated code supports distribution but does not constitute complete applications.

Some middleware supports component-based development by providing an infrastructure and development approach for producing components. Enterprise Java Beans (EJB), .NET, and the CORBA Component Model fall into this category and specifically support developing distributed components.

Middleware: Raising the Programming Abstraction Level

Some middleware has an additional function, namely to provide services that are not dependent on any particular operating system or programming language. Indeed this was one of the purposes of CORBA.

For example, the CORBA Concurrency Service provides an API that applications can invoke in order to obtain and release a lock on a resource. The Concurrency Service is not more powerful than similar services that operating systems supply, but it can be implemented over a variety of operating systems. Applications that use the Concurrency Service are more portable—and thus potentially have greater longevity—than ones that use operating-system-specific concurrency services.

CORBA provides a measure of programming language independence by allowing two programs written in different 3GLs, such as Java and C++, to communicate with each other in a well-defined manner. The degree of interoperability thus achieved also tends to improve longevity because it lowers the likelihood that an object developed in one language will have to be rewritten in order to function in an environment dominated by objects developed in other languages.

By raising the level of abstraction above the 3GL and operating system, CORBA made a modest but tangible improvement in the longevity variable. Microsoft's COM middleware also provided a measure of language independence via its own interface definition language, Microsoft IDL, but it was not operating-system-independent.

Declarative Specification

Declarative specification involves programming a system by setting the values of properties. It contrasts with imperative specification, which involves programming a system via sequential, procedural instructions.

Declarative programming improves productivity and quality because it is another form of reuse of preprogrammed, prevalidated logic. It has been in use for some time to reduce the labor intensiveness of producing database systems and graphical user interfaces (GUIs).

Sophisticated database systems are an integral part of enterprise computing. When we need a new database, we no longer code all of the logic of the database imperatively. Instead, we declaratively describe the formats of the various records. The database system uses these declarations to manage the database, allowing us to fine-tune the database via stored procedures and triggers.

Similarly, there was a time when a programmer had to code a graphical user interface (GUI) dialog entirely via laborious procedural instructions. Tools came along that allowed the programmer to simply draw a picture of the dialog, whereupon the tool would generate the bulk of the code for displaying and managing the dialog, with the programmer enhancing the generated code to produce the finished product. The tools for drawing the GUIs were called WYSIWYG (What You See Is What You Get) editors.

With EJB, .NET, and the CORBA Component Model, a descriptor contains declarations of various properties of a component. The middleware acts in accordance with the property declarations. For example, in order for a component to support ACID[6] transactions, a programmer need only declare such support in the descriptor, rather than write a set of procedural instructions to support transactional behavior. The middleware takes care of the rest.

We can classify two basic modes for processing declarations:

Code generation.   In this mode, the declarations drive a 3GL code generator. GUI development environments that generate code from a WYSIWYG declaration of GUI properties are an example.

Runtime interpretation.   In this mode, precompiled, predeployed executable code interprets the declarations at runtime. For example, a database engine does not generate new 3GL code when handed a new declarative data model. Instead, the database engine more or less interprets the model at runtime.

Enterprise Architecture and Separation of Concerns

Software architecture seeks to organize complex systems by separating concerns. Separating concerns tends to localize changes to one aspect of a system. When changes to one aspect do impact other aspects, separation of concerns makes it easier to trace the impact.

Separating concerns tends to have a positive effect on the viability variables. The localization of changes makes systems less brittle and thus improves their longevity. Once an architecture and a supporting infrastructure are in place, such localization also improves productivity because change can be effected more rapidly. Traceability tends to improve quality.

Multitiered architecture is one of the most well-known and widely accepted architectural approaches for distributed enterprise systems. Nevertheless, there is some variance in the industry with regard to the number of tiers, and the names and roles of the tiers. Since I use the concepts of multitiered architecture later in the book, it's worth spelling out the concepts and terminology that I employ.

---

[6] ACID transactions are atomic, consistent, isolated, and durable. See [GR 1993] for a definitive work on the subject.

As discussed above, corporate computing systems were originally located entirely on centralized mainframe computers. The terminals on users' desktops were *dumb* slaves; that is, they had only the minimal processing power necessary to support display and entry functions (see Figure 1.6), under the strict control of the central master.

Client-server architects separated concerns by relegating mainframes to database management while shifting display of the data—and business logic using the data—to client PCs, as illustrated by Figure 1.7. Local servers connected to groups of PCs via LANs held client-side code files and even some databases that were special to the concerns of local groups.

The industry began moving from two-tier client-server architecture to three-tier architecture because it recognized that programmers were coding similar business logic in multiple clients. For example, consider a client-server order entry system in which the client calls to a back-end order, inventory, and general ledger database. When the client software completes an order, it executes the following steps:

1. Add order record to the order table.

2. Relieve inventory table for the inventory items ordered.

3. Post credits to payables accounts in the general ledger table.

4. Post debits to inventory accounts in the general ledger table.

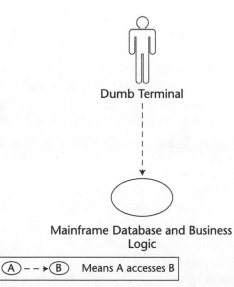

Dumb Terminal

Mainframe Database and Business Logic

(A) - - ▸(B)   Means A accesses B

Figure 1.6 One-tier architecture—all processing on centralized mainframe.

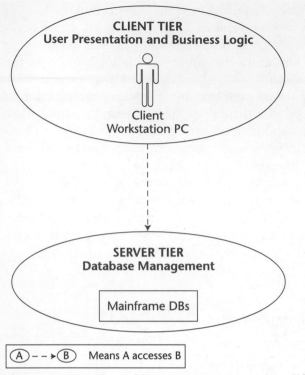

A) – – ➤ B)   Means A accesses B

Figure 1.7 Two-tier architecture—some processing off-loaded to client.

Gradually the industry realized that it was inefficient to program this kind of logic over and over again for the same database tables in many different client software modules. The inefficiency was due to a failure to separate the concerns of business logic and user presentation. Business logic needed to be encapsulated so many client modules could reuse it for various business use cases. Architects started creating a new tier between the database and the client that encapsulated this kind of business logic. They called this layer by various names, including *business tier, enterprise tier,* and *middle tier,* or *mid tier* for short. The other tiers were called the *client tier* or *front end* and the *database tier* or *back end.*

Thus, while two-tier architecture moved business logic from the mainframe to the client, three-tier moved business logic from the client to the mid tier (see Figure 1.8).

Tier separation is logical separation, not necessarily physical separation. It might make sense tactically in some cases to push middle-tier objects and components to client PCs for performance reasons. However, it became increasingly typical to place the middle tier on a separate server machine or set of machines. The advent of the Web solidified this trend because the Web demands that all logic except the basics of user presentation be off-loaded to a remote server.

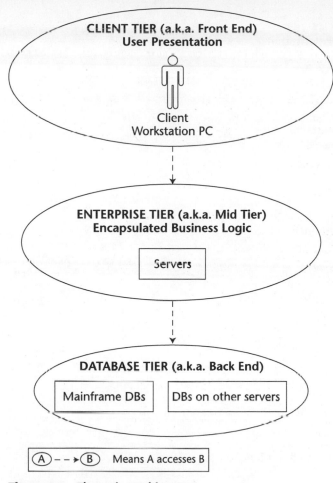

Figure 1.8   Three-tier architecture.

The *thin client* that thus became de rigueur for Web-based Internet and intranet applications spawned a variation of three-tier architecture in which the presentation facilities of the client machine were limited to a Web browser. Some of the user interaction and presentation facilities ran on remote Web servers, which dynamically generated HTML and sent it to the client; in that sense, Web servers spanned the client tier and mid tier, as illustrated by Figure 1.9. Well-architected systems carefully separated the Web server's GUI-oriented facilities from the mid tier's business logic, so that many user scenarios could use the business logic.

Three-tier architecture's concept of the database tier also evolved to include various enterprise information servers that are not mainframe-based.

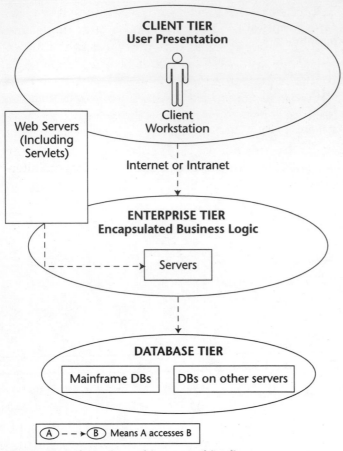

Figure 1.9   Three-tier architecture—thin client.

Three-tier architecture was a significant improvement over two-tier. However, architects and developers began to recognize that it had a limitation, namely its failure to separate business logic that involves interaction with the end user from business logic that is independent of user interaction.

Consider, for example, our order/inventory system now converted to three-tier architecture. The logic of interaction with the end user for one line item of an order might be:

1. Ask user to specify item desired.

2. Access database to get availability and price.

3. If unavailable, tell user.

4. If available, show user the price and give user the option to accept or reject.

5. If user accepts, call database to add a line item to the order.

Through the lessons of experience, architects began to realize that systems would be more scalable if the business logic that involves user interaction were separated from other business logic. Thus the mid tier was split into two tiers that separated these concerns: the *workspace tier* and the *enterprise tier*. The workspace tier is responsible for executing the logic of the pattern of interaction with the user. The interaction logic accesses the enterprise tier rather than going directly to the database.

Oliver Sims has been advocating four-tier architecture for the better part of a decade.[7] Herzum-Sims calls the four tiers *user tier*, *workspace tier*, *enterprise tier*, and *resource tier*, as Figure 1.10 illustrates. The figure also points out alternate names that some practitioners use for the tiers.

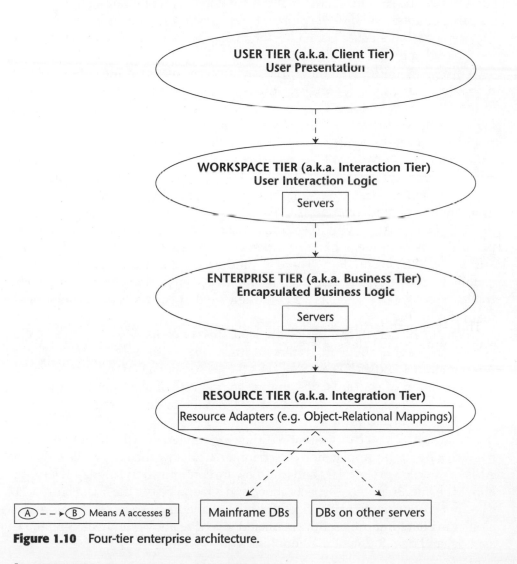

Figure 1.10 Four-tier enterprise architecture.

[7] See [HS 2000] for his most recent work on this subject.

The Herzum-Sims notion of a *business component* is a component composed of smaller components that are specific to individual tiers. A business component thus spans one or more tiers and can cover presentation, interaction, business logic, and data. An order entry component, for example, contains components that handle presentation, interaction, and so on for order entry.

Note that the Herzum-Sims resource tier is not quite the same as the database tier from three-tier systems. Instead, it represents the logic that provides the bridge between the enterprise tier and databases. Business components interact with but don't include databases, which is why Herzum-Sims does not define a tier to encompass databases. However, some enterprise architectures define the resource tier as including databases, while calling the tier that contains adapters the *integration tier*. Some practitioners define distinct tiers that separate client-side user interaction logic from server-side interaction logic handled by technology such as Java servlets.

In any case, multitiered enterprise architecture plays an important role in managing the complexity of distributed enterprise systems. The separation of different concerns in logical tiers promotes the reuse of data and logic and thus improves development productivity and quality.

There is more to enterprise architecture than organization by logical distribution tiers. For example, enterprise architecture also leverages middleware, layering the various tiers over middleware so as to minimize the degree to which basic functionality required by the tiers has to be programmed over and over again. There is middleware that supports GUI development, such as windows frameworks. There is middleware that supports the development of the workspace tier, such as J2EE servlets and analogous .NET technology. There is middleware that supports ACID transactions in the enterprise tier, such as the Java Transaction Service and .NET transaction support. There is also middleware that supports object-relational mapping for the resource tier.

Layering the tiers over middleware separates concerns into (1) aspects of the system that application programmers must deal with and (2) aspects that infrastructure handles. Oliver Sims uses the analogy of a water line to describe this separation of concerns, designating the aspects of a system that the programmer sees as *above the line* and aspects that the middleware infrastructure handles as *below the line*.

In Figure 1.11 you can see that middleware implementations that do much heavy lifting for the application programmer are below the line, while only the APIs to middleware services and middleware configuration languages surface above the line. 3GLs have aspects above and aspects below the line. Figure 1.11 does not exhaustively categorize all of the elements of an enterprise system along the water line. Other development tools have above- and below-the-line aspects, and development methodologies do as well.

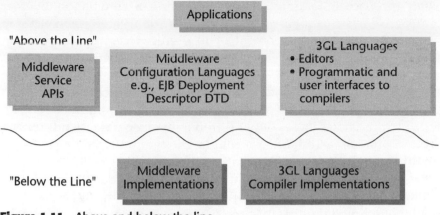

Figure 1.11 Above and below the line.

The notion of *viewpoints* is another enterprise computing concept that supports the idea of separation of concerns. A viewpoint is a projection of a system that filters out aspects of the system not relevant to that viewpoint. For example, we could define an application engineer's viewpoint of a system as revealing only the above-the-line aspects of the system. An infrastructure engineer's viewpoint, on the other hand, reveals the below-the-line aspects. The International Organization for Standardization's (ISO) RM-ODP makes a contribution to enterprise architecture by exploring the nature and ramifications of viewpoints. Each viewpoint is an abstraction of the system. RM-ODP defines abstraction as *the suppression of irrelevant detail*.[8]

Enterprise architecture also defines the separation of entity and process, defines levels of granularity of the various components of a system, and more.[9]

Multitiered architecture, granularity management, middleware layering, and so on are a common basis for enterprise architecture that most companies can adopt. However, it is always necessary for a business to customize these common contours to meet its own unique requirements.

Enterprise Application Integration (EAI)

Enterprise architecture makes it possible to design enterprise systems that by nature are well integrated. However, legacy systems and packaged applications are part of the IT landscape that cannot be ignored. By using enterprise architecture to develop new software, you can avoid creating more disconnected islands of automation, but existing islands need to be brought into the enterprise architecture as well.

---

[8] [RMODP]
[9] For an excellent treatment of enterprise architecture see [HRG 2000].

EAI is an approach to knitting preexisting islands of automation together within enterprise systems. Quite a few IT shops today are applying more resources to EAI than to development of new enterprise applications and components.

EAI adds the notion of *application adapters* to the resource tier. Application adapters wrap functionality islands such as packaged applications and other legacy systems. EAI systems support event-based communication among adapters, which promotes loose coupling among the disparate islands. Enterprise architects understand that loose coupling is the preferred way to integrate parts that were not designed to work with each other.[10]

Therefore, most EAI systems work by enabling disparate modules to send asynchronous messages when they complete various tasks and to handle messages sent by other modules that they receive from an event queue. Messages often consist of data that needs to be transformed, filtered, and/or routed to multiple destinations.

Figure 1.12 depicts the addition of adapters to the resource tier and the management of messages that flow among them.

There are a number of *messaging-oriented middleware* (MOM) platforms, including IBM's WebSphere MQ Integrator (formerly called MQSeries), Microsoft's MSMQ, and the Java Messaging Service (JMS).

Design by Contract

Design by Contract (DBC) is an approach to building reliable software that focuses on making the contract of a software module explicit and formal. It thus directly addresses the quality variable in the viability equation. E. W. Dijkstra formulated the basic foundations of Design by Contract in the 1970s.[11] Later advocates, such as Bertrand Meyer[12] and Haim Kilov,[13] built upon his work. Meyer's work laid the foundation for the Eiffel language.

DBC is based on a recognition that formal contract expression should go beyond merely the expression of the signatures of the operations that a module supports.

Design by Contract involves writing two kinds of formal constraints:

Pre-conditions and post-conditions.   Pre-conditions and post-conditions are assertions about operations. A pre-condition for an operation must be true when the operation begins executing. A post-condition must be true when the operation is finished executing.[14]

[10] In certain circumstances loose coupling can also be useful for integrating less disparate parts.
[11] [DIJK 1976]
[12] [MEYER 1997]
[13] [KR 1994]
[14] Some Design by Contract practitioners argue that it's more correct to say that if a pre- or post-condition isn't satisfied, then the behavior of the operation is undefined, rather than to say that the conditions must not be violated.

Invariants.   An invariant is an assertion about the state of a system that must always be true, except during the execution of an operation. In a sense, an invariant can be viewed as a universal pre- and post-condition for all operations. Invariants are generally stated as rules about classes or interfaces.

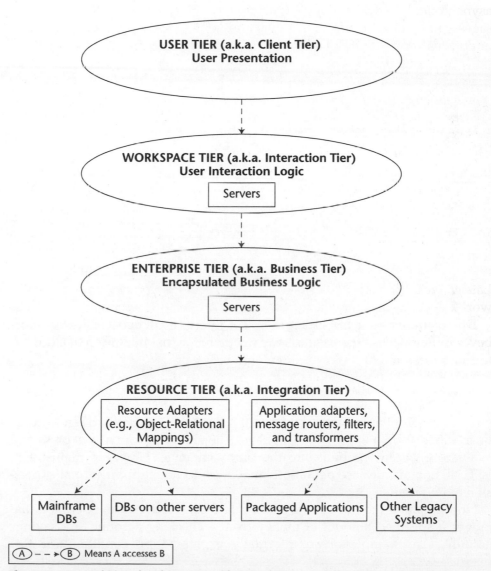

Figure 1.12   Multitiered architecture with EAI adapters and message management.

For example, consider the following Java interfaces:

```
Interface Customer
{
   String id;
   ...
}

interface Account
{
   double    balance;
   Customer customer;
   ...
}

interface CheckingAccount extends Account
{
   double minBalance;
   ...
}

interface SavingsAccount extends Account
{
   ...
}

interface FundsTransfer
{
   transferFromChecking(CheckingAccount fromAcct,
                        SavingsAccount toAcct,
                        double amount);
   ...
}
```

An invariant for the `CheckingAccount` interface might be expressed informally in English as "the balance may not go below the minimum balance." A formal expression of this invariant would be:

```
balance >= minBalance
```

The formal invariant is in the form of a Boolean assertion written in some unspecified formal expression language. The ability to formally express and evaluate invariants is built into the Eiffel language. However, mainstream 3GL, 4GL, and interface definition languages do not support formal expression of invariants.

Now consider the `FundsTransfer` interface, which has an operation that moves a specified amount of money from a checking account to a savings account. An example of an informally expressed pre-condition for this operation would be "the checking and savings accounts must have the same customer." It could be expressed formally as:

```
fromAcct.customer = toAcct.Customer
```

An informal post-condition for the operation is that the balance of the savings account is greater than its previous balance by the amount of the transfer. A formal expression of the post-condition might be:

```
toAcct.balance = toAcct.balance + amount
```

Where `toAcct.balance` on the left side of the equal sign refers to the balance after the operation executes, while on the right side it refers to the balance before it executes.

Mainstream languages do not support pre- and post-conditions any more than they support invariants. Therefore, most development organizations view invariants and pre- and post-conditions strictly as elements of design. Nevertheless, adherence to Design by Contract can have a significant impact on software quality.

Other Enterprise-Centric Technologies

4GLs such as Visual Basic are very popular. They provide higher-level environments for programming database-oriented functions and user interfaces. In order to provide this leverage, they restrict the range of problems that can be solved by the programmer.

XML supports interoperability between programs written in different 3GLs, so, like CORBA, it facilitates distribution.

Pressures on Enterprise-Centric Computing

Enterprise-centric computing advances made it possible to build new kinds of applications and to create true enterprise systems that are more than an amalgam of disconnected parts. However, the demands on enterprise software have continued to intensify (see Figure 1.13).

In the era that is now drawing to a close, companies expected enterprise software to manage information inside the business and to support end users on fairly uniform display devices. Now enterprise software is being pushed to also manage customer-to-business and business-to-business transactions over the Internet, accompanied by a wide array of end-user systems and devices, including fat clients, Web clients, telephone keypads, and wireless handhelds.

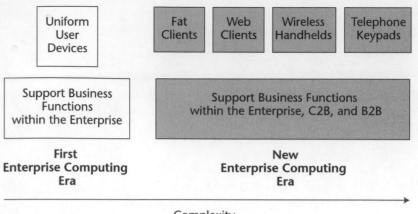

Figure 1.13 The pressure of increased complexity.

Business-to-business integration (B2Bi) adds a particularly demanding new dimension of complexity. The integration problem must now address not only disparate systems and data formats within the enterprise, but also differences between the enterprise's systems and the B2B message formats the industry is developing. The boundaries of the corporation from the standpoint of its computer systems are fluid, as companies virtually merge aspects of their systems via extranets and such partnerships undergo continual change.

Experience is proving that in these circumstances we are having trouble managing the viability equation. Just as increasing demand strained machine- and application-centric computing, it is now straining enterprise-centric computing. The problems facing the software industry that we outlined earlier stem from the increased demand being placed on enterprise software development and integration.

Pressure on Production Costs

Production costs are under pressure because of the level of labor-intensiveness required for enterprise programming to stand up to the more complex demand.

Adding a new data element to a customer-to-business transaction, for example, has ripple effects through code residing at multiple system tiers. The element has incarnations in multiple device GUIs, XML files, tier-specific components, databases, adapters, filters, routers, transformers, and so forth, and all these reflections of the element have to be synchronized. In fact, this is an oversimplified list of the different places where the element must be accounted for.

Development shops strain to get their arms around this complexity, which is difficult for the human programmer to manage and keep in synch manually.

Pressure on Quality

The inherent pressure of increased complexity on quality is aggravated by a fixation on coding that pervades much of the computer industry today. Far too often we code programs without rigorous architecture and design. This state of affairs developed over many years. Other engineering fields, such as civil, mechanical, electrical, and so forth, always require a rigorous and exhaustive architecture and technical product design before implementation. In the computer software industry there is a tendency to see coding as the only thing that really matters, all the rest being extraneous.

To be fair to programmers, it is they who bear the brunt of the pressure of the new complexity. They are asked to do the impossible—to produce increasingly complex software of high quality in Internet time. It's no wonder that they tend to look upon rigorous techniques such as Design by Contract as a luxury they can't afford.

The dot-com mania only made the situation more acute. Internet time drove startup companies that were garnering the best programming talent to release software of low quality. The idea of building software without design was now extended to building businesses without business plans. Inevitably, the bubble burst, bringing down a lot of Internet time software with it.

Imagine that architects and civil engineers failed in a significant percentage of their attempts to build modern high-rise buildings. This is very hard to imagine because such attempts rarely fail. Given the high rate of success in building high-rises, we might be tempted to say that building a high-rise is much simpler than building software. But a high-rise building is very complicated. It must be structurally sound to resist wind, rain, earthquakes, and extreme outdoor temperature variations. It has miles of heating and cooling system ducts, telephone and network cable, and power conduits. It has a multitude of junction boxes and switches of all sorts. It must meet stringent standards for soundproofing and indoor air quality.

Yet virtually all attempts to build high-rises succeed. Now imagine that we constructed such buildings without detailed architectural blueprints and engineering specifications. What would the success rate be?

Building corporate software is certainly at least as complicated as building high-rises. Yet the production pressures resulting from a compromised viability equation push us into trying to defy the laws of physics and build complex systems without first preparing detailed architectural blueprints and engineering specifications. The consequences of a poorly constructed sales order software system are not life-critical, as is the reliability of a high-rise. However, they are important to the health of companies and to our economy as a whole.

Michi Henning, one of the world's foremost distributed computing experts, has pointed out that the software book racks are filled with titles such as *Teach Yourself C++ in 14 Easy Lessons*, *Java for Morons*, *CORBA For Dummies*, *Complete Idiot's Guide to Win32*, and so on. He challenges us to imagine how odd it would seem to come upon books with titles such as *Brain Surgery in 14 Easy Lessons*, *Air Traffic Control for Morons*, *Bridge Design For Dummies*, or *Complete Idiot's Guide to Contract Law*.[15]

Building enterprise software is a serious undertaking requiring discipline and professionalism. But it is difficult for a culture of rigor to take hold in an environment where the viability equation is under pressure.

Nevertheless, some in the programming community have made efforts to come up with ways to manage the stressors. The Extreme Programming (XP) movement has tapped into the great need for programmers to get control of the situation. XP is known as a *lightweight* or *agile* development methodology. XP is helping to make formal process a bit more respectable among programmers. More comprehensive methodologies, such as the Unified Process, have had a tougher time penetrating the industry because developers see them as heavyweight, and thus as unaffordable by comparison.

In any case, the emergence of development processes mitigates the downward pressure on quality, but doesn't address the fundamental problem, which is that the complexity of enterprise systems is taxing developers' capacity to manage it. Anti-design attitudes are an exacerbating, rather than fundamental, factor.

Pressure on Longevity

The expanding reach of enterprise software drives a procession of new computing platforms. Changes in platform trends have blindsided many a development manager, proving their reading of industry directions wrong. Managers make informed guesses about which platforms will win the next round of industry battles. If their guesses turn out to be wrong, the cost of changing the platforms that their 3GL code writes to are enormous and often prohibitive.

The technology platforms receiving the most attention as this book goes to press in 2002 are Enterprise Java, .NET, and Web services. None of these platforms was even on the radar screen 5 years ago.

Here are just a few examples of platform changes in recent years:

- Java appeared in the mid-1990s as an object-oriented 3GL with some nice features for the Web, a worthy successor to the inscrutable C++. Today's Java 2 Enterprise Edition (J2EE) is a far cry from the Java of 1996. Furthermore, the EJB 2.0 specification is quite different from the EJB 1.X versions.

[15] [HENN 2002]

- XML's rate of change is also noteworthy. XML DTDs are evolving to XML Schemas. Simple XML data exchange is evolving to XML-based Web services using Web Services Description Language (WSDL) and Simple Object Access Protocol (SOAP) on top of XML, with registries such as Universal Description, Discovery and Integration (UDDI) on the next rung of the stack.

- The OMG's CORBA is constantly evolving. It has new features to allow invocations to carry security credentials. In addition, the OMG has released the CORBA Component Model (CCM), which supports application servers based on CORBA's language-neutral distribution framework. CCM was late to market, arriving after EJB was already entrenched. However, at least one large corporation with an internally developed CORBA ORB is now developing a CCM implementation for internal use. It may be too soon to write off this big evolution of CORBA.

- Microsoft's strategy for behind-the-firewall distributed components revolves around COM+, which is a significant evolution of the Distributed Component Object Model (DCOM) and the Microsoft Transaction Server (MTS). COM+ is now part of Microsoft's .NET platform.

- Until recently it looked as if Sun was going to compete head-on with CORBA's IIOP protocol when it defined Remote Method Invocation (RMI). However, Sun decided not to try to duplicate the features of CORBA and has now made IIOP support mandatory for J2EE application servers. Thus, Sun relegated RMI to the status of a higher-level protocol above the CORBA protocol.

We are forced to conclude that the only thing we can predict with confidence about the future of platforms is that things we can't predict will happen. Even if an IT manager makes a correct bet on a platform, the platform is unlikely to stay still; instead, it may morph over time into something almost completely new. Even when the manager's guess turns out to be right, code that is tied to the platform can become obsolete distressingly quickly. See Table 1.1.

Table 1.1 Platform Volatility

COMPANY	THEN	NOW
Sun	Java language	J2SE, J2EE
W3C	XML DTD	XML Schema, WSDL, etc.
OMG	CORBA	CORBA Component Model
Microsoft	MTS	COM+/.NET
Sun and OMG	RMI vs. IIOP	RMI over IIOP

Thus, a development manager with an ability to always pick platforms that survive the industry's competitive maelstrom will find that this gift does not protect her. She could easily find herself in a situation where the software her group has developed is not current technologically and won't be able to interface with third-party systems without very costly, hand-coded upgrading.

I call the tendency for the platform ground to shift under our feet *platform volatility*. We've mostly talked about platform volatility regarding enterprise tier technology, but it also rears its head in the sphere of interaction with the end user because of the proliferation of so many different end-user display and input frameworks.

A Modern Day Sisyphus

Homer tells the story of Sisyphus, who was fated to repeatedly push a rock up a hill, whereupon the rock would roll down the hill, forcing Sisyphus to push it up the hill again. An IT manager is a modern day Sisyphus, trying to manage the viability equation in the face of fast-changing technologies and increasingly complex demand.

Summary

Improvements in the way we develop software tend to keep the viability variables—quality, longevity, and the cost of production—in balance. Pushed by increasing demand, software has evolved from being a niche player in the corporate world to a point where it has a critical role in basic operations. The accumulated gains in enterprise computing help IT managers deal with growing complexity and volatility.

Major facets of enterprise computing include:

- Component-based development, which applies concepts honed in manufacturing industries to the development of software
- Design patterns, which also have analogues in manufacturing processes
- Middleware, which takes a step beyond operating systems in raising the level of abstraction of the computing platform
- Declarative specification, in which relatively brief declarations replace relatively complex procedural code
- Enterprise architecture, which organizes enterprise software by separating concerns
- Enterprise application integration, which ties disparate legacy systems into an overall enterprise system
- Design by Contract, which promotes high-quality software engineering

CHAPTER 2

Model Driven Enterprise Computing

MDA helps deal with pressures on enterprise computing by bringing a number of its trends together in new ways. MDA did not invent component-based development, design patterns, middleware, declarative specification, abstraction, multitiered systems, EAI, and Design by Contract; rather, it expands on them and helps them work better. This section examines how it does so.

Many of the points that this chapter discusses are treated more thoroughly in Parts Two and Three.

Bringing Model-Centrism to Intermediate Tiers, EAI, and B2Bi

The declarations of data formats that drive database engines, and the WYSI-WYG models of GUIs that drive the code generators in GUI development tools are harbingers of MDA. These declarative models of data and GUIs are not simply design artifacts. They are formal development artifacts that directly improve the viability variables in the development of the front and back ends of systems.

MDA brings this approach to the development of the intermediate tiers of enterprise systems, and into the sphere of EAI and B2B integration (B2Bi).

MDA uses standards-based modeling languages as formal development languages. Formal models drive generators that produce 3GL code, HTML, XML, WSDL, IDL, and other artifacts. MDA tools allow engineers to fine-tune the production of these artifacts. MDA sometimes uses dynamic execution engines—that is, virtual machines—to execute models directly.

Models as Development Artifacts

Most of us are used to looking upon software models as design artifacts and 3GL programs as development artifacts. Many companies separate the roles of modeler and programmer completely.

As a result, models, such as UML models, are often informal, meaning that they cannot be machine-processed. Programmers use them as guidelines and specifications, but not as something that directly contributes to production. Consequently many view them as peripheral to the production process.

MDA uses formal models that can be machine-processed. Such models are a direct part of the production process. In such an environment the roles of modeler and programmer are not nearly so distinct. The modeling activity is a programming activity.

This is not to say that there is no longer any role for informal modeling. Informal modeling remains useful for promoting communication among human beings about architecture and design. Informal modeling is a fine use for UML, but informal models cannot drive code generators or virtual machines.

Syntactic Abstraction versus Semantic Abstraction

The degree to which middleware such as CORBA and COM abstracts away 3GLs is quite limited. The code that a compiler generates from IDL declarations of object interfaces is skeletal, leaving the programmer with a lot of 3GL coding to do.

The reason for the limitation is that these IDLs are not very expressive. IDLs are pretty much limited to declaring the syntax of the interfaces. For example, CORBA interface declarations include declarations of attributes and operations. You can declare attribute types and operation signatures, but little more.

Consider the following CORBA IDL, which describes the interfaces exposed by some components. These interfaces are essentially programming-language-independent renditions of the Java declarations we looked at earlier.

```
interface Account
{
    attribute string id;
    attribute double balance;
};
```

```
interface Customer
{
    typedef sequence<Account> Accounts;
    attribute string    id;
    attribute Accounts accounts;
};

interface CheckingAccount : Account
{
    attribute double minimumBalance;
};

interface SavingsAccount : Account
{
    ...
};

interface FundsTransfer
{
    TransferFromChecking
        (in CheckingAccount fromAcct,
         in SavingsAccount  toAcct,
         in double          amount);
    ...
};
```

There is a lot of semantic information— that is, information about meaning rather than syntax—that this IDL can't express, and this information is likely to be important for a real banking application. For example, IDL can't express the fact that a customer owns its accounts, meaning that if the customer is removed from the system, then its accounts must be removed as well. IDL can't express the invariant rule discussed earlier that a checking account's balance cannot go below the minimum balance. Nor can IDL express the pre- and post- conditions for the funds transfer operation.

Therefore I refer to IDL as a *semantically thin* language. A set of IDL interfaces expresses little or nothing about the semantics of those interfaces. Semantic thinness sharply limits the value of IDL to serve as a formal specification of the system in question. It also limits the ability of an IDL compiler to generate code. The compiler generates code that supports distribution and that bridges the differences among 3GLs, but a programmer still has to hand-code the basic semantics of the system in some 3GL. The programmer must enforce the customer's ownership of its accounts. The programmer must enforce the invariant rules and pre- and post-conditions. Quality assurance teams must manually develop testing harnesses that validate that the required semantics are satisfied.

Modeling languages, on the other hand, are *semantically rich*. They can express syntax in a 3GL-independent fashion, but they can also express 3GL-independent semantics, much of it in declarative fashion.

For example, Figure 2.1 is a UML model of accounts and customers that is roughly equivalent to part of the IDL. The black diamond declares a composition, indicating that a customer owns its accounts. The model declares the invariant formally via UML's Object Constraint Language (OCL).

UML can also express pre- and post-conditions for operations. We'll look at some later in this chapter, and in Chapter 4 we'll thoroughly examine them and UML's overall support for Design by Contract.

Our semantically rich model is a more effective engineering specification than our semantically thin one. Furthermore, a code generator can do more with it. The generator can produce code that enforces a customer's ownership of its accounts and enforces the invariants and pre- and post-conditions. The generator can produce the parts of the testing harness that assess whether these constraints are satisfied.

Semantically rich, formal models and accompanying generators thus raise the programming abstraction level above 3GLs in a more profound fashion than IDL-based middleware does. Compact, semantic declarations correspond to many lines of generated, procedural 3GL code.

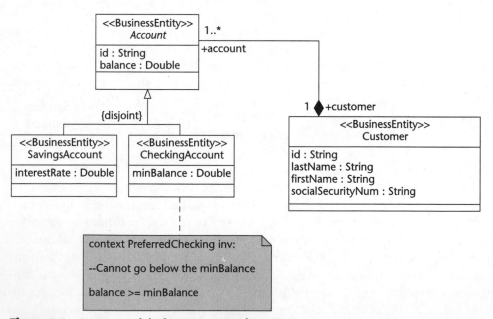

Figure 2.1 A UML model of customers and accounts.

As was the case when the programming abstraction level was raised from binary to assembly, and then from assembly to 3GLs, broadly raising the abstraction level above 3GLs tends to improve all three viability variables. Productivity increases because one language construct, such as composition, corresponds to many lines of 3GL code. Quality improves because generators reuse time-tested logic when they generate 3GL code that, for instance, enforces composition. Longevity increases because of the separation of 3GL concerns from the fundamental semantic concerns. This makes it possible to port models to different 3GLs by writing new generators, much as providing new compilers allows you to port COBOL and C++ programs to new machines with different processors and operating systems.

As was also the case with previous elevations of the programming abstraction level, the transition is encountering growing pains in its early stages. Generation algorithms and MDA tools will improve over time. Programmers will let go of 3GL-focused development techniques only when they have had time to adjust and to feel confident that the new tools and techniques work.

Furthermore, the need to deal with an enterprise's legacy systems complicates matters for MDA generators in a way that doesn't affect 3GL compilers. I'll return to this tricky issue later in this and subsequent chapters.

B2Bi and MDA

The parade of new technologies for B2Bi has tended to throw the software industry off kilter. Witness, for example, a recent article from the trade press that talked about the new Web services technologies:

> *The promise of Web Services depends heavily on vendors supporting the standards . . . analysts say that more standards will likely develop . . . If Web Services are to take off a significant [proportion] of the more than 20 million programmers in the world will have to write to UDDI, WSDL, XML and SOAP . . . The biggest issue may be translating current developer skills . . .*[1]

This approach will not scale, and is not viable in the long term, for several reasons.

It would be risky for 20 million programmers and countless development groups to retool so that they can write 3GL code for using UDDI, WSDL, XML, and SOAP. Once we completed this expensive process, we might discover that yet another unforeseen development has eclipsed those technologies or displaced it in some key environments.

---

[1] [INFW 2001]

First, the technologies for Web Services are in flux, and there are also several different ways of stacking these technologies, as we shall see later. The Simple Object Access Protocol (SOAP), Universal Description, Discovery and Integration (UDDI), and the Web Services Description Language (WSDL) are new and still evolving.

Some of the technologies implementing Web services depend on Port 80. There is some question as to whether Port 80 will remain what it was originally intended to be—a secure firewall peephole—when we begin multiplexing huge numbers of Web service messages through it.

Until just a few years ago, most industry observers thought that customer-to-business and business-to-business e-commerce would use CORBA and Microsoft DCOM for invoking services across the Internet.[2] However, it turned out that firewall administrators have been reluctant to open up new ports on the firewall for CORBA and DCOM, having already opened up a port for HTTP. Thus HTTP and technologies built on the HTTP stack, such as XML, now dominate transactions that involve communication through firewalls, while CORBA and the portions of .NET that evolved from DCOM stay behind firewalls.

The point is that platform volatility makes it likely that the technologies underlying Web services will change. Having developers program directly to these technologies invites rapid obsolescence and is also too labor-intensive.

We in the technical community have a tendency to fall in love with technology, in this case with SOAP, WSDL, and so on. Thus we may fail to see the forest for the trees. We must step back from the technology in order to understand that it is the information, and the services that use and create the information, that are of primary importance. The breakthrough concept of Web services is that such information and services can be presented and accessed over the Internet. While Web service implementation technologies are important, they must be kept in perspective, for they will change while the breakthrough concept survives.

Our goal should be to provide an environment in which individual Web services can be produced in a way that is as independent of these particular technologies as possible. The purpose of such an approach is to protect the investment in Web services as the underlying technologies change. Further, this approach promotes the ability to generate technology-specific Web service artifacts automatically or semiautomatically, rather than forcing programmers to construct them entirely by hand.

First- and Second-Generation Web Services Integration

The first generation of Web services has resulted in products that, in essence, project existing objects and components—for example, CORBA, Java, or COM

---

[2] See, for example, [GM 1995]

objects and components—as Web services. There are tools that generate the required WSDL, SOAP, and other XML files, and that also generate code (such as Java code) that binds the Web services to the objects and components that they wrap.

These tools relieve the programmer of much tedious work, and they meet the requirement of avoiding intensive hand-coding of technology-specific artifacts. Programmers turn the crank, so to speak, and the tool generates a great deal of the necessary XML, WSDL, SOAP, and 3GL artifacts.

However, Web services will be and must be coarser-grained than many of the already-existing objects and components because the business functions we need to expose to other businesses generally contain much more application logic than is present in any single existing object or component. Web services will often present abstractions of finer-grained functions that already exist; in other words, Web Services will be compositions of more primitive functionality.

Furthermore, for a company that publishes a Web service, it's more problematical to change the Web service than it is to change a service that only internal clients use. Impact control with external collaboration partners is difficult. Therefore, changes due to platform volatility have more serious ramifications in the B2Bi context.

Therefore, we must actually *design* Web services, and we must do so in a way that minimizes the impact of platform volatility. Second-generation Web services integration produces Web Services whose design is driven by business requirements and by the need to minimize network traffic from fine-grained interactions. We cannot limit ourselves to a mechanical approach that exposes as Web services the objects and components that we are already using because many of those individual objects are not likely to provide the level of function needed.

In order to identify and design a specific Web service according to these criteria, designers need to answer the following questions:

- What is the information that needs to be manipulated?
- What is the functionality that must be provided?

If we can capture the answers to these questions in a semantically rich, formal model, the model can be used to generate the artifacts that support the services over some set of technologies. The Web Services design vocabulary should let us describe the information and services in ways that are entirely independent of XML, WSDL, SOAP, UDDI, Java, and other Web Service implementation technologies. The trend is toward tools that can automate production of XML, WSDL, SOAP, UDDI, and artifacts and implementation code from design input.

It isn't necessary for business people to be able to construct such formal models. Technical people can create them, working with the business people.

In order for this approach to be viable, tools usually provide some mechanism that allows engineers who are intimately familiar with the Web services technologies to fine-tune the generation of the technology-specific artifacts. Such a mechanism plays a similar role to that of stored procedures and triggers that allow engineers to fine-tune the way database engines process data models.

One approach for supporting fine-tuning is to provide configurable generators that present engineers with a range of options for generating the necessary artifacts. Another approach, which is controversial, is to allow engineers some freedom to modify generated artifacts. The latter approach requires tools that are smart enough not to overwrite an engineer's modifications when the design is enhanced and the generator executes again.

As MDA matures and generators improve, the need for engineers to fine-tune the output of generators on a case-by-case basis will diminish. Chapter 8's section on synchronizing models and code examines the consequences of allowing engineers to intervene in the production of technology-specific artifacts.

Web Services and Enterprise Architecture

If we consider Web services in the context of an enterprise architecture, it's useful to define the notion of a *business service*, which might be presented as a Web service, a Web page, a fat-client application screen, a service for a wireless handheld device, or a Java API.[3] Business services are composed from lower-level, finer-grained business functions and information entities.

Because we want to reuse composed business services in these different contexts and separate them from presentation, we locate their core logic in the enterprise tier. This logic is independent of the implementation technologies used to expose the service, such as WSDL, HTML, WAP (Wireless Access Protocol), and so on.

When we decide to expose the business service as a Web service, there are still a number of technologies to choose from. We might expose it via WSDL bindings. WSDL itself has the ability to bind to SOAP, simple HTTP, or MIME, so there are several variants of WSDL-based implementation from which to select. We might decide not to use WSDL at all and instead expose the service via SOAP directly. Regardless of which technology stack we use, we still want to use the same enterprise-tier business services, as illustrated by Figure 2.2.

Early Web applications tended to wire Web front ends directly onto the back ends of existing systems, and in that way some companies have avoided building enterprise tiers. However, Web services and B2Bi require enterprise tiers to expose coarse-grained, reusable business services. By encapsulating these services in a fashion that is independent of the technical mechanisms we use to expose them, we make it possible to reuse them in any number of contexts.

---

[3] These ideas are based on original work by Mike Rosen.

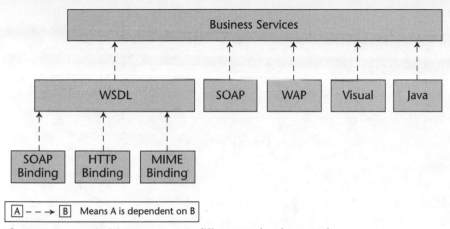

Figure 2.2 Maximizing reuse over different technology stacks.

This separation of the executable service functionality from the technologies used to access it dovetails with the requirement to formally capture the essence of a service in a fashion that is independent of WSDL, SOAP, and so forth. Let's examine how to meet this requirement.

Defining Abstract Business Services

Figure 2.3 is a semantically rich, formal model of a business service. The model is independent of Web service implementation technologies. It leverages the information model of Figure 2.1.

The service is called FundsXfer (funds transfer), and it has an operation called XferFromChecking (transfer from checking). This UML operation has three input parameters:

1. The checking account that is the source of the transfer.

2. The savings account that is the target of the transfer.

3. The amount to transfer from the checking to the savings account.

There are other approaches to creating this specification. For example, one might reify the operation into a class, and then make the parameters attributes of the class. Some approaches reify the operation into two classes, one for an input message that corresponds to the input parameters, and one for an output message that corresponds to the output parameters. There are advantages and disadvantages to each approach.

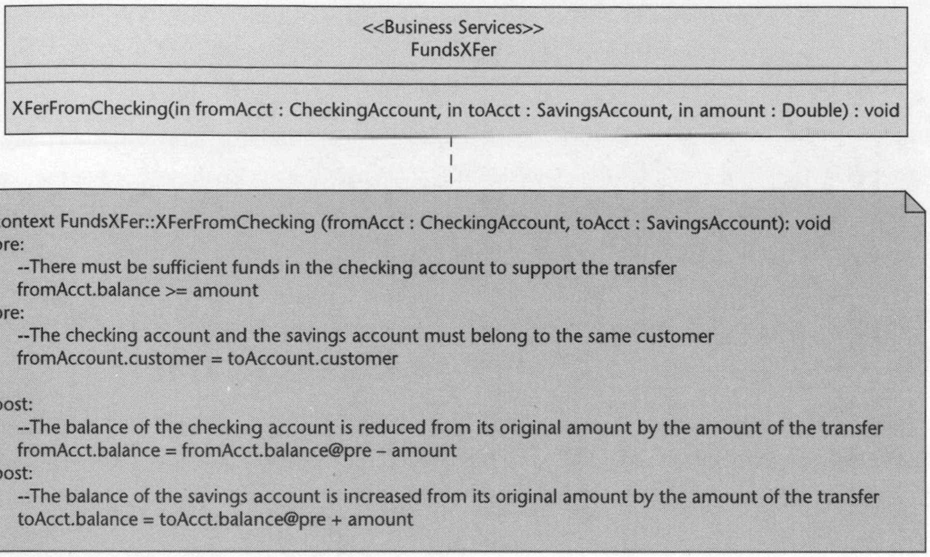

<<Business Services>> FundsXFer
XFerFromChecking(in fromAcct : CheckingAccount, in toAcct : SavingsAccount, in amount : Double) : void

context FundsXFer::XFerFromChecking (fromAcct : CheckingAccount, toAcct : SavingsAccount): void
pre:
    --There must be sufficient funds in the checking account to support the transfer
    fromAcct.balance >= amount
pre:
    --The checking account and the savings account must belong to the same customer
    fromAccount.customer = toAccount.customer

post:
    --The balance of the checking account is reduced from its original amount by the amount of the transfer
    fromAcct.balance = fromAcct.balance@pre – amount
post:
    --The balance of the savings account is increased from its original amount by the amount of the transfer
    toAcct.balance = toAcct.balance@pre + amount

Figure 2.3   A formal model of a business service.

In any case, the operation has two pre-conditions, which are expressed in OCL:

1. The balance in the source checking account must be greater than or equal to the amount to be transferred to the target savings account. Note that the source account's type is CheckingAccount, which we defined in our information model from Figure 2.1. The Checking Account.balance identifier in the constraint explicitly references the balance attribute of CheckingAccount in that information model.

2. Both accounts must be owned by the same customer. When this constraint specifies fromAccount.customer and toAccount. customer, the ".customer" traverses the association between Account and Customer shown in Figure 2.1. In other words, the expression treats customer as a property of the account.

The operation also has two post-conditions, that is, conditions that must be true when the operation is completed:

1. The source account's balance must be equal to what the balance was before this operation occurred, minus the amount of the transfer. The fromAccount.balance identifier to the left of the equal sign refers to the balance of the account after the operation executes;

fromAccount.balance@pre refers to the balance of the account before the operation executes.

2. The target account balance must be equal to what the balance was before the operation, plus the amount of the transfer.

The pre- and post-conditions are important not only because they provide generators with semantic information. They are also important in clarifying B2B contractual obligations. Chapter 4's section *Design by Contract* examines this point more closely.

Mapping Business Information Models to XML

There are a number of different approaches to mapping formal UML models to implementation technologies. An OMG standard called XML Metadata Interchange (XMI) exemplifies one approach. This standard defines mapping rules that specify how to generate an XML Document Type Definition (DTD) or Schema from a class model. The generated DTD or Schema defines a format for representing instances of the classes in XML documents.[4]

Figure 2.4 shows the results of running the class model of Figure 2.1 through an XMI-generating tool. The result is a DTD, and the lower-right portion of Figure 2.4 shows a fragment of the generated DTD that corresponds to the Customer class. It shows XML DTD definitions for the attributes of Customer, namely id, lastName, firstName, and socialSecurity Number. Although it isn't evident from the small fragment of the generated DTD shown here, the various semantic elements of the model, such as the properties of associations, affect how the DTD is generated.

Parameterized Mappings

XMI gives the engineer a number of choices governing XML production. It defines each of these choices as a *mapping parameter*. A mapping that provides such choices is called a *parameterized mapping*. The engineer indicates choices by tagging the model with actual values of those parameters.

For example, one of the parameters determines whether an attribute of a class maps to an XML attribute or to an XML element. Mapping to an XML attribute is more intuitive. However, some engineering groups prefer to reserve XML attributes for ancillary metadata, such as internally generated ID numbers.

As mentioned earlier, this fine-tuning capability is especially necessary during MDA's early stages, but will become less so over time.

---

[4] See [XMI] for the formal specifications and [GDB 2002] for a full-length book on the subject.

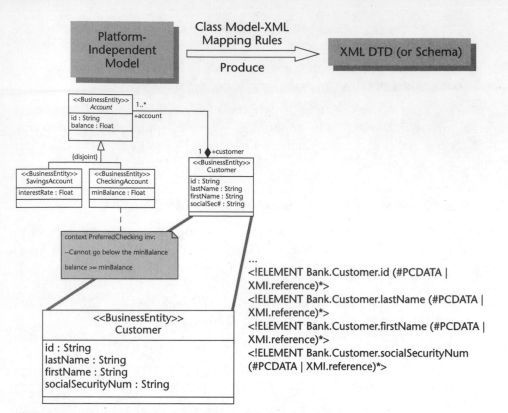

Figure 2.4   Mapping the business information model to XML.

Mapping Business Service Models to WSDL

Mapping a business service model to WSDL is an exercise in mapping the input parameters to WSDL input messages and the output parameters to WSDL output messages. Figure 2.5 illustrates this mapping and expands our business service example to include the declaration of two output parameters representing the ending balances of the two accounts.

The boxes in the lower part of Figure 2.5 correspond to fragments of a formal model of WSDL itself. Here we see that WSDL defines port types, which own operations. Operation definitions reference, but do not own, message definitions, with some messages playing the role of inputs for the operation and some playing the role of outputs.

By applying XMI for XML Schema to the information model of Figure 2.1, we can derive the XML formats of the input and output message payloads, since that model defines all of the business service's input and output parameter types.

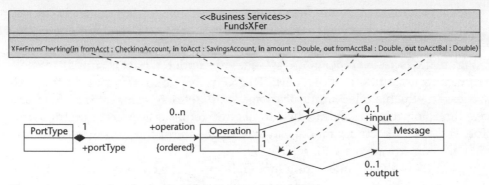

Figure 2.5 Mapping the business service model to WSDL.

Eventually there will be generators that automatically implement mappings to WSDL, but for now we apply them manually. However, tools that automatically produce a DTD from a class model, as shown in Figure 2.4, exist today.

Generators that implement mappings to different technologies can process the formal models as well. That is the key to promoting longevity of B2Bi systems.

Automating Business Processes and B2B Collaborations

The automation of business processes and collaborations is at the frontier of B2Bi. A *collaboration* is a coordinated set of interactions among two or more parties called *collaboration partners*.[5]

Defining and supporting business processes and collaborations is a more complex problem than defining and supporting Web services. Collaborations may in fact be compositions of a number of Web services that collaborating partners supply, where each Web Service plays a particular role in the collaboration.

The specific messages exchanged as part of a collaboration trigger business processes within the collaborating partners' own systems. In order to do B2Bi, we therefore must be able to specify both business processes and collaborations. Hence, both business process and collaboration definitions are important in this technology.

Here again we have a mix of concrete technologies for describing processes and collaborations, including ebXML's Business Process Specification Schema, RosettaNet's Partner Interface Processes (PIPs), Web services Flow Language (WSFL), Web services Conversation Language (WSCL), XLANG, and so on. What is central here is the processes and collaborations, rather than these specific technologies.

---

[5] The collaboration partners might be different companies or might be different administrative domains of the same company.

We can use UML activity and interaction models to define processes and collaborations in a manner that is independent of these B2B technologies. We can also define mappings to the various implementation technologies.

Figure 2.6 is an example of a UML activity model, which is similar in some respects to a traditional flowchart. This activity model describes a business process in which a telecommunications company determines which field service time slots are available to a customer and requests a reservation for a time slot. This type of activity model can drive a generator that produces code and XML for some implementation technology.

Figure 2.7 is a UML interaction model. It specifies a collaboration composed of a sequence of messages among various parties in support of the business activity shown in Figure 2.6. This kind of interaction pattern is crucial to B2B commerce. Such interaction models can provide additional input to generators.

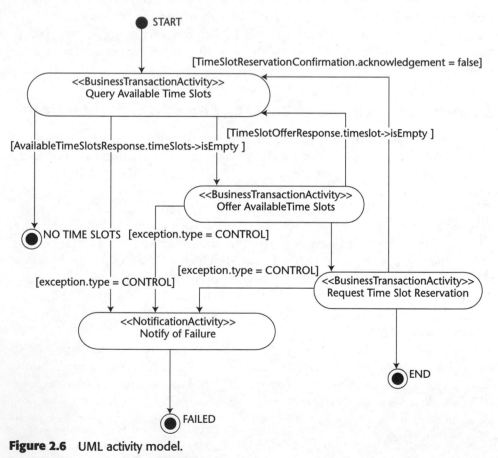

Figure 2.6 UML activity model.
Reused, with permission, from [CLARK 2001].

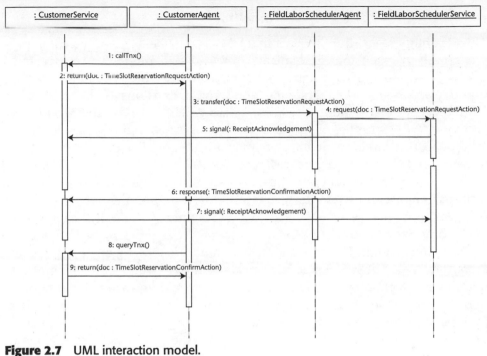

Figure 2.7 UML interaction model.
Reused, with permission, from [CLARK 2001].

Various organizations are laying a foundation of standards for defining business processes and collaborations in an implementation-technology-independent fashion. They are also developing standard mappings that specify how to map these definitions to various implementation technologies.

If you aren't convinced that UML is the best language for modeling B2B collaborations and business processes, note that it's possible to use alternate notations while still conforming to UML's XMI-based interchange format. MDA can even support modeling languages that are quite different from UML. We'll revisit this point in several contexts later in this book, particularly in Chapters 5 and 6.

Flexibility in Choosing the Abstraction Level

MDA is not limited to abstracting away 3GLs, operating systems, and B2B description formats such as WSDL. UML models can be 3GL-specific, middleware-specific, middleware-independent, and so forth.

Modeling Language Extensibility

This flexibility stems from the fact that UML is a malleable language that provides built-in extension mechanisms. You can add modeling constructs to UML to support 3GL-specific modeling, middleware-specific modeling, middleware-independent modeling, and so on. Extensions of UML are called *UML profiles*. Furthermore, a sister standard to UML, called the *Meta Object Facility (MOF)*[6], supplies even more power to define languages for whatever level of abstraction is suitable for the purpose at hand. Chapter 5 covers MOF in detail, and Chapter 6 covers UML profiles.

This flexibility is an important part of MDA. It means that a development team can choose, for example, to use a middleware-independent model of a business entity and generate at least part of an enterprise-tier EJB component, .NET component, and/or CORBA component (see Figure 2.8).

The value of a middleware-independent model is that, together with generators, it raises the abstraction level even above middleware. Now that multiple middleware technologies have proliferated, developing directly to specific middleware carries platform volatility risks. In many cases, therefore, it is preferable to define a middleware-independent model that can be mapped to particular middleware. As we've seen, raising the abstraction level tends to improve all of the viability variables.

Even so, component models that are specific to particular middleware are useful because they provide a snapshot of the system from the viewpoint of that level of abstraction. Thus, for instance, when an EJB generator produces an EJB component from the middleware-independent model, it can also produce an EJB-specific model of the generated EJB component. Such a model is helpful for understanding the generated code during debugging because, in most cases, interactive debugging still requires 3GL-specific source-level debugging tools.

Some MDA methodologies use the middleware-specific models as more than convenient views. They allow engineers to fine-tune such models before generating code. There are different opinions in the industry about whether this is good practice, and different MDA products that are emerging reflect these different opinions. In Chapter 8 we will discuss the trade-offs and provide an example of a middleware-independent component model, analyzing how such a model relates to middleware-specific models.

Figure 2.9 depicts a generator producing a middleware-specific component and a middleware-specific UML model of the component at the same time.

[6][MOF]

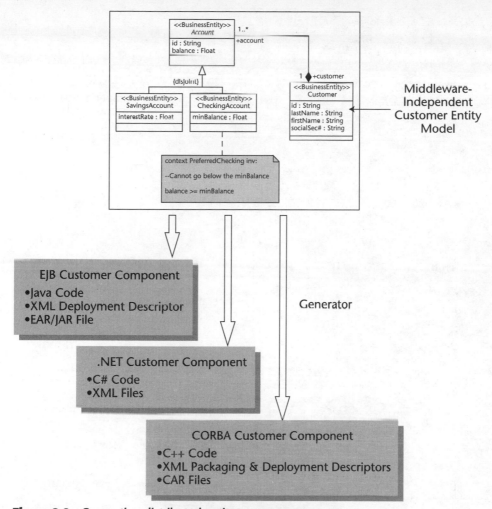

Figure 2.8 Generating distributed entity components.

The extensibility of the MDA modeling language environment is key to supporting modeling at different levels of abstraction. The Java Community Process standards initiative is defining a UML profile for EJB-specific modeling.[7] The OMG has defined a UML profile for CORBA-specific modeling.[8] A number of initiatives are underway to define UML profiles for middleware-independent modeling.

[7] [JSR26]
[8] [UML4CORBA]

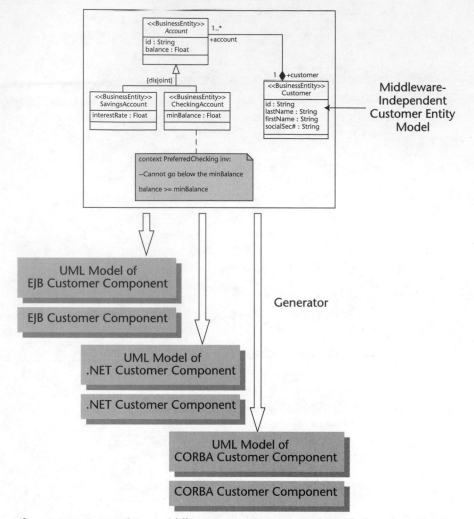

Figure 2.9 Generating a middleware-specific UML model with the component.

Platform Independence: A Relative Concept

The OMG has defined the terms *Platform-Independent Model (PIM)* and *Platform-Specific Model (PSM)*. It is important to understand that platform independence is a relative concept. It has meaning only with respect to some specified platform or platforms.

For example, when CORBA was first introduced, it was considered to be platform-independent because it was independent of 3GLs and operating systems. However, now that there are several major middleware technologies, CORBA can be considered to be a platform, and some are calling middleware-independent models platform-independent.

Thus, it makes no sense to call a model or a modeling language platform-independent without specifying the platform or platforms from which it is independent. If we state that by *platform* we mean middleware, we can call a middleware-independent component model *platform-independent*, as in Figure 2.10.

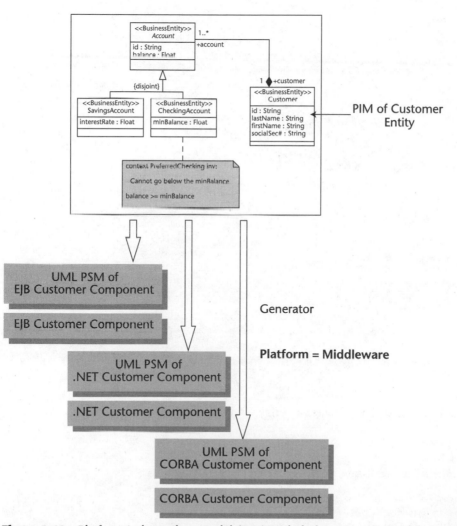

Figure 2.10   Platform-Independent Model (PIM) and Platform-Specific Models (PSMs).

EAI and MDA

The OMG has defined a standard UML profile for modeling event-driven EAI[9] in a manner that is independent of specific message-oriented middleware such as WebSphere MQ Integrator (MQSeries), MSMQ, and JMS.

The specification also includes preliminary mappings to WebSphere MQ Integrator and JMS. Such mappings can be the basis for generators that read a middleware-independent model of an EAI solution and produce code and other artifacts specific to particular message-oriented middleware technologies (see Figure 2.11). Figure 2.12 and Figure 2.13 are fragments of a middleware-independent model of an EAI adapter for a back-end brokerage system.[10]

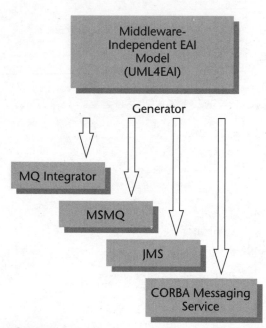

Figure 2.11   Mapping a middleware-independent model of an EAI solution.

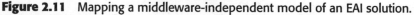

[9] [UML4EAI]

[10] Adapted, with permission, from [UML4EAI] Figures 123 and 124.

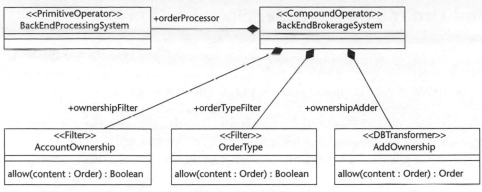

Figure 2.12 Middleware-independent EAI model (part 1).

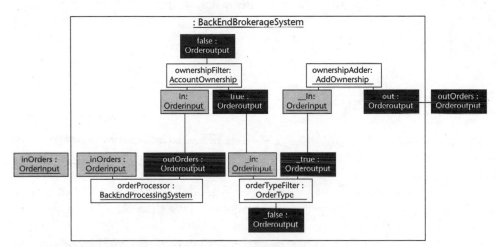

Figure 2.13 Middleware-independent EAI model (part 2).

The first draft of the UML Profile for EAI does not make entirely clear how to use the profile to create models that are sufficiently precise to drive generators. However, as this book goes to press, the standard is still in its official finalization phase and should shed light on this matter when it becomes officially available.

The Limits of Declarative Specification

For most kinds of systems, it is impossible to generate a complete implementation from a declarative model of the system. There are two ways to deal with this limitation. One is for programmers to enhance the generated code. The other is to raise the level of abstraction for imperative programming as well, which means defining a language for imperative programming whose abstraction level is higher than that of 3GLs.

Allowing programmers to enhance generated code complicates the synchronization of model and code. It raises questions such as: Are enhancements to the code reflected in the model? What happens to the programmer's enhancements when, inevitably, the model needs to be changed and code regenerated? The discussion about synchronizing models and code in Chapter 8 delves into these issues extensively.

UML has defined a language for abstract imperative programming called Action Semantics. UML models can include action statements that more fully specify a system implementation. Discussions of UML Action Semantics appear in several places later in this book.

Metadata Integration

As stated, middleware technologies such as EJB use declarative programming to replace some detailed 3GL coding. However, EJB's declarative XML-based component descriptors are not particularly well integrated with Java. Moreover, an EJB component may also have CORBA IDL that is used to expose the component as a CORBA object. In that case we have three languages that are used to describe different aspects of the component—Java, XML, and CORBA IDL. Furthermore, database schemas that describe the data that the component binds to are expressed in data-modeling languages. There are data-modeling languages for describing relational database schemas and different languages for describing multidimensional schemas. Object-relational mapping tools require additional resource-tier declarations that describe mappings between the enterprise tier and the relational schema. Furthermore, there may be UML models that describe the component as well.

Each of these descriptions constitutes metadata about the component. We express these specifications in disparate languages that we knit together on an ad hoc basis (see Figure 2.14).

The problem is *not* that we use different languages to describe different aspects of a component. It isn't realistic to expect that one language can describe all aspects of a system. The problem is that we have no overall architecture for integrating specifications made in different languages.

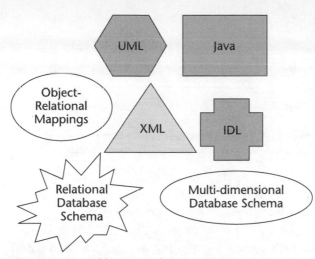

Figure 2.14 Ad hoc metadata integration.

One of the most important improvements that MDA brings to this picture is an architecture for managing metadata in an integrated fashion, even when the metadata is expressed in widely varying languages, as depicted by Figure 2.15.

Chapter 5 explores how the Meta Object Facility (MOF) uses model-based technology to support the managing of disparate metadata in a coordinated way. The basic idea is to define a formal model of each language. These models drive MOF-based metadata management facilities. MOF doesn't guarantee that the way an application developer combines different kinds of metadata for a specific purpose is sensible. However, it ensures that the means for accessing and manipulating the metadata is consistent.

UML	Java
XML	IDL
Object-Relational Mappings	Relational Database Schema
Multi-dimensional Database Schema	B2B Collaboration Descriptions

Figure 2.15 Coordinated metadata integration.

Metadata figures prominently in B2Bi, where descriptions of business services and collaborations at various levels of abstraction feed metadata-driven tools. MOF-based technology is being woven into the fabric of IBM's enterprise software offerings, into Oracle's data-warehousing products, and into the Unisys software product line.

MDA and Component-Based Development

MDA amplifies CBD's application of the principles of industrial production to software development by seeking to automate more of the process of developing components and of assembling applications from components.

The Herzum-Sims approach to CBD presages MDA by including design artifacts in the definition of the contents of a business component. Herzum and Sims understand that a component's reusability depends on more than technical pluggability. A component's design must be understood by those who intend to reuse it. While it's critical to package a component's runtime artifacts so that they can be deployed at runtime, it's also important to package the design artifacts so as to make them accessible to those who wish to reuse them.

With MDA, some of the models of a business component that were formerly viewed as design artifacts become highly formalized and acquire the characteristics of development artifacts. They drive generators that automate the production of the APIs for the workspace and enterprise tiers of a business component, and automate at least some of the implementation of the APIs as well.

Furthermore, in the MDA context, component implementations need not be fully generated prior to generating applications that use them. A possible scenario is as follows: The programmer reuses the models of components, declaring values for various component configuration parameters. The application generator produces customized components that satisfy the configuration parameters. The footprint of the component is kept to the minimum necessary to satisfy the customization requirements. This contrasts with a pre-generated component that contains all of the component's *potential* functionality. An MDA generator only needs to generate the *actual* functionality required by the configuration parameters.

Automatic Pattern Replication

MDA generators have the capacity to encapsulate knowledge of design patterns and apply them automatically. This strengthens the role that design patterns play in applying industrial production methods to software development.

A J2EE Example

For example, consider again the J2EE Value Object pattern. Recall that the basic idea of the Value Object pattern is to make it possible to get or set the values of multiple component attributes with only one remote invocation. Instead of having one object that has remote get and set operations for each attribute, the pattern uses multiple objects, including façade objects and Value Objects.

Having programmers apply this pattern over and over for each entity component can be tedious and error-prone. An MDA approach entails creating a platform-independent model (where platform = middleware) of the component that simply declares the attributes of the entity component. A generator then does the work of creating the multiple Java objects that the pattern requires, as illustrated by Figure 2.16. From the entity component attribute declarations, a generator can produce the following:

- The façade interface and a complete class that implements it
- A complete Value Object class
- The bean interface
- A skeletal class that implements the bean interface

Except for some of the bean implementation class, all of this code is completely mechanical. That is why a generator can automate its production. Furthermore, the Value Object pattern is not really Java-specific. A generator tailored to a different middleware target, such as .NET, can start with the same platform-independent model and replicate the pattern in a manner that makes sense for .NET.

The example in Chapter 8 includes automated replication of the Value Object pattern.

This kind of automated pattern replication is one of the benefits of raising the development environment's level of abstraction above the middleware and, as such, it improves all of the viability variables. It increases productivity by relieving programmers of the mechanical aspects of replicating the pattern, and it improves quality because it is less error-prone than manual replication. Finally, it improves longevity because of the PIM's portability, in that generators can replicate a pattern in somewhat different ways in different middleware environments.

Note that it is appropriate to employ some patterns at the PIM level. For instance, the Observer pattern, one of Gamma et al.'s most well-known patterns,[11] often captures real business semantics and thus properly surfaces, at least in simplified form, at high levels of abstraction. The Value Object pattern, on the other hand, is a more technical pattern that makes no contribution to describing the semantics of business logic.

[11] [GHJV 1995]

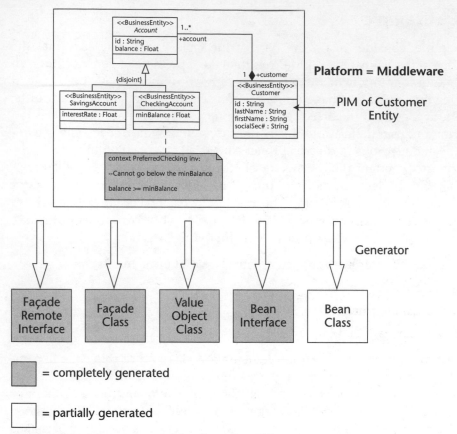

Figure 2.16   A generator applying the Value Object pattern.

Architectural Styles

Richard Hubert, in his important book *Convergent Architecture*,[12] coins the term *architectural style* to refer to a way of structuring systems, development processes, and tools that is dictated by an enterprise architecture. An architectural style determines, among other things, a coordinated set of design patterns.

MDA generators enforce architectural styles by replicating the design patterns automatically. This makes it easier to adhere to architectural principles when building and integrating systems. Programmers may have to fill in many details, but it can be very helpful to have tools enforce basic system structure.

[12] [HUBE 2002]

Pushing More below the Line

Automatic pattern replication illustrates MDA's effect on what lies above and below the water line. Recall that the water line analogy characterizes the application programmer's concerns as above the line, and those that the infrastructure handles as below the line.

MDA tends to push more system knowledge, such as knowledge of the Value Object pattern, below the line into a generator. The generator encapsulates the knowledge, along with knowledge of other patterns consistent with the enterprise's architectural styles (see Figure 2.17).

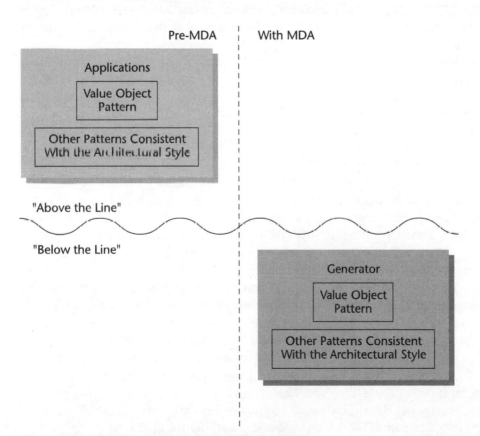

Figure 2.17   Pushing pattern knowledge below the line.

In practice, a generator's encapsulation of pattern knowledge might not be complete, especially during the early stages of applying MDA to enterprise computing. In our Value Object example, where the programmer has to manually enhance the code for the bean class, the development tools may not be smart enough to hide the rest of the code that reveals the pattern. Furthermore, unless tools are available for debugging at the model level, programmers have to see all the generated code in order to debug the system.

Model Driven Enterprise Architecture

UML out-of-the-box is not rich enough to support modeling the various tiers, middleware layers, and levels of granularity that are crucial to the separation of concerns in an enterprise architecture. A mature, model driven enterprise architecture requires distinct but coordinated modeling languages to support the formal specification of these aspects of enterprise systems at various levels of abstraction. UML profiling and the Meta Object Facility are the mechanisms for defining these languages.

The separation of modeling languages corresponds to the separation of concerns at the architectural level. Furthermore, we need languages not only for describing the functional characteristics of the various tiers of a system, but for defining nonfunctional aspects of systems as well, such as transactional behavior, security, and persistence.

Languages designated as platform-independent require mappings down to platforms. For instance, middleware-independent languages require mappings to specific middleware technologies such as J2EE, .NET, and CORBA.

Standards organizations are defining some of these languages and mappings. Enterprises will have to extend this work by defining their own languages and mappings, which satisfy their unique requirements. A model driven enterprise architecture must identify, define, and position languages and mappings in the overall architecture.

Standard and proprietary languages, mappings, and generators that implement the mappings form an important part of the infrastructure supporting a model driven enterprise architecture. Figure 2.18 indicates where these resources fall in terms of the above-and-below-the-line concept.

This book does not define a complete model driven enterprise architecture, and thus does not definitively specify languages and mappings. Instead, it concentrates—in Parts Two and Three—on explaining (1) the MDA technologies that support the definition of languages and mappings, and (2) the general principles that MDA-based languages and mappings share.

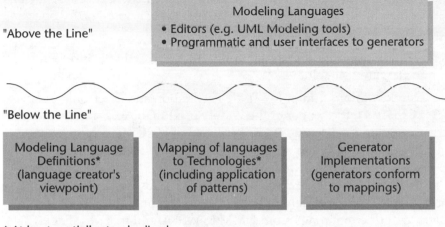

"Above the Line"

Modeling Languages
- Editors (e.g. UML Modeling tools)
- Programmatic and user interfaces to generators

"Below the Line"

| Modeling Language Definitions* (language creator's viewpoint) | Mapping of languages to Technologies* (including application of patterns) | Generator Implementations (generators conform to mappings) |

* At least partially standardized

Figure 2.18   MDA architectural resources, above and below the line.

Standardized MDA-Based Modeling Languages

The OMG has defined a standard language for data modeling, data warehousing, data transformation, and data analysis. This language is called the *Common Warehouse Metamodel.*[13] As we've seen, the database aspects of enterprise systems have been model driven for some time.

The Common Warehouse Metamodel (CWM) advances model-centrism by standardizing database modeling languages so that tools from different vendors can exchange data models, data transformation rules, and data analysis specifications. CWM makes such exchange possible even if vendors use their own proprietary GUIs for interactively displaying the models and rules to a user.

CWM is defined via the Meta Object Facility (MOF). Therefore, CWM-compliant data models and transformation rules constitute metadata that MOF-based metadata management facilities can handle in an integrated fashion, along with metadata that specifies other aspects of enterprise systems. We will return to CWM in Chapter 5 and Chapter 9.

---

[13] [CWM]

We've already mentioned a number of standardized UML profiles, such as the EJB, CORBA, and EAI profiles. There are some other noteworthy ones:

- The OMG's UML Profile for EDOC is a language for modeling component collaboration and business processes in a way that is independent of middleware technologies.[14]

- The United Nations Center for Trade Facilitation and Electronic Business (UN/CEFACT), the keeper of the widely used EDIFACT standard for electronic data interchange (EDI), is developing a UML profile for use with the ebXML B2Bi standards. The profile is called the *UN/CEFACT Modeling Methodology* (*UMM*). It supports specifying business information, business services, B2B collaborations, and business processes in a fashion that is independent of specific B2Bi technologies. There are plans to define mappings from UMM to WSDL and to EDI.[15] The RosettaNet B2Bi standards group is also planning to use UMM.

Some authors have published UML profiles that, while not standardized, address the modeling of specific aspects or kinds of systems. For example, Jim Conallen of Rational published a UML profile for modeling Web applications.[16] Although he doesn't use our tier terminology, he essentially covers the user and workspace (interaction) tiers of such applications.

Synchronizing among Multiple Tiers

As described earlier, programming the synchronization of the tiers in multi-tiered systems can be rather labor-intensive. Adding one attribute to the definition of a customer can ripple across all of the tiers of a system.

MDA can help with such synchronization by automating at least some of the ripple effect. Chapter 8's section on synchronizing models and code covers this topic in detail.

Middleware and the Abstraction Gap

Middleware is a key enabler of MDA because raising the level of abstraction of computing platforms makes the job of a generator easier.

Consider the task of writing a generator that processes the model fragment of Figure 2.1. If the generator has to produce machine code, it's harder to write than if it has to produce 3GL code. Similarly, if it has to produce 3GL code from scratch to implement basic services such as transactions, naming, security, and so on, it's more difficult to write than if the generated 3GL code can leverage middleware services.

---

[14] [UML4EDOC]
[15] [UMM]
[16] [CONN 2000]

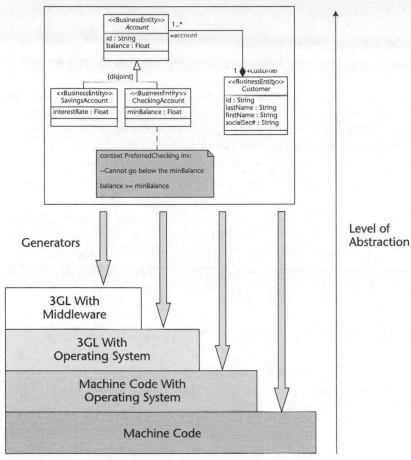

Figure 2.19   Middleware narrows the abstraction gap.

Thus, without middleware in the picture, MDA would be harder to implement. Figure 2.19 illustrates how middleware narrows the abstraction gap that the generator has to fill.

Design by Contract Revisited

Design by Contract (DBC) has not gained much of a following in the software development industry. As discussed, production pressures lead development groups to view this kind of rigorous design as too time-consuming to be practical.

Advocates of disciplined design techniques typically counter that, although such techniques take more time up front, they save time in the long run by producing software that has fewer problems and is easier to maintain. This argument usually fails to move development managers, who are in no position to dismiss the short-term pressures facing them.

MDA changes the terms of this debate. Since generators can use invariant rules and pre- and post-conditions to produce a good deal of the assertion-checking code, exception-handling code, and testing harnesses required to successfully complete a development project, Design by Contract in the MDA context can actually speed project completion. Invariants and pre- and post-conditions are now development artifacts rather than simply design artifacts, just as is the case with the models to which they belong.

Developers who are skeptical about MDA often relax when they realize that MDA uses highly formalized models. Lack of formality frequently is one of the factors that turns them off to modeling. Formal modeling that includes Design by Contract, with a mathematically precise constraint language such as UML's OCL, is less likely to alienate someone with a development background.

MDA and Other New Development Approaches

There are some design and development methodologies that have garnered staunch supporters in recent years. Thus, it is worth considering the relationship between these approaches and MDA.

Interactive Design

Alan Cooper, the father of Interactive Design, decries the lack of design in software in his book *The Inmates Are Running the Asylum*.[17] He focuses on the interaction of software with human users and points out that the lack of design in the way software interacts with human beings has resulted in computer-based products that are far too difficult to use. In that context, he states, "End-product interaction design is the only part of the design that I want to take away from programmers and put into the hands of dedicated interaction designers."

Following Cooper's lead, I go further: Programmers also should not be defining the fundamental business behavior of software modules that *don't* interact with human beings. Some software modules talk only to other software modules, a phenomenon that is spreading due to the move toward componentization, Web Services, and B2Bi. As we have seen in our B2Bi example, many such modules have basic business behavior that has nothing to do with the details of specific technology platforms.

[17] [COOP 1999]

For another example, in which the required business behavior is less obvious, consider an accounts receivable component whose API provides an operation to perform an end-of-month roll over. The operation rolls 120-day balances over to collections, 90-day balances to 120, 30-day balances to 60, and new invoices to 30 days. These rules are fairly routine, yet there are also rules that differ among businesses. In some businesses it's critical to run all new invoices through invoice processing before starting the end-of-month roll over, whereas in others it's not vital. If the rule hasn't been specified, the programmer might make a unilateral decision that turns out to be wrong. The programmer may not realize how crucial the decision is. For a Web Service, clearly specifying the contract is even more critical, as the client has no way of knowing the assumptions behind the operation.

This fundamental business behavior does not depend on whether it is actually implemented via CORBA, EJB, IMS, or something else. An accounts receivable business expert should specify this fundamental behavior, not a programmer. Yet programmers who are not qualified to do so sometimes make these kinds of business decisions because the requirements specification is sparse and informal. Failure to make and capture such decisions in the appropriate place means that the decisions will be made in inappropriate places—in the mind and the code of the programmer. Formal models using techniques such as Design by Contract capture the decisions so that they are readily accessible to human auditing and to generators.

Extreme Programming

At first glance, many people assume that MDA and Extreme Programming (XP) are opposing approaches to software development. This reaction rests on the assumption that models are merely design artifacts and on the fact that XP places more emphasis on development artifacts than on design artifacts.

However, formal models that drive generators and virtual machines are development artifacts that fit the XP scheme quite well. For example, a key XP practice is pair programming—that is, programmers always work in pairs. This practice can be applied to the creation of formal models. The models are development artifacts, so, in an XP shop, those who create them should work in pairs. We can extend the XP principle of common code ownership to include common ownership of formal models. MDA is also in synch with XP's rejection of waterfall development processes, since MDA assumes iterative development. In this manner we can readily extend most of the principles of XP for the MDA context.

XP also advocates delaying design decisions as much as possible because factors that influence the design change rapidly. Thus, XP advocates that it is ideal to put off working out aspects of a design until just before it is time to program those aspects of the system. To some extent MDA accommodates this approach, since designing a component of a system in a way that is abstracted from implementation does in a sense defer detailed implementation decisions. However, in iterative development all levels of abstraction are revisited frequently, so abstraction is not really deferral in the XP sense.

There is also a danger that the practice of delaying design can be taken as a license to develop software without architecture. This may work for individual applications, but it does not scale up to developing enterprise-scale systems that encompass many applications and components.

Summary

Model driven approaches to database and GUI development have been entrenched in enterprise computing for some time. MDA builds on this and other gains made in enterprise computing by bringing a model driven approach to the intermediate tiers of enterprise systems and to EAI and B2Bi.

Major aspects of MDA's impact on enterprise computing include:

- Raising the level of abstraction of the programming environment
- Using formal models that drive code generators and also raise the bar of engineering discipline
- Integrating metadata based on different specification languages
- Encapsulating pattern knowledge in generators
- Generating components on demand
- Using Design by Contract to drive generation of assertion checking, exception handling, and testing harnesses

UML, UML profiles, and the Meta Object Facility (MOF) make up an extensible MDA modeling language environment. A mature model driven enterprise architecture must include properly positioned standardized and company-specific MDA-based languages. It also must include mappings from those languages to technologies of concern.

MDA extends Interactive Design's notion of putting interaction design in the hands of interaction experts. It does so by putting the specification of business semantics in the hands of business experts.

MDA is compatible with XP in many respects, although the two will diverge if XP is misused by an IT shop as an excuse to avoid defining a real enterprise architecture.

PART

Two

The Base MDA Technologies

Several bodies are defining standards that form the base upon which MDA will be constructed and that are gradually being implemented in the industry. This part of the book looks at these technologies in some detail and provides some insights into how to use them effectively.

CHAPTER 3

The Role of UML in MDA

This chapter provides an overview of the role that the Unified Modeling Language (UML) plays in MDA. Rather than provide a primer on the basics of UML, I refer the reader to the many books on the subject.[1] However, subsequent chapters delve into specific UML topics that are particularly important for MDA.

Origins and Evolution

As object-oriented analysis and design (OOAD) techniques spread during the early 1990s, the OOAD industry balkanized into three camps, roughly corresponding to the followers of Grady Booch, Ivar Jacobson, and Jim Rumbaugh. Each had its own notation, methodological approaches, and tools.

In the late 1990s the camps merged to create UML. The merger began when Rational Software Corporation brought Rumbaugh and Jacobson into the company to join Booch. The three pioneers—now known as the "three amigos"—wrote the first UML specification. Later, they decided to submit UML to the Object Management Group (OMG) for standardization.

---

[1] For an excellent and concise UML primer see [FOW 1997].

UML has become a widely used standard for object-oriented modeling. UML tools are available from a number of vendors. The OMG now owns the UML trademark and logo and manages the standard's evolution.

As of this writing, the current version of UML is 1.4. There may be one more minor revision in the UML 1.X[2] series before UML 2.0 takes shape. When this book refers to features of UML, the reference is to UML 1.X unless otherwise stated.

Strengths

This section outlines some of the key features of UML that help support MDA.

Separation of Abstract Syntax from Concrete Syntax

Early versions of UML focused mostly on the graphical notation, specifying the semantics (meaning) of the various graphical shapes and lines. More recent versions include a formal model of UML's own semantics. This model defines the concepts that UML modelers use and associates them with an *abstract syntax* rather than with the syntax of the graphical notation. The graphical notation is a concrete syntax for expressing the abstract syntax. Other concrete syntaxes are possible.

This formal model of UML is referred to as the *metamodel* of UML. We can think of a metamodel as a model of a model. A model of a bank includes elements named Account, Customer, Fund, and so on because these are the things that make up a bank. A model of a model includes elements named Class, Attribute, Operation, Parameter, Association, and so on because these are the things that make up a model. A metamodel models those things that constitute models as shown in Figure 3.1, which is part of the abstract syntax for the UML metamodel. Notice that the abstract syntax looks like an ordinary UML class model, except for the fact that the names of the elements refer to UML concepts rather than user concepts such as accounts and customers.

To understand how the metamodel works, consider how it models an operation. `Operation` has a set of properties, some of which it inherits from its parent, `BehavioralFeature`, and some from more distant ancestors. (Because of space limitations, the diagram doesn't show all of `Operation`'s properties). The sum total of these properties are what the metamodel allows you to say logically about an operation, regardless of whether you say it graphically or by some other means.

For example, the `visibility` property, which `Operation` inherits from `Feature`, has the possible values `public`, `private`, `protected`, and `package`. The graphical notation expresses visibility in a model by prepending a plus (+) symbol to the operation name (indicating that the operation is public), a

---

[2] "UML 1.X" means all versions of UML that precede UML 2.0.

minus sign (indicating that it is private), a pound sign for protected, or a "~" for package. For example, +UpdateInvoices() denotes a public operation.

However, the OMG also defines an XML syntax (based on XMI) for expressing UML models. This XML syntax encodes the value of the visibility property for an operation as a word, such as public, private, and so on. The OMG is developing a more human-friendly textual syntax to complement the graphical and XMI syntaxes.[3] The JCP and OMG have also defined how to represent UML models as Java objects or CORBA objects.

The key to this flexibility is the fact that the metamodel defines UML's modeling properties in terms of abstract syntax and semantics. As long as you have a consistent way to encode values of these properties in some concrete technology, you can describe models in terms of UML's semantics.

The metamodel describes the semantics of the modeling constructs via informal text and formal constraints. The descriptions of the semantics of the visibility property hold regardless of the concrete syntax used to encode values of the property in models.

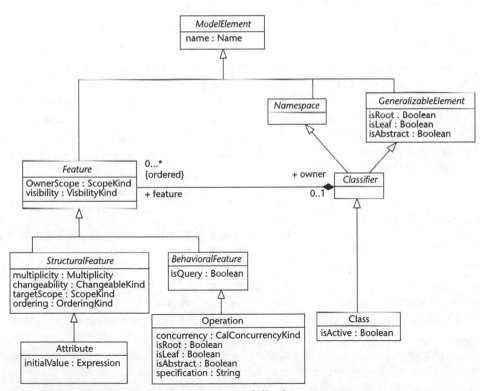

Figure 3.1 A fragment of the UML metamodel's abstract syntax.

Adapted, with permission from [UML], figure 2-5.

[3] [HUTN]

The following is a fragment of the metamodel[4] that describes the semantics of the `visibility` property in informal English:

Visibility Specifies whether the Feature can be used by other Classifiers.

Visibilities of nested Classifiers combine so that the most restrictive visibility is the result.

Possibilities include:

- *public—Any outside Classifier with visibility to the Classifier can use the Feature.*
- *protected—Any descendent of the Classifier can use the Feature.*
- *private—Only the Classifier itself can use the Feature.*
- *package—Any Classifier declared in the same package (or a nested subpackage, at any level) as the owner of the Feature can use the Feature.*

The following excerpt is another fragment that expresses a constraint about the visibility property in informal English and formally using UML's Object Constraint Language (OCL):

```
The visibility of the Method should be the same as for
the realized Operation.
self.visibility = self.specification.visibility⁵
```

The clear separation of concern between abstract syntax and concrete syntax is a major strength of UML and is a key requirement of MDA. It means that UML models encoded in a particular concrete syntax are not inextricably bound to that concrete syntax. From the standpoint of MDA, it is the properties of a model that matter most, not the layout of the diagrams used to visualize the model nor the particular way the model is encoded in an XML document.

We explore the subject of metamodels, abstract syntax, and concrete syntax more fully in Chapter 5.

Extensibility

Another UML strength is that it has built-in extension mechanisms that allow the creation of specialized, UML-based languages called *UML Profiles*. As mentioned previously, the ability to define specialized languages for various aspects of systems is one of the key requirements for an MDA environment, with each language supporting the specification of a particular aspect of a system. This is UML profiling's contribution to MDA.

As also mentioned, when one defines a profile, it's common MDA practice to also define mappings that specify how to transform models conforming to

---

[4] Reused, with permission, from [UML], p. 2-37.
[5] Reused, with permission, from [UML], p. 2-62.

the profile into artifacts appropriate to the kinds of systems that the profile addresses. For example, a UML profile for modeling distributed components in a middleware-independent fashion suggests the need for a mapping that defines how to transform a model expressed via that profile into artifacts appropriate for EJB, .NET, and/or CORBA. Generators implement such mappings.

Chapter 6 describes UML's profiling mechanisms in more detail.

Support for Platform-Independent Modeling

UML, by its nature, supports the creation of system specifications that are platform-independent, yet formal and precise enough to drive generators.

In Chapter 2, I established that platform independence is a relative concept that means independence from some specific execution and development domains. Thus, when one uses the term, the context must be set by specifying the domains from which independence is being asserted. I adhere to this principle by stating that, within the remainder of this book, when we use the term platform-independent, I mean independent of the following:

- Information-formatting technologies, such as XML DTD and XML Schema

- 3GLs and 4GLs, such as Java, C++, C#, and Visual Basic

- Distributed component middleware, such as J2EE, CORBA, and .NET

- Messaging middleware, such as WebSphere MQ Integrator (MQSeries) and MSMQ

This particular level of abstraction has a special role to play because it is essentially one rung above the level of abstraction of today's mainstream development environments. As we've seen, raising the level of abstraction for development tends to improve all of the viability variables.

One way in which UML supports formal, platform-independent modeling is by making it possible to separate the specification of semantics from the specification of implementation.

For example, aggregation makes it possible to directly express concepts related to object grouping and ownership, such as specifying that a well-formed invoice must have a header and a collection of line items, and that the header and line items are owned by the invoice and thus must be deleted if the invoice is deleted. UML can specify this requirement formally, succinctly, and declaratively, without specifying how to implement it. Figure 3.2 expresses this requirement via the strong variant of aggregation known as *composite aggregation* or sometimes simply as *composition* (described briefly in Chapter 2).

As we've also seen, invariants, pre-conditions, and post-conditions that are platform-independent can be expressed in UML.

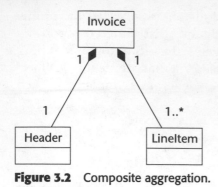

Figure 3.2 Composite aggregation.

UML's extensibility also contributes to support for platform-independent modeling. The profiling mechanisms can define customized languages specifically geared to platform-independent modeling. Chapter 6 and Chapter 8 provide an example of a profile for the platform-independent modeling of distributed components.

Maintained by a Standards Organization

The fact that UML is not a proprietary technology is one of its strengths. UML's basis as a standard enables the marketing of different but complimentary UML tools that users can combine to tailor their development environments.

A profile that a third party develops can plug into a UML tool that supports the UML profiling mechanisms. Associated generators also take advantage of standards. Because there are standards for concretely representing UML models as XML documents, Java objects, and CORBA objects, generators can use those representations to read models that are inputs to transformations. Therefore, generators can plug into UML environments as well.

A profile or set of profiles, along with an associated generator or generators, constitutes a *modeling framework*. Standards make the notion of pluggable modeling frameworks a reality.

For instance, a development team might combine one vendor's generic UML modeling tool with modeling frameworks from other vendors. One vendor may offer a modeling framework for the security aspects of a system, another for financial systems, and so forth.

In theory, a de facto standard established by a major company could also serve as a basis for a Model-Driven Architecture. In the case of UML, however, companies willing to expend the resources to influence UML's direction can do so via the OMG.

It's worth noting that the adoption of UML as an OMG standard was a milestone for the OMG, marking the first time that the organization adopted a standard that was not based on CORBA.

Weaknesses

While UML has many good qualities, it also has a number of limitations that affect its role in MDA. Some, but not all, of these shortcomings will likely be addressed by UML 2.0.

To be fair, some of the limitations that observers cite are actually limitations of tools that purport to implement UML, rather than limitations of the specification. However, the management of UML by a standards body, cited as a strength in the preceding section, is also a weakness. The development of the standard has at times been only loosely connected to the development of products that implement the standard. As a result, there are parts of UML that cannot be implemented efficiently, and there are few, if any, tools on the market that implement UML exactly as specified. We summarize below some of the problems with the specification that have the most impact on MDA.

Large and Poorly Partitioned

The UML metamodel is large, with concerns not well separated. The interdependencies are too numerous and are hard to trace. Thus, it is difficult, if not impossible, to use just one part of UML without the interdependencies pulling in more than what is actually needed for the purpose at hand.

The XMI-based XML DTD that is the OMG's official XML-based concrete syntax for UML[6] reflects this problem. It's difficult to use part of it without pulling in other parts by reference that are not truly semantically related.

A practical ramification of this problem arose in the course of the drafting of the ebXML standards. ebXML is a B2B commerce standards body supported by the United Nations and OASIS. It defines a profile of UML activity models for defining business processes. It specifies that business process models can be exchanged using the OMG's XML DTD for UML. However, encoding business processes as UML activity models in a manner that can be validated against the DTD is complicated because of the large and complex nature of the DTD. The part of UML, and therefore of the DTD, that supports activity models is not well separated, so it's not possible to use just the apparently relevant part of the DTD. Thus, the encoding is problematical from a practical standpoint. For this reason, ebXML specified a second DTD that focuses exclusively on the semantics of business processes.[7] The encoding it mandates is more straightforward.

---

[6] [UML], Chapter 5.
[7] [BPSS]

Weak Support for Viewpoints

It's possible to create different viewpoints of a UML model, but the metamodel and notation provide no *direct* support for viewpoints, such as allowing a modeler to indicate which viewpoint or viewpoints include a particular model element. Thus, it's not possible for a UML tool to support viewpoint filtering in a standardized fashion.

Not Current with Industry Developments in Components and Patterns

UML is behind the curve on some key advances in software, particularly with respect to components and patterns.

The UML notion of a component is fairly primitive. It's possible to create profiles that provide basic support for modeling components such as EJBs or that support more abstract component concepts, but the results are not entirely satisfactory.

UML supports patterns to some extent via UML templates and collaborations, but support could be more robust.

Vagueness about Relationships

Despite the fact that UML provides some powerful high-level modeling constructs, it's vague about some basic things.

For example, it says little about the actual semantics of aggregation and whole-part relationships in general. Its sister standard, the Meta Object Facility (MOF), had to define the semantics in order to define various technology mappings. In my earlier examples using composition (strong aggregation), my description of the semantics is actually drawn from MOF. Chapter 7 covers the semantics of aggregation in more detail.

UML is incapable of distinguishing between topological inclusion—that is, something being inside something else temporarily—and something being a part of something.[8] Furthermore, there is a substantial body of knowledge about relationships that UML ignores, such as the ISO's General Relationship Model.[9]

Limitations of Profiling

UML's extensibility mechanisms are quite restrictive. Both the typing mechanism for new language constructs defined by profiles and the ability to define relationships among such constructs are very limited.

---

[8] [U2 DSTC]

[9] See [GRM]. Also see [UML4EDOC], Chapter 3, section 6 for a UML profile that provides some limited enhancement to UML's relationship constructs, based on the General Relationship Model and the work of Haim Kilov and James Ross [KR 1994].

Therefore, despite the fact that UML supports the definition of new modeling constructs to some extent, without MOF it would be insufficient for MDA.

Misalignment of UML and MOF

UML and MOF, which are sister standards, both defined by the OMG, are subtly out of synch with each other. This causes problems for vendors trying to build MDA tools based on these standards and can complicate matters for users, as well. Chapter 6 and Chapter 9 delve into this issue.

Lack of Standard Diagram Interchange

UML does not define a standard way for tools to exchange diagrams created with its graphical notation. This is the case because it has no metamodel for diagrammatic information.

Thus, if one tool wishes to export a UML model to another tool, it can export the semantic properties of the model in a standard way but not the graphical properties.

For example, consider Figure 3.2 again. UML defines a standard way for different tools to exchange the semantic properties of this model, which specify that an invoice is a strong aggregation of one header and one or more line items. All the element names, multiplicities, and relationships can be exported in a standard fashion. However, it isn't possible to export, in a standard way, the fact that there is a particular diagram that provides a view of the semantic information (one in which the invoice box is above the header and line item boxes, with the association lines drawn at specific, symmetrical angles to the boxes). Thus, a modeler using a tool that imports the model may have to manually reconstruct the diagram.

Generators that transform models into other artifacts do not need the diagrammatic information. They require only the semantic properties. Regardless of how powerful MDA tools become, however, from a practical perspective people will still have a role to play in constructing models and in using human judgment as to the best way to arrange model elements in diagrams. The investment made in creating model diagrams is therefore too important to be lost so easily.

Lack of a Metamodel for Object Constraint Language

UML's Object Constraint Language (OCL) is a crucial element in UML's support for Design by Contract. Yet UML has no metamodel for OCL. Thus, although OCL has a concrete syntax, it has no abstract syntax.

There is therefore no way for tools to exchange abstract syntax trees (that is, parse trees) for OCL expressions in a standard fashion. The importing tool must have a parser that understands the concrete syntax. This will not scale when multiple, specialized tools collaborate in the context of MDA.

In addition, there are subtle differences between the semantics of OCL and the semantics of UML. These differences create challenges for tool vendors seeking to compile or interpret OCL expressions to enforce semantic consistency in UML models.

Future Directions

UML 2.0 will fix some of the flaws that I have pointed out. Others may persist for some time.

UML 2.0

In 2000 and 2001, the OMG issued a series of four Request for Proposals (RFPs) for UML 2.0. As of this writing, the OMG has received initial submissions for all four.

UML 2.0 Infrastructure.[10]   The UML 2.0 Infrastructure RFP mandates:

- More modular packaging and refactoring of inheritance hierarchies in the metamodel in order to make it easier to reuse parts of UML without reusing other parts

- Improvements in the extension (profiling) mechanisms

- Correction of the misalignment between UML and MOF

UML 2.0 Diagram Interchange.[11]   The UML 2.0 Diagram Interchange RFP mandates the definition of a mechanism by which tools can exchange diagrammatic information.

UML 2.0 Object Constraint Language.[12]   The UML 2.0 Object Constraint Language RFP mandates the definition of a metamodel for OCL.

UML 2.0 Superstructure.[13]   The UML 2.0 Superstructure RFP calls for upgrades to the language not covered by the other, more tightly focused UML 2.0 RFPs.

Expected Outcomes

UML 2.0 is likely to yield at least adequate solutions to some of the problems that we have described. However, its final shape is still uncertain. Some of the problems we cited, as well as a number of others that we have not mentioned, will persist. Submitters are working hard on improving support for components,

[10] [U2 INFRA]
[11] [U2 DIAG]
[12] [U2 OCL]
[13] [U2 SUPER]

patterns, and whole-part relationships, but as of this writing it's still too early to tell what the results will be. In the case of some of the RFPs there are competing submissions that take different approaches.

The uneven progress of UML is probably inevitable given the pull of competing forces on it. As I have said, MDA will not sweep the industry overnight. The speed at which UML improves, both as a set of formal specifications and as a technology realized in commercial development tools, will be an important factor in determining the pace at which MDA advances.

What You Can Do Now

As we shall see in subsequent chapters, UML is not the only language that MDA employs. However, quite a bit of MDA technology will use UML. It's a good idea to ensure that development personnel are conversant with UML. They should also understand that there is a trend toward using UML models as engineering artifacts that contribute directly to development, rather than using them only as design artifacts.

Summary

UML arose as a compromise between three major object-oriented modeling languages. Its greatest strengths, from the standpoint of MDA are:

- It separates abstract syntax from concrete syntax.
- It is not one fixed language but, rather, supports the definition of extended UML languages called profiles.
- It makes it possible to raise the level of abstraction for software development.
- It is managed by an open standards body.

Some noteworthy UML weaknesses are:

- The metamodel has too many unnecessary cross-dependencies among its elements.
- It has weak support for viewpoints.
- UML and MOF, which should be tightly coordinated, are somewhat out of synch with each other.
- There is no standard way for tools to exchange diagrams.

The UML 2.0 initiative underway in the OMG will address many of UML's shortcomings, although it will take some time to play out and for commercial implementations to appear.

CHAPTER 4

Beyond Basic Class Modeling

A significant number of UML modelers use UML for class modeling exclusively and even then do not use the full power UML offers for class modeling. From an MDA perspective, this approach to modeling is limited in some important ways. This chapter provides some insights into the territory that lies beyond basic class modeling.

Design by Contract

Most software has features that few people use. This is true for UML tools in that many people use only a fraction of UML's power. In some cases, the non-use of a UML feature is the result of lack of support by tools. However, there are reasonably well-supported but often-unused UML constructs that are crucial for exploiting UML's ability to express specifications. The most important of these is a set of constructs that support Design by Contract (DBC).

The Basics

As explained earlier, DBC involves writing two basic kinds of constraints:

Pre-conditions and post-conditions.   A pre-condition for an operation must be true when the operation is invoked. A post-condition must be true when the operation is finished executing.

Invariants.   An invariant is an assertion about the state of a system that must always be true.

UML fully supports writing these kinds of constraints. Tool support is somewhat uneven, but generally it's possible to work around the limitations.

An Example

Consider the simple UML class model shown in Figure 4.1. Many UML modelers would consider this fragment to be quite complete within its limited scope. The attributes of ARProcessor and ReceivablesAccount are spelled out. The multiplicities of the associations between Receivables Account and Invoice are specified.

However, from the perspective of DBC, if the model stops there, it is only 50 percent complete at best. The model as is tells us little about the expected behavior of ARProcessor's operations; it only specifies the operations' signatures, that is, the types of its parameters. It fails to express the constraint that an invoice cannot be both unprocessed and processed. In sum, the model is semantically thin.

Now, consider the enhancement of the simple model by the declaration of invariants, pre-conditions, and post-conditions, as delineated in Figure 4.2. In the example that uses OCL in Chapter 2, I placed the constraints in notes attached to the associated model elements in the class diagram. That is not always practical because it clutters the class diagram. Different tools have different user interfaces for entering constraints. Here I simply write them out as text.

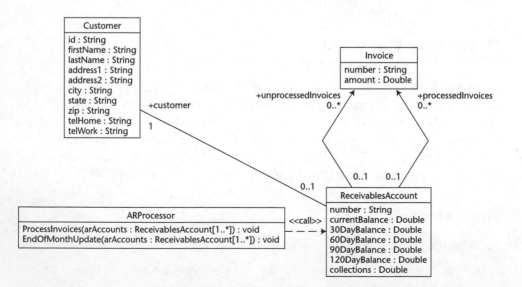

Figure 4.1 Simple UML class model.

```
-----------------------------------
--ReceivablesAccount invariants
-----------------------------------
--An invoice cannot be both unprocessed and processed.

context ReceivablesAccount inv:

   unprocessedInvoices->intersection(processedInvoices)->isEmpty ()

--An invoice number must be six characters in length.

context ReceivablesAccount inv:

   self.number->size () = 6

-----------------------------------------------
--ARProcessor::ProcessInvoices pre-conditions
-----------------------------------------------
--There must be some unprocessedInvoices.

context ARProcessor::ProcessInvoices (arAccounts : Set
(ReceivablesAccount)) pre:

   arAccounts->forAll (unprocessedInvoices->notEmpty () )

-----------------------------------------------
-- ARProcessor::ProcessInvoices post-conditions
-----------------------------------------------

--unprocessedInvoices become processedInvoices.

context ARProcessor::ProcessInvoices (arAccounts : Set
(ReceivablesAccount)) post:

   arAccounts->forAll
   (
     unProcessedInvoices->isEmpty () and
     processedInvoices->includes (unprocessedInvoices@pre)
   )
-----------------------------------------------
--ARProcessor::EndOfMonthUpdate pre-conditions
-----------------------------------------------
--There are no unprocessed invoices.

context ARProcessor::EndOfMonthUpdate (arAccounts : Set
(ReceivablesAccount)) pre:

   arAccounts->forAll (unprocessedInvoices->isEmpty () )
```

Figure 4.2 Design by Contract enhancements to the simple model. *(continues)*

```
--------------------------------------------------
--ARProcessor::EndOfMonthUpdate post-conditions
--------------------------------------------------
--For all of the ARaccounts the following holds:
   --The Collections value is its previous value plus the previous
120DayBalance and
   --the 120DayBalance is the previous 90DayBalance and
   --the 90DayBalance is the previous 60DayBalance and
   --the 60DayBalance is the previous 30DayBalance and
   --the 30DayBalance is the previous currentBalance
   --the currentBalance is 0.

context ARProcessor::EndOfMonthUpdate (arAccounts : Set
(ReceivablesAccount)) post:

   arAccounts->forAll
   (
      -- @pre modifies an identifier to refer to the value it had
      -- before the operation executed.
      currentBalance = 0 and
      30DayBalance =  currentBalance@pre and
      60DayBalance =  30DayBalance@pre and
      90DayBalance =  60DayBalance@pre and
      120DayBalance = 90DayBalance@pre and
      Collections = collections@pre + 120DayBalance@pre
   )
```

Figure 4.2 Design by Contract enhancements to the simple model. *(continued)*

I've written the constraints in English and, more formally, in OCL.[1] Note that in OCL two consecutive hyphen characters ("--") denote a comment. If you're not familiar with OCL, you should be able to decipher it by first reading the English rendition of the assertion, then reading the OCL.

The OCL references properties of the model. Specifically, it uses a <ClassName.AttributeName> syntax to refer to an attribute and a <ClassName. AssociationEndName> syntax to refer to something that is linked to a class through an association. Thus a model's class names, attribute names, and association end names (also sometimes called *role names*) are the declared identifiers to which OCL expressions can refer. Misspellings of these identifiers are errors, just as is misspelling an identifier in a traditional programming language.

[1] For a comprehensive treatment of OCL, see [WK 1998]. The formal OCL specification is part of the UML specification; see [UML], Chapter 6.

Tools are starting to appear that validate OCL against a model, and some have generators that transform the OCL into executable constraint-checking code. Marking the English renditions of the constraints as comments prevents tools from rejecting them.

Constraints have two fundamental purposes:

- Spelling out corner cases that are unacceptable
- Expressing key semantics of the class or operation to which they apply

For example, the `ReceivablesAccount` invariant, stating that an invoice cannot be both unprocessed and processed, rules out a corner case.

On the other hand, the post-conditions for the `ARProcessor::End OfMonthUpdate` operation express, in a platform-independent fashion, the fundamental logic of the operation, such as the fact that current balances need to be rolled over to 30 day balances.[2] This reflects a business rule.

Similarly, the pre-condition for `ARProcessor::EndOfMonthUpdate` that there should be no unprocessed invoices reflects a business rule. Technically, you could construct a software system that would perform an end of month update prior to processing all invoices generated during the month. A business could even be organized to allow it. However, the business that *this* software supports does not allow it.

UML supports the declaration of constraints for any element in a model, be it an operation, a class, an attribute, an operation parameter, or any other type of model element. In practice, as long as a tool supports pre-conditions, post-conditions, and invariants for classes, DBC can be practiced without serious restriction. A constraint on an attribute can always be written as a constraint on the class that owns it. For example, in Figure 4.2 the second invariant is actually a constraint on the `number` attribute of the `ReceivablesAccount` class, but I phrased it as a constraint on the class.

Contracts, Reuse, and Interoperability

A UML class model that declares invariants, pre-conditions, and post-conditions for its classes and operations is more precise and rigorous than one that does not. In the sample model, the constraints nail down the properties of the classes without predetermining platform-specific techniques for implementing them.

Our DBC-enhanced model quite precisely specifies usage contracts for `ARProcessor` and `ReceivablesAccount`. These contracts are relevant to clients and to generators.

---

[2] The *@pre* suffix in the post-conditions modifies an identifier to refer to the value it had *before* the operation executed.

Modeling without DBC is like a civil engineer specifying that a junction box is needed without a formal blueprint that states which electrical lines will run through it. The blueprint forces the civil engineer to connect all the dots for the contractor, and, crucially, the process of creating the blueprint exposes flaws in the general design. Similarly, writing OCL in terms of the properties of the model connects the dots for generators and programmers and flushes out design flaws.

The more precisely a class's properties are specified, the easier it is to reuse the class. Object-oriented and component-based development promise reuse as a major advantage. Yet developers often find reusing an object or component difficult without access to its source code because its usage contract is not well specified.

Furthermore, it's difficult to achieve interoperability among components developed by different companies, even when the components support standardized interfaces, messages, and protocols, unless there is a good understanding of the contract that implementations of an interface must honor. This has important ramifications for interoperability efforts such as the Java Community Process, the OMG, and various B2Bi initiatives.

The level of interoperability is based on the degree of shared understanding among the interoperating objects and components. *Syntactic interoperability* is the ability of a set of objects to coordinate their activities based on a shared understanding of the syntax—that is, the signature—of requests and messages that flow among them. Remote request protocols such as CORBA's IIOP permit a client and server, though residing in dramatically different environments, to have a shared understanding of the signature of the operation. For example, in Figure 4.3 the client and server have a shared understanding that the first parameter is an unsigned integer and that the second is an unsigned, double-precision floating point number. CORBA ensures syntactic interoperability, that is, that the values transmitted between client and server will pass through all the transport layers and emerge in the correct form.

Semantic interoperability, on the other hand, is the ability of a set of objects to coordinate their functioning based on a shared understanding of the semantics—that is, the meaning—of the requests and messages that flow among them. Syntactic interoperability is a necessary pre-condition for semantic interoperability.

Protocols such as transaction protocols rely on semantic interoperability. There is a shared understanding of the semantics of a commit, abort, rollback, and other such messages that are part of the protocol (see Figure 4.4). B2Bi collaboration protocols will rely on semantic interoperability as well.

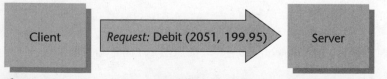

Figure 4.3   Syntactic interoperability—shared understanding of syntax.

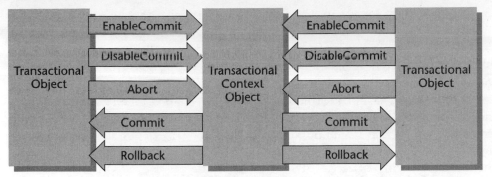

Figure 4.4 Semantic interoperability—shared understanding of semantics.

Formal, DBC-based contracts improve semantic interoperability, regardless of the degree of automation used to produce the software that honors the contracts. Hence, DBC can make an important contribution to B2Bi's scalability.

A good deal of B2Bi use will be among parties whose human languages (for example, English, French, and so on) are different. Mathematically precise contracts are less subject to misinterpretation than is informal text, even among parties who speak the same language. We will not be able to do away entirely with informal text as part of contracts. However, we can reduce our dependence on it considerably.

As Precise as Programming[3]

Who writes the constraints? It's not reasonable to expect a business domain expert to write OCL. The business expert knows the business rules, but a technical person, working with the business expert, creates a precise, DBC-based model.

DBC constraint writing in a formal language like OCL is a form of coding. The coding is more abstract than traditional programming because it omits many implementation details that 3GL code would include. But, at its level of abstraction, this new kind of coding is no less precise.

Precision and detail are not the same. If you find this hard to fathom, consider an electric motor that a company manufactures and sells to other companies for use inside mixers, juicers, and other household appliances. The companies that buy the motors might not care about their internal workings, which are not part of the contract. They only care about the characteristics that affect a motor's interaction with the rest of the appliance, such as its horsepower at various rotational speeds, the physical dimensions of the motor's outer casing, the strength of the electromagnetic field when it operates, and so forth.

[3] Kilov and Ross speak of "making analysis as disciplined as programming." [KR 1994], p. xv.

A specification for the motor could be very precise at that level of abstraction, while not being very detailed with regard to the insides of the motor. In other words, it might specify the horsepower, physical dimensions, and field strength to a high level of precision, while suppressing detail about the motor's insides.

As mentioned earlier, abstraction is the suppression of irrelevant detail. It is not a license to be vague. Thus, a model that is at a higher level of abstraction than a 3GL program need not be imprecise.

Constraints and Exceptions

Many of the exceptions for operations can be inferred directly from DBC constraints. An operation pre-condition maps directly to a specific exception to be raised when the operation is invoked and the pre-condition is not satisfied. Invariants declared for a class map to exceptions that should be raised when the invariant is not satisfied. UML out of the box does not define the point in time when the invariants should be checked. A UML profile may define a point in time for checking invariants, or it may provide a way to specify when they should be checked. The more frequent the invariant checking, the more expensive such validation becomes.

Tools are emerging that generate code that checks at runtime whether invariants and pre- and post-conditions expressed in OCL are satisfied. They need to provide options, on a global and per constraint basis, as to when the invariants should be evaluated. For example, in business systems, it is apt to be less expensive to evaluate invariants only when ACID transactions are being started and committed than to do so upon every operation invocation.

A Framework for Quality

DBC also provides a framework for quality assurance (QA). The pre-conditions, post-conditions, and invariants represent a good deal of what QA engineers must validate. As mentioned earlier, DBC constraints can drive a generator that produces test harnesses that exercise the system and test whether the constraints are satisfied. Even when not used to automatically generate test harnesses, DBC constraints provide value as precise guides to QA engineers regarding what they must test.

There are additional nonfunctional factors, such as scalability and performance, that are not covered by DBC assertions based on business rules, but DBC gives QA a significant head start. UML extensions for such nonfunctional aspects of a system can be used to enrich a system specification further and drive the generation of additional validation code.

DBC and UML Tools

Figure 4.2's linear, textual layout of all the assertions for the model is not the only way to capture invariants and pre- and post-conditions. UML tools typically have dialogs for classes and operations, with slots for inserting constraints. Tools that follow the UML metamodel fastidiously actually have slots for inserting constraints for any model element.

Some tools have neglected to provide slots for all three kinds of DBC constraints. Vendors that use constraints as input to generators usually supply plug-ins for such tools to provide a well-defined way to enter constraints.

Overcoming Barriers to Use

Even modelers who are aware of the extent of UML's support for DBC often don't use it. Yet for anyone with a modest programming background, OCL is not difficult to learn. In addition, MDA tools are starting to include editing assistants for building OCL expressions. These are similar to the editing assistants for 3GL code that Integrated Development Environments (IDEs) provide, and may even include context-sensitive graphical model browsers to help developers locate the model elements they need to complete an expression under construction. The learning curve is therefore not the problem.

The primary barrier is the amount of time it takes to practice DBC conscientiously. As we have discussed, the production pressures on software development projects discourage the use of rigorous but time-consuming engineering techniques. As mentioned earlier, with MDA DBC promises to be a time*saving* technique, since generators elaborate each formally declared constraint into many lines application and testing harness code.

Without MDA, DBC addresses only the quality variable in the viability equation. With MDA, it addresses the cost of production variable as well.

Another Look at Constraints

Everything expressed formally in a model is actually a constraint. A class declaration containing a set of attributes constrains instances to support those attributes. Multiplicities on relationships constrain the number of class instances that can be linked in an association. Designating an association as a composition constrains the lifetime of a component not to extend beyond the lifetime of the composite to which it is linked.

In this sense, OCL is not special. It is used for declaring constraints, as are all constructs that UML makes available for defining a model. OCL is special only in the sense that it provides a means for declaring constraints that UML's other modeling constructs can't express.

Behavioral Modeling

Class models that use DBC do a very thorough job of delineating the usage contract that class implementations must honor. However, they do not describe the flow of control and state changes *inside* the code that implements the contracts. They also do not say much about how sets of objects interact with each other to perform tasks.

For this reason, UML officially calls class models *static structure models* as distinguished from *behavioral models*. What UML refers to as behavioral models includes state machine models, activity models, use case models, and interaction models. In a sense, a DBC-based class model does describe behavior when it specifies pre- and post-conditions for operations, but it confines itself strictly to aspects of behavior that are interesting to a client.

In this section, I provide a high-level survey of the different forms of UML behavioral modeling and comment briefly upon the role these forms can play in MDA.

The portions of this book that examine MDA implementation issues in some detail overwhelmingly emphasize static structure modeling for two reasons. One is that I have more MDA implementation experience using static structure modeling. The other reason is that industry standards for MDA have progressed more with respect to static structure modeling. The MOF technology mappings described in Chapter 5 all concern the transformation of MOF models, which are static structure models.

However, behavioral modeling is at least as important to MDA as static structure modeling. Some of the most advanced industrial MDA work is based mainly on behavioral modeling. Shlaer-Mellor-based systems, for example, have used state machine models for some time to generate embedded code for machinery ranging from photocopiers to complex telecommunications switches. Similarly, activity graphs have been used for some time to specify workflow systems.

My lean treatment of this subject is not intended to demean its value. I leave it to others to explore the subject of MDA and behavioral modeling in depth.

State Machines

State machine models can be roughly divided into two categories. The first kind of state machine deals with the state transitions of public class attributes, that is, attributes that are visible to the client and thus are part of the contract. Such state machines are usually called *protocol state machines*. If the class model is DBC-based, then all of the information in this kind of state model should also be available in the class model. In such a case, the state model doesn't add anything to the client-visible contract other than a different representation of the same information.

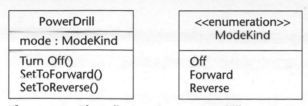

Figure 4.5 Class diagram for a power drill.

The simplistic class diagram for a power drill shown by Figure 4.5 and the associated protocol state machine in Figure 4.6 illustrate this point. The state machine apparently provides information that the class model does not. In particular the state machine says that, while transitions directly from Off to Forward, Forward to Off, Off to Reverse, and Reverse to Off are permitted, there can be no direct transition from the Forward mode to the Reverse mode nor vice versa.

If Figure 4.5 were the sum total of the power drill class model, we could say that the state machine diagram provides additional information that is relevant to the client. As we have seen, however, a DBC-based class model contains extra declarations, namely invariants and pre- and post-conditions. Figure 4.7 is a complete set of pre- and post-conditions for the PowerDrill class's operations. These constraints are logically equivalent to the information in the state machine diagram.

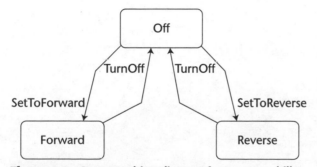

Figure 4.6 State machine diagram for a power drill.

```
-------------------------------------
--PowerDrill::TurnOff pre-conditions
-------------------------------------
--The drill must be in Forward or Reverse mode.

context PowerDrill::TurnOff () pre:

    self.mode = ModeKind::#Forward or self.mode = ModeKind::#Reverse


------------------------------------
--PowerDrill::TurnOff post-conditions
------------------------------------
--The drill is off.

context PowerDrill::TurnOff () post:

    self.mode = ModeKind::#Off


----------------------------------------
--PowerDrill::SetToForward pre-conditions
----------------------------------------
--The drill must be off.

context PowerDrill::SetToForward () pre:

    self.mode = ModeKind::#Off


-----------------------------------------
--PowerDrill::SetToForward post-conditions
-----------------------------------------
--The drill is in Forward mode.

context PowerDrill::SetToForward () post:

    self.mode = ModeKind::#Forward


----------------------------------------
--PowerDrill::SetToReverse pre-conditions
----------------------------------------
--The drill must be off.

context PowerDrill::SetToReverse () pre:

    self.mode = ModeKind::#Off


-----------------------------------------
--PowerDrill::SetToReverse post-conditions
-----------------------------------------
--The drill is in Reverse mode.
```

Figure 4.7 Pre- and post-conditions for the `PowerDrill` class model.

```
context PowerDrill::SetToReverse () post:

  self.mode = ModeKind::#Reverse
```

Figure 4.7 Pre- and post-conditions for the `PowerDrill` class model. *(continued)*

Thus, a protocol state machine—the kind that deals with the state of public class attributes—is merely another representation of information that a proper DBC-based class model already provides. This does not mean that this kind of state model isn't valuable. The visual metaphor of a state diagram is often more easily constructed, grasped, and modified than textually expressed constraints.

Note, however, that protocol state machines can't express *all* information that DBC constraints can because DBC constraints can be more complex than what a state model can convey. In particular, an invariant or pre- or post-condition can make assertions about state pertaining to more than one object. For example, a post-condition for invoice processing can assert state changes in a receivables account *and* in a general ledger account. State models express information about the state of one object only.

The second category of state machine deals with state that is not visible to the client. There may be states and state transitions going on *inside* our power drill. For instance, the gear mechanism may be interested in the state of the motor. However, the drill *user* only cares about the Off, Forward, and Reverse states, as well as how to change from one of these states to another. State models that deal with internal state are relevant to implementation designers and to programmers who must implement the design in 3GL-centric development environments. State models can also be input to generators. Therefore, although they are irrelevant to the client contract, they can play an important role in MDA.

Both types of state machine models can include constraints called *guards*. They express constraints on the permissibility of a state transition. Guards can be expressed via OCL.[4]

Activity Models

Activity models are basically flowcharts, specifying the flow of control among *activities*. We saw some examples of activity models in Chapter 2. Activity models have two basic uses: One is to express the flow of control inside the

---

[4] [WK 1998], Section 4.1.4

implementation of an operation. The other is to express business processes and workflow. Thus, activity models have uses at different levels of granularity, which we can think of as micro- and macrolevels.

- At the microlevel, the flow of control inside an operation's implementation constitutes inner workings that are not relevant to a client. Microlevel activity models have typically been used to provide good, detailed specifications to programmers, but can be processed by generators if it they are formal enough. There are some robust products on the market that feature generators that process such activity models.

- At the macrolevel, a business process or workflow expressed as an activity model may be used for communication among human beings, may provide input to a generator, or in some cases may be directly executed by a virtual machine. In an executable activity model, the activities are executable modules whose contracts and implementation are modeled elsewhere. Products that directly execute activity models describing workflows have been available for some time, and products that directly execute activity models describing business processes are starting to appear, particularly in the B2Bi and EAI space.

Interaction Models

Interaction models describe how several objects interact with each other to perform a task. There are two kinds of interaction diagrams. One is called a *sequence diagram* and the other a *collaboration diagram*. The two kinds of diagrams provide different ways to convey similar information.

In some cases and from certain viewpoints, interactions are an implementation detail best hidden from sight. In our accounts receivable example, a client of an ARProcessor that invokes the EndOfMonthUpdate operation should not be interested in the fact that the operation is performed by sequentially invoking operations on some helper objects. From the viewpoint of the ARProcessor, however, the specification of such interactions is relevant.

On the other hand, an interaction model can describe a protocol whereby a request from a customer to a vendor for a price quotation is answered by a quotation that, in turn, is answered by an acceptance, a counteroffer, or a rejection. This kind of interaction is relevant to both parties.

An interaction model can provide guidance to a programmer, or can drive a generator if it is formal enough. Currently, interaction models don't provide enough information to support the generation of complete implementations for most kinds of systems. Additions to the interaction model semantics proposed for UML 2 will most likely address this shortcoming by allowing modelers to describe conditional execution and loops.

Use Case Models

A *use case* is a description of the behavior of a part of the system in terms of its interaction with human and computerized actors. A *use case model* describes the relationships between use cases and actors and among use cases themselves. One use case may be an extension of another or may include another.

Some of the better-known software development methodologies center around use cases. For example, in the *Unified Process* each use case represents a task. Each use case's realization is described by an interaction model that specifies how objects interact to accomplish the task. Class models describe the contracts of the collaborating objects, and state machines and activity models describe the implementations.[5]

It should be noted that some methodologies are not use case driven and some do not employ use cases at all. Some start with class models and look upon interaction models, state machines, and activity models as refinements of the class models. Some start with interaction models.

Generally, use case models are not input to compilers. Rather, their purpose is to make the overall structure of a system intellectually manageable for human beings. Tools can use them to generate skeletal interaction models, however. Tools can also maintain traceability links between use cases and the artifacts that describe their implementations, and can use these links to provide limited forms of synchronization.

Action Semantics

The OMG recently completed work on the UML Action Semantics specification.[6] It defines a metamodel for an action language. Unlike OCL, which is basically restricted to declarative assertions, action semantics expressions describe imperative—that is, dynamic—behavior.

This new specification creates a standard way to use UML to describe dynamic actions completely, increasing the potential to generate complete implementations from UML models.

Action languages have existed for some time. They have been used mostly for real-time and embedded systems development. Although they haven't been used much for enterprise systems, the advent of the UML Action Semantics standard makes the action language approach more attractive in the enterprise arena.

The Action Semantics standard does not define a standard concrete syntax for action statements. Standardization of the abstract syntax in the metamodel makes it possible for tools to exchange models containing action statements even if they use different concrete syntaxes. However, the lack of at least one standard concrete syntax may restrain the degree of penetration that the standard achieves.

[5] [JBR 1999]
[6] [ACTION]

What You Can Do Now

Make sure that your development groups understand that models that do not formally declare known constraints are incomplete. If development pressures force constraint declaration to be skipped, everyone should understand exactly what is being glossed over. As tools come online that use models to automate system production, groups that have produced models with precise semantic declaration will be best positioned to take advantage of the productivity boost such tools offer.

Some groups that practice modeling are very class-model-oriented and some are more oriented toward behavioral modeling. Managers should expose their staff to the broad range of different kinds of formal modeling that industry standards now support.

Summary

Abstraction is the suppression of irrelevant detail. Raising the level of abstraction does not mean lowering the level of precision. From an MDA standpoint, class models that don't use UML's Design by Contract (DBC) facilities are insufficiently precise.

Syntactic interoperability is a necessary but insufficient condition for widespread B2B commerce. Semantic interoperability, which DBC enhances, is required.

A generator can use invariants, pre-conditions, and post-conditions in order to produce:

- Assertion-checking code
- Exception-handling code
- Testing harnesses

While development managers have tended to see DBC as a quality improvement design technique they can't afford, MDA casts DBC constraints in the role of development artifacts that not only improve quality, but also improve productivity.

Class models are called "static structure" models in UML parlance. State, activity, interaction, and use case models are called "behavioral" models. This book focuses mostly on static structure models, but behavioral models are at least as important.

UML Action Semantics defines the abstract syntax for an action language that supports putting imperative—as opposed to merely declarative—expressions in UML models. Action Semantics makes it possible to produce UML models that generators can use to produce complete implementations.

CHAPTER 5

The Meta Object Facility (MOF)

The Meta Object Facility (MOF) is a sister standard to UML, maintained by the same standards organization, the OMG. This chapter explains the roles it plays as a foundation for MDA and as an application of MDA to the domain of metadata management.

A Key MDA Foundation

As we mentioned earlier, the ability to define specialized languages appropriate for the various aspects of systems and for different abstraction levels is key for MDA. We also explained that MOF and UML profiling are MDA's language definition mechanisms. MOF is more fundamental to MDA because even UML is defined via MOF.[1]

Figure 5.1 is a fragment of the abstract syntax of the UML metamodel that we saw in Chapter 3. This particular fragment defines some of the

---

[1] MDA experts know that it is a slight oversimplification to say that UML is defined via MOF. In fact, UML has two metamodels. One is what the UML specification calls the "logical" metamodel, and the other is called the "physical" metamodel. The physical metamodel is defined via MOF and is the metamodel to which MOF technology mappings are applied. UML 2.0 will probably have just one metamodel, which will be defined via MOF. I don't use the terms "logical" and "physical" to describe metamodels.

class-modeling constructs. We mentioned earlier that the UML metamodel defines the abstract syntax of UML, from which many concrete syntaxes can be derived, but we did not mention that MOF is the language used to define the UML metamodel.

A metamodel uses MOF to formally define the abstract syntax of a set of modeling constructs. In other words, with MOF we define such constructs formally. A metamodel also specifies some semantics informally via natural language. We call the combination of these formal and informal definitions a *MOF metamodel*. Sometimes in the industry a MOF metamodel is referred to simply as a "MOF model."

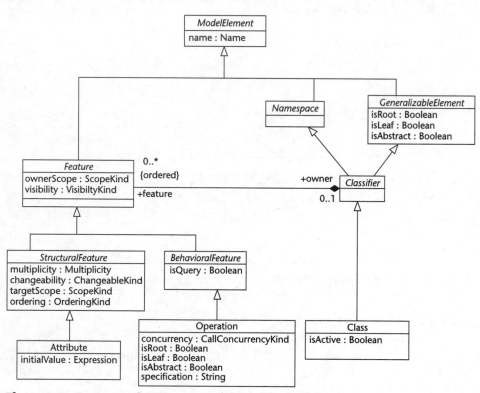

Figure 5.1   Fragment of UML metamodel for class modeling.

A Basic Premise

The OMG ratified MOF in 1997. MOF proceeds from the basic premise that there will be more than one kind of model and therefore that there must be more than one modeling language.

I have already established that we need different sets of modeling constructs for different functions. The set of modeling constructs we need for relational data modeling includes table, column, key, and so on. The set of modeling constructs we need for workflow includes activity, performer, transition, split, join, and so on. The set of modeling constructs we need for UML class modeling includes class, attribute, operation, association, and so on. The set of modeling constructs we need for defining CORBA interfaces includes interface, valuetype, and so on.

So in order to describe a particular kind of model we have to describe the set of modeling constructs that make up models of that kind. The MOF architects understood a crucial point that has also been understood by ontology experts for some time, namely that it is useful to have a consistent means to describe language constructs.

The MOF architects saw that the industry was using completely different means for describing the nature of different kinds of modeling constructs. For example, the mechanisms used to express the fact that a table owns its columns were different from the mechanisms used to express the fact that an object-oriented (OO) class owns its operations.

The architects rejected the idea of trying to merge these different sets of modeling constructs into one set, because that would entail merging all languages into one. So they decided to define a universal way to *describe* the different kinds of modeling constructs. This would result in a common way of describing the properties of and relationships among the modeling constructs that make up a given kind of model.

MOF is that universal way of describing modeling constructs. MOF has been used to describe the modeling constructs used by relational data models. It has been used to describe the modeling constructs used by UML class models. It has been used to describe the constructs used for other kinds of modeling as well.

Borrowing from UML

MOF borrows OO class-modeling constructs from UML and presents them as the common means for describing the abstract syntax of modeling constructs, that is, for defining a metamodel's abstract syntax. Thus, MOF metamodels look like UML class models, and you can use UML class-modeling tools to create them. With MOF, you model a modeling construct as a class and the properties of the construct as the attributes of the class. You model the relationships between constructs as associations. You use OCL to increase a metamodel's precision. It's all very UML-like.

The fact that MOF can support the definition of diverse modeling constructs for different domains is evident from looking at the abstract syntax of some of the other metamodels that the OMG has standardized.

Figure 5.2 is a part of the abstract syntax for the OMG's *Common Warehouse Metamodel (CWM)*. CWM actually contains quite a number of metamodels. We'll focus on CWM later, but here we look at a fragment of CWM's relational data metamodel just to get a feel for the shape of it. It defines familiar classes of relational modeling constructs such as table and column and defines the associations among those classes. Table, column, and so forth are the constructs used to specify data models. The CWM metamodel defines their abstract syntax and semantics.

Figure 5.3 shows a part of the abstract syntax for the metamodel for the OMG's *CORBA Component Model (CCM)*. The part shown covers the extensions to IDL that CCM defined. CCM is very similar to EJB except that it is programming-language-independent, and it has some capabilities that EJB does not have.

Figure 5.4 exhibits a portion of the abstract syntax for the metamodel for state charts that is part of the UML metamodel. State charts are different from class models, and thus this fragment of the UML metamodel is different from the part that covers class modeling that we saw in Figure 5.1.

These metamodels are diverse because they describe the constructs that make up different kinds of models. However, they have an important commonality—they are all defined using MOF's UML-like modeling constructs. For example:

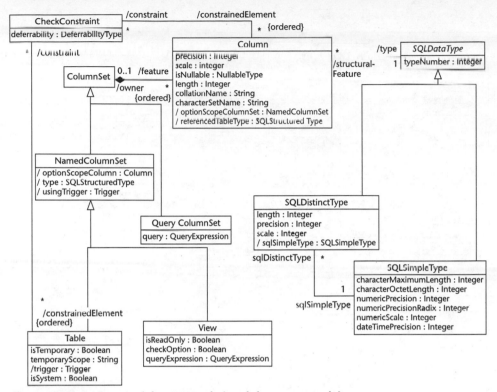

Figure 5.2   Fragment of the CWM relational data metamodel.

Reused with permission from [CWM], Figure 9-3.

- The UML metamodel for class modeling uses composite aggregation (black diamond) to express the fact that a *BehavioralFeature* (such as an operation) owns its parameters.

- The CWM relational data metamodel uses composite aggregation to express the fact that a table owns its columns.

- The CCM metamodel uses it to say that a home owns its factory and finder operations.

- The UML state chart metamodel uses it to convey that a state transition owns the actions that are defined as effects of the transition.

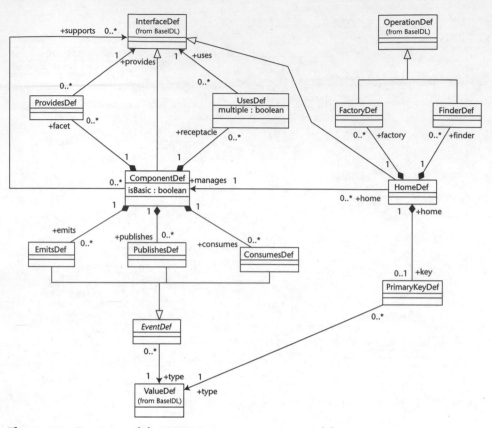

Figure 5.3 Fragment of the CORBA component metamodel.
Reused with permission from [CCM], figure 2-13.

All of the metamodels use subclassing to express the fact that certain constructs have common properties. They also all use attributes, ordinary (nonaggregation) associations, and association navigability. All of these meta-modeling constructs are familiar to UML modelers.

Note that the UML metamodel specification makes a distinction between abstract syntax and OCL-based constraints, putting them in separate sections of the document.[2] I, however, consider OCL that specifies constraints on a metamodel's elements to be part of the abstract syntax because it is expressed formally and thus can be used by a generator.

[2] [UML], chapter 2. UML 2.0 may eliminate the distinction.

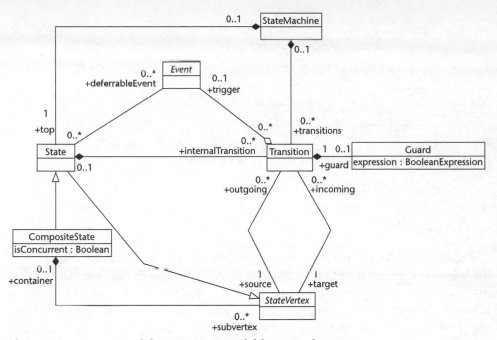

Figure 5.4 Fragment of the UML metamodel for state charts.

Adapted with permission from [UML], figure 2-24.

MOF Isn't Just for OO

MOF's constructs for defining metamodels, having been borrowed from UML, are object-oriented (OO). However, they can be used to define non-OO metamodels.

When you use UML to make class models, you can use OO-style subclassing, but this is not a consequence of the fact that the UML metamodel is defined via MOF. It is a consequence of the fact that subclassing constructs are explicitly defined in the UML metamodel.

Figure 5.5 is a simple metamodel for simple data modeling. It uses MOF's subclassing capability to capture the fact that `Table` and `Column` have a name attribute in common. It does this by defining `Table` and `Column` as subclasses of a common superclass[3] containing a `name` attribute. The key point is that, despite the fact that the metamodel uses OO-style subclassing to define the `Table` and `Column` constructs, a conforming data model cannot subclass a definition of a `Table` or `Column` because the metamodel does not specifically define what subclassing would mean for a data model.

[3] The italicization of the name of the superclass indicates that the class is abstract. The implications of abstract classes for generators are examined in Chapter 7.

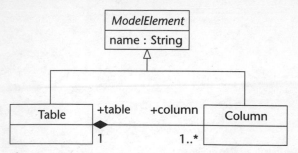

Figure 5.5 Using MOF subclassing to define a metamodel.

Figure 5.6 and Figure 5.7, on the other hand, show a further enhancement of the metamodel that says that a table can have superclasses and subclasses. Figure 5.7 uses OCL to declare an invariant that nails down the fact that a table inherits the columns of its superclasses. This metamodel supports OO-style subclassing of tables. Note that if the multiplicity on the superClass end of the new association were 0..1, then the metamodel would support single inheritance but not multiple inheritance.

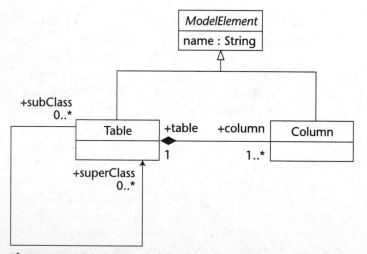

Figure 5.6 Using MOF to define subclassing in a metamodel.

```
--A Table inherits the columns of its superClasses.

context Table inv:
   superclass.column->forAll
      (superClassColumn | self.column->includes (superClassColumn) )
```

Figure 5.7 Invariant refining the definition of subclassing.

There is nothing sacred about the names subClass and superclass in the enhanced metamodel. I could just as well have named these association ends child and parent or subType and superType or specialization and generalization. The existence of these properties, regardless of their name, plus the inheritance invariant, are what make this metamodel support OO-style subclassing of tables.

There are other ways to define OO subclassing. The UML metamodel uses the term *generalization* and defines Generalization as a full-blown class rather than as the name of an association end.[4] Again, it is only the fact that the metamodel explicitly *defines* subclassing that makes it *support* subclassing.

Thus, it is perfectly legitimate to define a MOF metamodel that does not support subclassing but that uses MOF subclassing to define itself. This is important because there are many kinds of models that do not support subclassing or other object-oriented mechanisms. A key architectural goal of MOF is to support highly varied kinds of modeling, including non-OO modeling.

Abstract Syntax Trees

Traditional compilers decode a specification written in a concrete syntax, create a parse tree corresponding to the specification, use the parse tree to generate code, and discard the parse tree.

A metamodel's abstract syntax tells tools how to construct abstract syntax trees to represent models of the kind defined by the metamodel (see Figure 5.8). Just as there are many possible models that conform to a given metamodel, there are many possible abstract syntax trees that conform to a given abstract syntax.

---

[4] The UML metamodel also defines a class named GeneralizableElement, but that detail is not important to this discussion.

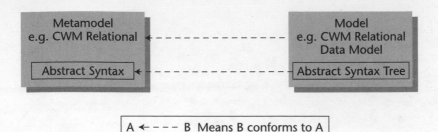

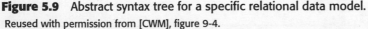

Figure 5.8 Abstract syntax and abstract syntax trees.

Because MDA uses MOF to define abstract syntax, and because MOF's constructs for describing abstract syntax are similar to UML's constructs for class modeling, we can use UML object diagrams to roughly visualize an abstract syntax tree.

Figure 5.9 is a UML object diagram showing instances of the constructs that CWM defines for relational data modeling that we saw in Figure 5.2. We can consider Figure 5.9 to be a depiction of the abstract syntax tree for a particular data model.

We shall return to the subject of abstract syntax tress shortly.

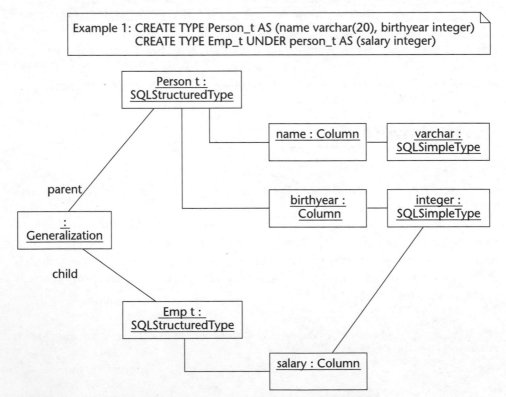

Figure 5.9 Abstract syntax tree for a specific relational data model.

Reused with permission from [CWM], figure 9-4.

Metalevels

MOF architecture conceives of four "metalevels." In order to be MDA literate, you should be conversant about these levels. They are named M3, M2, M1, and M0, as seen in Table 5.1. (This table is duplicated on the last page of the book for easy reference.)

Level M3

Level M3 is MOF, whose elements are the constructs MOF supplies for defining metamodels. These elements include Class, Attribute, Association, and so on. Conceptually there is only one MOF. Some call MOF the *meta-metamodel* because it is essentially the model of what a metamodel is. The double meta can be confusing, but the term is technically correct. If you find "meta-metamodel" awkward to manage intellectually, simply think of MOF as the set of constructs used to define metamodels.

Table 5.1   MDA Metalevels

METALEVEL	DESCRIPTION	ELEMENTS
M3	MOF, i.e., the set of constructs used to define metamodels	MOF Class, MOF Attribute, MOF Association, etc.
M2	Metamodels, consisting of instances of MOF constructs	UML Class, UML Association, UML Attribute, UML State, UML Activity, etc.
		CWM Table, CWM Column, etc.
M1	Models, consisting of instances of M2 metamodel constructs	Class "Customer," Class "Account"
		Table "Employee," Table "Vendor," etc.
M0	Objects and data, i.e., instances of M1 model constructs	Customer Jane Smith, Customer Joe Jones, Account 2989, Account 2344, Employee A3949, Vendor 78988, etc.

Level M2

Level M2 is populated by metamodels defined via the MOF constructs. We have seen a number of these metamodels, including standardized ones such as UML, CWM, and CCM, as well as some simplistic ones we used as examples. These metamodels' constructs are defined using MOF `Class`, MOF `Attribute`, MOF `Association`, and so on. Thus, M2 constructs are actually instances of M3 constructs. In other words, the constructs defined by metamodels are instances of the MOF constructs, as illustrated in Figure 5.10.

Level M1

Level M1 is populated by models that consist of instances of M2 constructs. Figure 5.11 uses a UML object diagram based on our simple data metamodel of Figure 5.10 to provide an example of an M1 model consisting of instances of M2 constructs. The instance model portrays a data model that defines a table named `Employee` with three columns named `Number`, `Name`, and `Address`. The table is an instance of the metamodel's M2 `table` element, and its columns are instances of the metamodel's M2 `Column` element. The links between the `Employee` table and its columns are instances of the M2 association between `Table` and `Column` defined in the metamodel.

So, `Employee` (M1) is an instance of `Table` (M2), which is an instance of MOF `Class` (M3).

`Address` (M1) is an instance of `Column` (M2), which is an instance of MOF `Class` (M3).

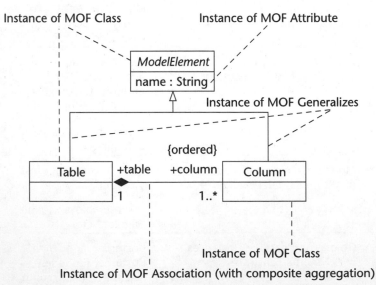

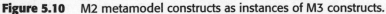

Figure 5.10 M2 metamodel constructs as instances of M3 constructs.

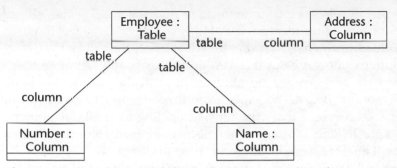

Figure 5.11 M1 data model elements as instances of M2 data metamodel elements.

The link between `Employee` and `Address` (M1) is an instance of the meta-model's association between `Table` and `Column` (M2), which is an instance of MOF `Association` (M3).

If you're thinking that this looks like an abstract syntax tree, you're right. I'll address that shortly.

Level M0

Level M0 is populated by objects and data, which are instances of M1 elements. Using our data model example, consider employee number A3949, named "Susan Smith," with address "111 Main St. USA." This is an M0 element that is an instance of the M1 element `Employee`.

So, this particular employee (M0) is an instance of `Employee` (M1), which is an instance of `Table` (M2), which is an instance of MOF `Class` (M3).

The employee's number, A3949, is an instance of `Number` (M1), which is an instance of `Column` (M2), which is an instance of MOF `Class` (M3).[5]

How Meaningful Are Metalevels?

From a certain point of view, the metalevels are arbitrary. After all, if we use a UML tool to construct an M2 MOF metamodel with classes such as `Table`, `Column`, `View`, and so on, and then use the tool to construct an M1 UML class model with classes such as `Customer`, `Account`, and so on, the tool may not understand the difference in the metalevel of the two models.

---

[5] Some MOF practitioners maintain that the instantiation relationship between M0 and M1 elements is fundamentally different from the instantiation relationships between M1 and M2 elements and between M2 and M3 elements. This argument is based on the observation that M0 elements represent real-world elements, whereas the elements at other levels only represent models of the real world.

This view of metalevels has led some to claim that absolute metalevels are completely arbitrary and thus meaningless. However, despite the fact that this is true in some theoretical sense, there are practical issues that make the designation of absolute metalevels helpful in certain contexts. You will note that I refer to the absolute metalevels a number of times in the rest of this book because doing so makes it easier to explain certain concepts. It also turns out that there are special concerns that arise when modeling accounts, customers, and so on that typically don't surface when modeling tables, columns, classes, and so forth. We'll analyze some of these concerns in Chapter 7.

On the other hand, there are circumstances in which there are distinct technical advantages to treating the absolute metalevels as arbitrary. We encounter one such case later in this chapter.

Self-Description

If M0 elements are instances of M1 model elements, M1 model elements are instances of M2 metamodel elements, and M2 metamodel elements are instances of M3 elements—that is, instances of MOF elements—then what are the MOF M3 elements instances of? Do we need an M4? If we define an M4, what would the M4 elements be instances of? Do we need an M5? Does this have an end?

The answer is that M3 is the end of the line. The levels stop there because the MOF M3 elements are instances of the M3 MOF elements. In other words, the MOF uses the MOF to describe itself. In technical terms, the MOF is *self-describing*. The MOF defines a MOF-compliant model of its own constructs. This model is often called *"the"* MOF Model. "The" MOF Model is subtly distinct from any arbitrary MOF metamodel. It is a MOF metamodel of MOF. Figure 5.12 shows a fragment of its abstract syntax.

I explore some of the implications of self-description later in this chapter.

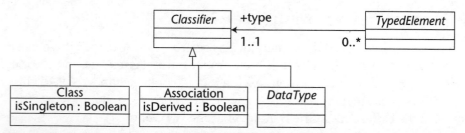

Figure 5.12 A fragment of "the" MOF Model's abstract syntax (for MOF 1.4).

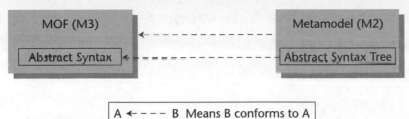

Figure 5.13   M3, M2, and abstract syntax.

Metalevels and Abstract Syntax

We can also look at the relationships between the various metalevels using the concepts of abstract syntax and abstract syntax trees. Since M3 defines an abstract syntax for metamodels, a particular metamodel at M2 can be represented as an abstract syntax tree in terms of that abstract syntax (see Figure 5.13). Because of MOF self-description, "the" MOF Model can be represented as an abstract syntax tree in terms of that abstract syntax as well (see Figure 5.14).

On the other hand, we have already seen (see Figure 5.8) that the abstract syntax tree that represents a metamodel at M2 is the abstract syntax for a domain of conforming M1 models. Thus, what is an abstract syntax from the viewpoint of one metalevel is an abstract syntax *tree* from the viewpoint of another metalevel. For example, the abstract syntax of the CWM relational metamodel is an abstract syntax tree from the viewpoint of M3.

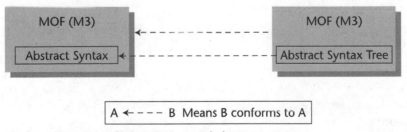

Figure 5.14   M3, self-description, and abstract syntax.

Model Driven Metadata Management

MOF's significance goes beyond metaprogramming. Along with some related standards, MOF is also the basis for a model driven metadata management architecture.

What Is Metadata?

A software development organization that uses MDA will accumulate many models. In addition to UML models and MOF metamodels, companies also must maintain data models; data transformation rules; CORBA and COM interfaces, expressed in CORBA IDL and Microsoft IDL; APIs[6] expressed as C# or Java interfaces; descriptions of Web services, expressed via WSDL and SOAP; and models of processes, expressed via RosettaNet, ebXML, and so on. All of these models are metadata.

Originally the term metadata strictly meant "data about data." It referred to data models, that is, database schemas. The information that describes the format of a database record, such as the names, types, and lengths of each of the columns in a customer record, is of a fundamentally different character than the rows of customer records that contain values for each of the columns. The database industry was, therefore, one of the first communities to distinguish between data and metadata in everyday practice.

This distinction and the term metadata have now expanded to include the kinds of models mentioned above:

- A UML model of customer and account classes is fundamentally different from actual instances of those classes. Therefore, we consider it to be metadata.

- A UML model of an executable business process or workflow is different from an actual executable process or runtime workflow instance. Therefore, we consider it to be metadata.

- Data transformation rules are not the customer and account records themselves; they are an extended form of metadata concerning those records.

- APIs expressed via Microsoft IDL, CORBA IDL, C#, Java, WSDL, and so on are models of services rather than the actual services. Therefore, they are metadata.

The metadata term now also encompasses various kinds of standardized and proprietary product configuration information, such as component packaging and deployment descriptors and product tuning parameters.

---

[6] I use the terms *interfaces* and *APIs* interchangeably.

Volume and Value

A good deal of the newer kind of metadata is buried in source code files, and thus is not as readily accessible as the traditional forms of metadata. Much of the value of MDA is in capturing this metadata in an explicit form that can be used to automate development. We already have a proliferation of source code files and rely on tools to manage them that do not understand the semantics they contain.

Companies are still in the early phases of amassing these newer kinds of models. However, they have been accumulating data models for quite some time, so a look at the volume of data models in today's Global 1000 companies should give us some idea of the magnitude of the metadata explosion that we face. It is not uncommon for a large company's data models to contain *tens of thousands* of columns.

Thus, we are dealing with serious amounts of metadata, even before we start adding other, newer kinds of models. MDA increases the volume of explicitly captured metadata available to an enterprise because of its use of multiple models for various levels of abstraction and for different aspects of a system.

At the same time, the new metadata spawned by MDA is of high *value*. UML models for MDA don't simply enhance human understanding; they also drive generators that produce other models, 3GL code, and XML, and even drive execution engines at runtime. In other words, MDA uses metadata computationally. Computational metadata usage is not a brand new concept because GUI, database, and workflow engines have been metadata-driven for some time. Moreover, CORBA and COM compilers have been generating code from interface descriptions for years. MDA merely accelerates the trend toward a mission-critical role for metadata.

Increasing volumes of increasingly valuable metadata—this is the specter facing development managers. Typically today, the computer industry manages these different kinds of metadata in highly disparate, and in many cases proprietary, ways with little integration, as mentioned earlier.

Previous Attempts at Metadata Integration

The idea of an integrated approach to metadata management may worry veterans of the metadata repository efforts of the late 1980s and early 1990s. Some ambitious metadata unification projects in the corporate world fell apart during that era.

Typically, those projects began with a correct diagnosis of the metadata problem. Even then, it was apparent that data models were not the only kinds of metadata and that different kinds of models, such as workflow and object models, were appearing on the scene. Software architects were concerned that each kind of metadata was being conceptualized and managed without any overall coordination.

Again, there was nothing wrong with this diagnosis. The proposed solution, however, was to define one grand modeling paradigm that would encompass all the disparate forms of models. In other words, the solution to the problem of having multiple kinds of models was to eliminate the different kinds and replace them with one kind. This would make it easy to be consistent about how to store metadata in repositories. The "one kind of model" was typically object-oriented (OO), of course, since OO was considered the most advanced form of modeling.

This prescription proved unworkable. The key flaw results from the fact that different stakeholders have different viewpoints of computing systems, and the constructs they use to model their views of the systems differ accordingly.

For example, attempts to force data modelers to use OO modeling were often unsuccessful. Object models did not give people a clear view of the data to be managed. The object models served a different group of stakeholders, viewing the system at a different level of abstraction.

Thus, as we have seen, there are good reasons that there are multiple kinds of models. Modeling a service API really *is* different from modeling a work-flow. There are legacy modeling languages that are not object-oriented and later ones that are. Trying to have one universal set of modeling constructs often required a shoehorn—the fit just wasn't right in many cases.

The collapse of the early metadata repository initiatives left the industry's management of metadata disjointed and without a common thread. MOF arose in this context.

An Additional Premise

Earlier, we stated that MOF's fundamental premise is that there will and should be more than one kind of model. The MOF architects asserted another important principle, namely that it is possible to achieve a significant degree of commonality in the management of metadata without sacrificing the ability to use very different kinds of models or the ability to invent new kinds of modeling languages. Having a common way to describe the modeling constructs that make up various modeling languages is the key to making this possible.

If there is a common way to describe different kinds of modeling constructs, it means that a metadata management tool that understands such descriptions can infer how to manage models that use those constructs. If the same terms are used to describe the fact that a table owns its columns and that a class owns its operations, a metadata management tool can apply a consistent set of rules as to how to manage metadata owned by other metadata. If the same terms are used to describe the properties of a column and the properties of an operation, a metadata management tool can be consistent in how it manages the property information.

Since MOF is a common means for describing such properties,[7] it turns out that you can feed a MOF metamodel to a generator that produces software for managing models that conform to the metamodel. In fact, in this sense, MOF is one of the purest applications of MDA to emerge so far. MOF mapping standards support the creation of generators that produce metadata management software. A MOF repository tool provides generators that conform to the mappings and an execution platform on which generated metadata management software runs.

What Is the Benefit?

When the OMG ratified MOF in 1997, XML had not yet become prominent and Java was still in its early stages. Yet, without compromising its architecture, MOF has embraced XML and Java, will soon encompass WSDL, and could work with C# as well. How does MOF deal with technology volatility so well?

Platform Independence

The MOF metamodels we have just looked at are platform-independent. In Chapter 3 we established that, for the context of this book, this means that MOF metamodels are independent of:

- Information-formatting technologies, such as XML DTD and XML Schema
- 3GLs and 4GLs, such as Java, C++, C#, and Visual Basic
- Distributed component middleware, such as J2EE, CORBA, and .NET
- Messaging middleware, such as MQSeries and MSMQ

Industry-standardized mappings of the MOF to specific middleware, 3GLs, and information formats tell MOF-based generators how to automatically transform a metamodel's abstract syntax into concrete representations based on XML DTD, XML Schema, Java, and CORBA technology.

For example (see Figure 5.15), the MOF-XML mapping, when applied to CWM, tells generators how to automatically transform the metamodel's abstract syntax into an XML-based concrete syntax for CWM. The XML-based concrete syntax is the format for XML documents that encode CWM data models.

Similarly, when applied to the UML metamodel (see Figure 5.16), the MOF-XML mapping tells generators how to automatically transform the UML metamodel's abstract syntax into an XML-based concrete syntax for encoding UML models.

---

[7] Another way of saying that the MOF provides a common way to describe different kinds of modeling constructs is to say that it defines a common way to model metadata. In this sense, metamodels are models of metadata.

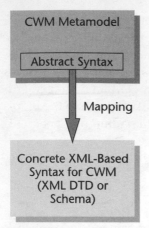

Figure 5.15　Applying the MOF-XML technology mapping to CWM.

The XML mapping can be reused with any properly defined MOF meta-model to automatically generate a concrete XML syntax for that metamodel. There are actually several MOF technology mappings:

- The MOF-XML mapping, defined by the OMG, is called *XML Metadata Interchange (XMI)*, and we looked at it briefly in Chapter 2.

- There is a MOF-Java mapping defined by the Java Community Process. This mapping is called *Java Metadata Interface (JMI)*.

- There is also an OMG MOF-CORBA mapping that does not have a special name.

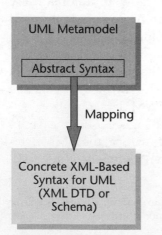

Figure 5.16　Applying the MOF-XML technology mapping to UML.

We examine each of these mappings more fully later in this chapter. MOF-based generators employ these mappings when they read metamodels and produce XML DTDs, XML Schemas, Java APIs, and CORBA APIs for representing metadata in terms used by these different languages and middleware systems.

Enforcing Semantics

Autoproduction of the APIs and XML formats is important, but MOF generators also produce *implementations* of the APIs and formats. For example, if a metamodel says, via composite aggregation, that a table owns its columns, a MOF metadata management tool may not really understand what a table is nor what a column is, but it does understand what composite aggregation is because it is one of the MOF metamodeling constructs. The metadata management software generated by the MOF tool from the metamodel is thus able to enforce ownership by making sure that, when a table is deleted from a repository, its columns are deleted too. It uses the same reasoning to enforce the ownership by a UML operation of its parameters because the UML metamodel also declares the ownership via composite aggregation—this despite the fact that UML models and data models are quite different.

Composite aggregation is just one example of the standardized MOF metamodeling constructs that provide a common means to describe the semantics of modeling constructs and that allow MOF tools to use their understanding of these semantics to automate the production of metadata management software.

Furthermore, MOF metadata management tools increasingly are able to generate implementation code that understands and enforces a metamodel's OCL-based invariant rules. All of the standardized OMG metamodels make extensive use of Design by Contract by declaring invariants for the various classes of metadata that they define. The UML metamodel, for example, has hundreds of OCL-based invariant rules. By generating code to check assertions and raise exceptions when violations are detected, MOF tools relieve programmers of yet another tedious coding task and ensure that assertion checking is handled in a consistent fashion.

Metadata Management Scenarios

Figure 5.17 illustrates a MOF repository holding many different kinds of models. The repository represents the metadata in the repository as Java and/or CORBA objects by exposing Java and/or CORBA interfaces. Repository clients use these interfaces to manipulate the metadata, that is, to create new metadata in the repository, read metadata already in the repository, update metadata in the repository, and delete metadata from the repository (CRUD = create, read, update, delete).

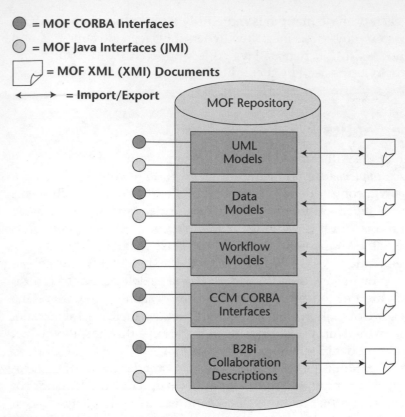

● = MOF CORBA Interfaces

○ = MOF Java Interfaces (JMI)

▢ = MOF XML (XMI) Documents

◄──► = Import/Export

Figure 5.17   Integrated MOF repository.

For example, a data-modeling tool might use the Java APIs to populate the repository when the modeler saves a model and to retrieve a model when a modeler wishes to load it. Alternately, the tool might export an XMI-based XML document to the repository in order to save a model and import such a document from the repository in order to retrieve it.

Since formal models that can be transformed by generators are central to MDA, and because such models are metadata, this kind of automated metadata management is not simply about managing analysis and design artifacts. It is also about managing development artifacts. Furthermore, since formal deployment models help automate aspects of deployment and such models are metadata too, metadata management applies to the entire development life cycle.

The APIs used to manipulate models in the repository are specific to each kind of model. For any particular kind of model, a MOF tool's generator produces the APIs, along with their implementations, from a MOF metamodel that describes that kind of model. Generators also produce the XML DTDs and Schemas that describe the format of XML documents used to import and export models, along with the code that actually does the importing and exporting.

The MOF standard is agnostic as to how the models are physically stored in the repository. They could be stored in an Oracle or DB2 database, an OO database, a flat file system, directly as XML files, in memory only, and so on—it is up to the MOF repository tool. Some MOF tools isolate the persistence layer, providing a default persistence implementation but making it possible to plug in other persistence implementations. Some provide several persistence options. In any case, the standardized MOF technology mappings determine the APIs and XML formats used to interact with the repository but are deliberately silent about the physical format of the metadata store.

Figure 5.18 demonstrates the federation of separate MOF repositories living in different business system domains.[8] XML import and export is typically the best means for exchanging metadata among repositories living in different business system domains because transactional interaction via CORBA or Java interfaces can be problematic due to firewalls and other restrictions.

MOF repositories could even be exposed as Web services. The OMG is currently working on a MOF-WSDL mapping that will make this possible. It is also developing a related technology for grouping fine-grained metadata requests into coarse-grained ones that are more economical in a Web services environment.

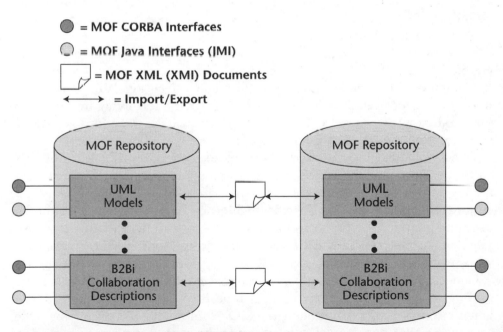

Figure 5.18   Federating MOF repositories.

[8] Fred Cummins defines the notion of a *business system domain* in [CUMMINS 2002]. A business system domain is a domain of control managed by a business unit, within which that unit can maintain a consistent, recoverable representation of state.

Generic MOF Code

It is possible for generic MOF code to manipulate metadata that lives in the repository. The same code that manipulates UML models can manipulate data models, workflow models, and so on. This generic code is *not* statically generated for each metamodel. How is this possible?

All APIs generated from metamodels inherit from a fixed set of interfaces called the *MOF Reflective Interfaces*. Figure 5.19 illustrates this inheritance via a conceptual UML diagram. There are MOF Reflective Interfaces for CORBA and a similar set for Java. The Reflective Interfaces have all the functionality that the generated, metamodel-specific interfaces have, although they are less convenient to use since their signatures are not tailored to the specific metamodels.

For example, a client using the Java interfaces specific to the UML metamodel makes the following invocation to determine whether a class is abstract:

```
boolean isAbstract = myClass.getIsAbstract ( );
```

Things are not nearly so straightforward for a client using the Reflective Interfaces. We don't show the code here, but the client has to build a Java object containing a definition of the metamodel's `isAbstract` attribute, pass that object to a generic `refGetValue` operation, and cast the return value to a boolean.

A generic MOF client uses the Reflective Interfaces. But, in our example, how could a generic client possibly know how to build a Java object that defines the `isAbstract` attribute of a UML class, since it has no prior knowledge of the UML metamodel?

The answer is that it reads the UML metamodel dynamically at runtime. By reading the metamodel, the generic client can discover the abstract syntax of the metamodel "on the fly." As long as the metamodel is available in the repository for it to peruse, the client can browse UML models living in the repository and provide a generic but fully functional GUI for performing CRUD operations on metadata that makes up UML models in the repository.

This is how MOF repository products provide generic repository editors. The editors use only the Reflective Interfaces and are driven at runtime by metamodels that reside in the repository along with models. A generic repository editor that doesn't have any specific intelligence about particular metamodels uses one generic GUI for all metadata. It does not know how to show UML metadata in the form of UML diagrams, for example. Generic editors, therefore, while useful, are also limited.

Generic code can execute the import and export of XML documents representing models to and from a MOF repository. For example, consider a generic code module that is handed a MOF-compliant XML document representing a CWM data model to import into the repository. The module does not need the CWM-specific XML DTD or Schema generated from the CWM metamodel. It is sufficient for it to have access to the metamodel itself. If it understands the MOF-XML mapping rules, it can use them to make sense of the XML document representing the data model.

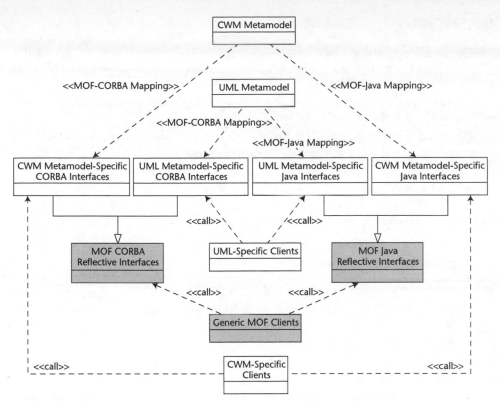

Figure 5.19   Generic MOF repository clients use the Reflective Interfaces.

MOF Is Not CORBA-Based

When the MOF standard was issued in 1997, CORBA looked to be the "up and coming" programming model. It still dominated the OMG, as UML was just entering the scene. There was, therefore, strong interest within the organization in tying MOF closely to CORBA.

However, the architects of MOF wanted to avoid tying MOF to *any* particular technology platform. They understood technology volatility. When they chose instead to borrow some of the UML class-modeling constructs to be MOF's constructs for modeling metadata, they committed the OMG to yet another CORBA-independent standard, one that complements UML.[9]

[9] There was actually one concession to CORBA. In early versions of the MOF, the primitive data types were the same as those of CORBA. However, MOF 1.4 changed this, defining a more neutral set of primitive data types.

Appearances versus Intent

The architects' intention all along was to map MOF to multiple technologies. The first one they mapped it to was CORBA. In fact, the mapping to CORBA is part of the MOF specification itself. This gives many people who look at the MOF superficially the impression that it is a CORBA-based standard. You have to actually read the specification to discover that it is CORBA-independent. Certainly CORBA is an important platform and the MOF mapping to CORBA is important—you just have to keep this in perspective.

The mapping to CORBA defines rules for representing metadata as CORBA objects. The mapping specifies how to transform a metamodel's abstract syntax into CORBA IDL-based APIs. The APIs provide a way to represent models as CORBA objects for the domain of models that conform to the metamodel.

Mapping beyond Syntax

The MOF-CORBA mapping does not limit itself to specifying only the *syntax* of the CORBA IDL–based APIs that should be produced from a metamodel's abstract syntax. If it stopped there, we would know the IDL signatures of the generated CORBA operations; but we would not know their semantics, that is, what those operations are supposed to do. Thus, the mapping also spells out the semantics of those APIs, including all of their required behaviors, such as the fact that the implementation of an operation to delete an object representing a piece of metadata should also delete any objects owned via composite aggregation.

By specifying the semantics of the APIs in addition to the syntax, the mapping makes it possible for MOF compilers to generate not only the APIs themselves in a standard fashion, but also their implementations. This promotes interoperability among different implementations of the APIs. It follows the general industry pattern for defining APIs. It is never enough to simply standardize the signature of an API. A signature alone is not sufficient to define a contract. A combination of formal declarations and informal text stipulate the syntax and semantics of the API.

Applying the MOF-CORBA Mapping

The first MOF metamodel that the OMG standardized was the UML metamodel. The OMG then applied the MOF-CORBA mapping to the metamodel. The result of applying the mapping was a specification of how to represent UML metadata (that is, UML models) as CORBA objects via a set of CORBA IDL interfaces. The interfaces support CRUD operations on UML models. The idea was that CORBA-based clients of a metadata repository would use the interfaces.

Figure 5.20 illustrates the application of the mapping to one piece of the UML metamodel. One of the classes in the metamodel is `Classifier`, which is a superclass of several UML modeling constructs, including `Class`, `DataType`, and `Interface`. The figure includes a fragment of the metamodel that defines `Classifier` alongside the CORBA IDL interface generated for representing a `Classifier` as a CORBA object. For purposes of the current discussion, don't try too hard to decipher the generated IDL. We'll talk more about the principles behind API generation in Chapter 7. If you wish to understand the mapping in detail, refer to the MOF specification.[10]

Later, the OMG standardized more metamodels and applied the MOF-CORBA mapping to them. For example, it applied the mapping to CWM's relational data metamodel and thus produced standard CORBA IDL–based APIs for representing relational metadata as CORBA objects.

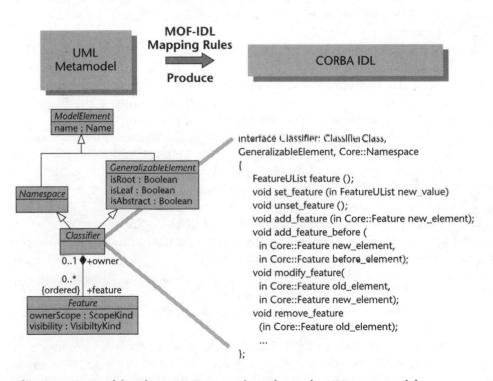

Figure 5.20 Applying the MOF-IDL mapping rules to the UML metamodel.

[10] [MOF]

A Closer Look at XMI

XMI is an important MOF-based standard due to the prominence of XML in today's distributed systems. This section provides a closer look at its architecture.

Return on Investment

XML became popular after the MOF specification was written. As XML's popularity grew, a business case developed for representing metadata as XML documents. XML presented an excellent medium for tools to exchange models in a standard way. The rise of XML was a classic case of a new, unforeseen technology emerging.

It was at this point that the farsightedness of the MOF's architects began to pay dividends. Had the MOF been inextricably hard-wired to CORBA, adapting it to XML would have been painful. However, MOF's platform independence made doing so relatively straightforward. In late 1998, the OMG adopted a MOF-XML mapping, which, as previously noted, is called XML Metadata Interchange (XMI).

When the OMG applied XMI to the UML metamodel, it produced a DTD for exchanging UML models. Figure 5.21 illustrates how XMI is applied to the `Classifier` element of the UML metamodel, which we looked at earlier in the discussion of the MOF-CORBA mapping. The figure shows only a fragment of the generated DTD element for representing a `Classifier`. For purposes of this discussion, the mapping details are not important. In Chapter 7 we discuss general principles for generating information formats from class models and how XMI puts those principles into practice. If you want to understand XMI's mapping rules in detail, refer to the XMI specifications.[11]

XMI also defines a set of rules for producing XML documents that validate against the generated DTDs. These rules are necessary because the DTD production rules specify only the syntax of the XML for representing models. If XMI stopped there, it would be as if the MOF-IDL mapping only specified the syntax and not the semantics of generated CORBA IDL-based APIs. XMI's document production rules specify the semantics of the XML information that goes into the slots defined by an XMI DTD.[12]

The XMI rules for producing DTDs and documents make it possible not only to generate DTDs from a metamodel automatically, but also to generate implementation code that imports models to and from a metadata repository.

---

[11] [XMI] and [XMI SCHEMA]

[12] "XMI DTD" means an XML DTD generated via XMI's MOF-XML mapping rules.

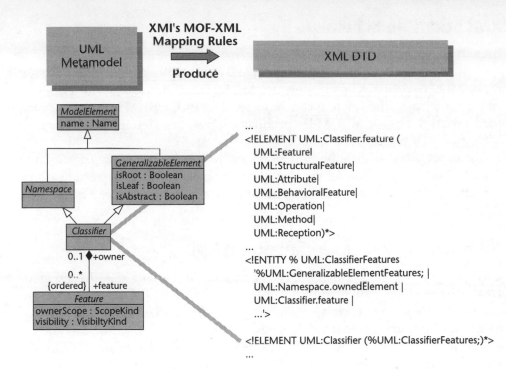

Figure 5.21   Applying XMI's MOF-XML mapping rules to the UML metamodel.

For example, a MOF generator that knows the MOF-CORBA and MOF-XML mapping rules can produce code that:

- Reads models from a CORBA-based metadata repository via the MOF-derived CORBA APIs

- Exports them via XMI

A MOF generator can also produce code that:

- Imports an XMI document representing a model

- Uses the CORBA APIs to populate the repository with the model

The generated XMI import and export code might, on the other hand, use proprietary means to save and load the metadata to and from the repository if the generator is intimate with the repository.

Such generated code is an alternative to generic code that, as explained earlier, reads the metamodel dynamically at runtime, uses the mappings to determine the XML format, and talks to the repository via the generic Reflective Interfaces.

XMI and XML Schema

In 2001 the W3C, owner of the XML specification, approved *XML Schema* as the successor to XML DTDs. Once again, MDA principles paid off. XMI did not make MOF dependent in any way on XML DTD technology, just as the MOF-CORBA mapping did not make MOF dependent on CORBA. In the same year, the OMG adopted a new XMI specification,[13] which defines a mapping of MOF to XML Schema.

The new XMI specification also increases the degree of parameterization of the MOF-XML transformation. As mentioned in Chapter 2, by setting transformation parameters engineers can control a number of aspects of XML Schema production.

A Common Misconception about XMI

UML is the most well-known MOF metamodel. As a result, the XMI DTD for UML that was generated from the UML metamodel is the most well-known XMI DTD. Most UML tools now support importing and exporting UML models via XMI documents that validate against this DTD. By the time this book is available, there may already be an XMI Schema for UML; generated from the UML metamodel via the new XML Schema production rules.

Some people in the industry have only encountered XMI when exchanging UML models among tools. Therefore, they believe that XMI simply is a specific DTD for exchanging UML models. They haven't had the opportunity to see that XMI is more than that; that is, that it is a mapping that determines DTD production. We have found it to be prudent to be respectfully skeptical when someone claims to know what XMI is because often it turns out that they harbor this common misconception.

Furthermore, it pays to treat with caution claims by vendors that their products support XMI. You need to know exactly what this means. It might only mean that the product supports the XMI DTD for UML, that is, it can import and export UML models via documents that validate against *that* DTD. More comprehensive compliance would entail being able to act as a generator that produces an XML DTD or Schema from any arbitrary metamodel's abstract syntax. The most far-reaching XMI support would also generate code that implements import and export, to and from a MOF repository, of XMI documents that conform to the generated DTD or Schema.

Hand-Coded DTDs and Schemas

XMI DTDs look ugly to XML aficionados. For one thing, they start with a slew of standard XMI type declarations. Many also have a liberal sprinkling of legal but strange looking XML entity declarations.

[13] [XMI SCHEMA]

So XMI DTDs are not as elegant looking as hand-coded DTDs and Schemas. The key question is: How important is this? Remember that a key point of MDA is to relieve programmers of repetitive coding tasks where the code can be generated. Thus, XMI DTDs and Schema are not *meant* to be written and read by human beings. They are meant to be *machine* written and read.

The assembly code produced by 3GL compilers in the early phases of 3GL adoption looked bad compared to hand-coded assembly language written by a skilled assembly language programmer. But we don't care much about that anymore because we've long since raised the level of abstraction above assembly language for all but the most specialized systems programming.

This argument does not entirely assuage a tool vendor who wants neither to use nor build a MOF engine but simply to import and export metadata that validates against a particular XMI DTD. The good news is that the schema produced by XMI are more elegant than the DTDs produced by earlier versions. But to some extent there is a trade-off between the elegance of hand-coded artifacts and the potential productivity gains of raising the level of abstraction. Furthermore, UML tools that do not understand MOF may find themselves at a disadvantage in the marketplace over the course of the next few years.

XMI Complexity versus UML Complexity

XMI has another public relations problem that stems from the fact that the XMI DTD for UML is enormous and not well modularized. The basic tendency of machine-generated XML to be less compact than hand-coded XML is not the main cause of this complexity. As discussed in Chapter 3, the cause is the fact that the UML 1.X metamodel is complex and does not manage cross dependencies among its elements very well. If you give an XMI compiler a large metamodel, it will generate a large DTD. If there are excessive cross-dependencies among metamodel elements, this will be the case with the generated DTD as well.

So when engineers wish to use just part of the UML XMI DTD—say the part for activity modeling, for example—they find themselves having to pull in a large number of elements that are not relevant to their concern. This indeed is a problem, but it's not XMI's fault. The same problem exists with the CORBA IDL generated from the UML metamodel because the problem lies with the UML metamodel.

To be fair to UML's original architects, it is only with the benefit of some years of experience with UML that the cross-dependency problem in the metamodel has come to be understood. Many of those same architects are working to fix the problem in UML 2.0. UML 2.0 will still be quite large because its coverage is broad. But hopefully it will be better modularized and, if so, then the XMI DTD and Schema generated for the new metamodel will be better modularized as a consequence.

XMI as Input to Generators

Up to now I've talked about XMI being generated *by* MOF metadata management tools. We've seen how MOF generators take metamodels as input and produce XMI DTDs and Schemas and that they also produce code capable of importing and exporting XMI documents that validate against those DTDs and schemas.

There is also a case for generators that take XMI documents *as input*. There are generators on the market that take UML models as input and produce various artifacts such as code and relational data models. Some of these products require a proprietary representation of a UML model, such as a Rational Rose UML model file, as input.

However, increasingly such generators expect as input an XMI document that represents a UML model. This decouples the generators from dependency on a proprietary representation of a model. You can use such generators along with any UML tool capable of exporting UML models as XMI documents. Some products accept a Rose file as input to a preprocessor that transforms the Rose file into an XMI document, which, in turn, is handed to the main generator (see Figure 5.22).

Figure 5.22 oversimplifies in an important way. Figure 5.23 provides an expanded view that highlights the fact that, in a generator that properly separates concerns, the main generation logic uses an abstract syntax tree as the source for the transformation that it performs. The formal specification of the mapping that the generator executes is independent of any particular concrete representation of the model on the source side of the transformation. Thus, the main generator is independent of XMI, with XMI-specific knowledge isolated in an XMI parser that produces an abstract syntax tree representing the model.

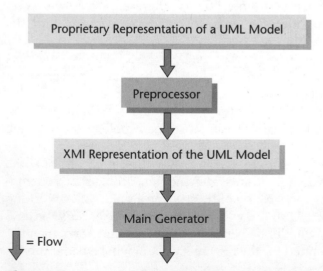

Figure 5.22   Preprocessing a proprietary representation of a UML model.

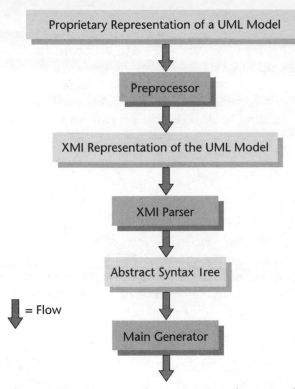

Figure 5.23   More complete separation of concerns in a generator.

XMI and UML Diagram Interchange

As discussed in Chapter 3, the UML metamodel does not cover the UML graphical notation. The metamodel does not contain elements such as box, line, coordinate, and so on. Thus, the XMI DTD for UML does not specify a format for encoding the graphical information contained in UML diagrams.

Let's look at this issue again from a slightly different angle. For example, suppose you define the class Customer in a model and use it in several class diagrams, each of which provides a different view of Customer. Perhaps one diagram shows all of Customer's superclasses while another shows all of the associations in which it participates. Despite the fact that Customer appears in more than one diagram, there really is only one *definition* of its properties. That single definition includes the specification of all of its properties, including its superclasses and associations, and that definition is what is encoded in an XMI document representing the model.

It is important to understand that a generator that produces code and other artifacts from a UML model *does not need the diagram information*. In our example, the generator needs only the single definition of Customer.

Although not required by code generators, the ability to exchange diagrams in addition to definitions is useful. If there were a metamodel for UML diagrams, then XMI would provide a means to encode UML diagrams in XMI documents as well, so that they could be exchanged among tools. As we discussed, the OMG is in the process of enhancing UML to include a diagram metamodel as part of UML 2.0. Thus, when the UML 2.0 metamodel is run through an XMI generator, the resulting XML DTD and Schema for UML will support the exchange of diagrams.

A Closer Look at JMI

In some industries, such as telecommunications, CORBA is a very popular programming model. However, in many respects J2EE has eclipsed CORBA as a programming model for distributed applications. CORBA plays a crucial role in J2EE, but primarily as plumbing not visible to the application programmer. This is yet another example of technology volatility, and it makes the MOF-CORBA mapping less interesting than we thought it would be a few years ago.

Here again MOF's platform independence is paying off. Sun's Java Community Process (JCP) recently finished its MOF-Java mapping. As I mentioned earlier, this mapping is known as the *Java Metadata Interface (JMI)*.[14] Products that implement JMI are starting to appear.

A MOF-Java Mapping

JMI defines rules for representing metadata as Java objects. The mapping specifies how to transform a metamodel's abstract syntax into Java APIs. The APIs provide a way to represent models as Java objects, for the domain of models that conform to the metamodel.

Thus, JMI is analogous to the MOF-CORBA mapping. The basic difference is that, instead of specifying the production of CORBA IDL–based APIs, it specifies production of Java APIs. The APIs are typically exposed to Java clients of a metadata repository. Like the MOF-CORBA mapping, JMI not only specifies the syntax of the generated APIs but also specifies their semantics, making it possible for different vendors' MOF generators to produce interoperable implementations of the generated APIs.

JMI rounds out the set of MOF technology mappings that have been standardized so far, as illustrated by Figure 5.24. As mentioned earlier, the OMG is developing a MOF-WSDL mapping. Mappings to new Microsoft .NET technologies, such as a MOF-C# mapping, may be defined as well.

---

[14] [JSR40]

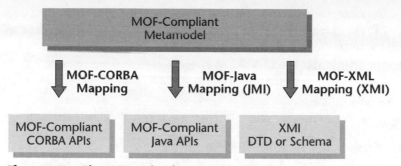

Figure 5.24   The MOF technology mappings.

Now that JMI is finalized, the OMG and the Sun JCP will apply it to some of the OMG's standard metamodels, such as UML and CWM, to produce standard Java APIs for representing UML models, data models, and other warehouse metadata as Java objects. At press time the JCP has already issued some Java Standards Requests (JSRs) for this purpose.

Aren't XML and DOM Enough?

Architects who are learning about MOF sometimes ask an important question at this juncture: What benefits do XMI and JMI afford that are not provided by XML and a Java implementation of W3C's Document Object Model (DOM).[15] After all, a Java-based DOM tool provides a read/write Java API for accessing XML-based information.

The short answer is that a MOF metamodel is richer semantically than an XML DTD or Schema. A MOF tool can use the additional semantic information to automate more of the metadata management than a DOM tool can.

In order to understand this delta, suppose we define again a simple MOF metamodel for data modeling. This metamodel is so simple that the only data modeling constructs it defines are tables and the columns that make up those tables (see Figure 5.25). To keep things uncomplicated, we don't even use inheritance in our metamodel, even though we could have defined a common supertype for Table and Column to capture the common name attribute.

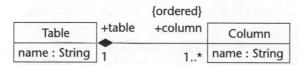

Figure 5.25   Simplistic metamodel for data modeling.

[15] [W3C DOM]

A MOF tool can generate Java APIs for manipulating this metadata and can generate an XMI DTD or Schema defining how to represent this metadata in XML. In our example the table interface generated via JMI's MOF-Java mapping rules includes or inherits the following operations:

getName   Returns the name.

setName   Sets the name.

getColumn   Returns a Java `List` of the columns. Uses `List` because of the `{ordered}` specification in the model. The `List` can also be used to add, modify, and remove columns.

refDelete   Deletes the table.

The MOF metamodel, although its coverage is limited to only the most basic data modeling constructs, is still rich semantically when it comes to defining those constructs. For example, the metamodel uses composite aggregation to express the fact that a table owns its columns. By following MOF's semantic rules and JMI's mapping of those rules to Java, a generator can produce an implementation of the table interface that knows to delete owned columns automatically when the table is deleted.

Another example of MOF's semantic power is that it provides a way to indicate in the model whether the `List` of columns may contain duplicates, and the generated implementation can enforce a specification that no duplicates are allowed (more on this in Chapter 7). Furthermore, the model can declare precise invariant rules via OCL. For example, suppose it were illegal for a column to have the same name as its owning table. We could express this constraint with mathematical precision in OCL as follows:

```
context Table inv:
    column->forAll (col | col.name <> self.name)
```

A generator that understands OCL could produce code in the implementation that enforces this constraint.

Thus, from the information in the metamodel, it is possible for a generator to produce a rather intelligent implementation of the Java APIs.

Furthermore, a generator can also produce the code for importing a data model represented by an XMI document. The XMI format for such a document conforms to the MOF-XML mapping rules as applied to our simple metamodel. The generated import code could also enforce the semantics of the model, such as detecting that a column has the same name as its owning table and raising an exception when it detects a violation.

Now, suppose that instead of using the MOF approach, we directly define an XML DTD that specifies the format for representing the properties of tables and columns as follows:

```
<xml version="1.0" encoding="UTF-8"?>
<!ELEMENT TABLE (NAME,COLUMN+)>
<!ELEMENT NAME (#PCDATA)>
<!ELEMENT COLUMN (NAME)>
```

In this scenario we use a DOM tool that parses XML documents conforming to that DTD and allows us to access the document via Java DOM APIs. This DTD is thin semantically compared with the MOF metamodel. For example, it does not express the fact that a table owns its columns because XML cannot express that. It also does not express the fact that a column cannot have the same name as its owning table. Since the DTD does not and cannot express these and many other rules that the MOF metamodel expresses, a DOM tool cannot enforce them.

Thus, the implementations of the Java APIs that a DOM tool provides permit a client to delete a table without deleting its columns. They permit a client using the Java DOM APIs to add a column to a table that has the same name as the table. Programmers have to write extra Java code on top of DOM to enforce these rules. Furthermore, programmers may well have to write the enforcement code *again* when technology volatility forces them to port to environments other than Java and XML.

It may appear that the DOM tool has an advantage in that it parses the XML dynamically, rather than reading the DTD and then generating the parsing code, which has to be compiled and deployed. However, some MOF tools *can* read metamodels dynamically at runtime to drive their management of metadata. So far, we have talked mostly about scenarios in which MOF tools read metamodels at design time and statically generate code; however, dynamic interpretation of metamodels at runtime is also possible, as we mentioned earlier.

A side benefit of the MOF approach is that the programming model presented by the generated Java APIs reflects the structure of the metadata. Operations such as `getColumn` make metadata manipulation rather intuitive for the client programmer. By contrast, the DOM APIs are totally generic and their semantics are all about DOM parse trees.

What we have said about DOM can be said about the other popular XML parsing API, SAX. SAX is also driven by XML DTDs that are semantically thin in comparison to the metamodels that drive MOF tools. This limits the intelligence of SAX tools. SAX is also no different from DOM when it comes to managing technology volatility.

Another Look at MOF Self-Description

MOF self-description—that is, the fact that MOF is defined via MOF—has some interesting practical consequences. As we've discussed, when we apply XMI's MOF-XML mapping to a MOF-compliant metamodel, we get an XMI DTD for representing *models* that conform to that metamodel. But when we apply XMI's

MOF-XML mapping to "the" MOF Model—that is, to the MOF model of MOF itself—we get an XMI DTD for representing MOF-compliant *metamodels*. This DTD is often called *"the" MOF DTD*, and it is an official OMG standard DTD. For each of the OMG's standard metamodels, the OMG has a standard XMI document that represents the metamodel and that validates against "the" MOF DTD.

Figure 5.26 shows the fragment of "the" MOF DTD that defines the format for representing an instance of MOF `Class`. Note the `isSingleton` property, which is visible in Figure 5.12's fragment of "the" MOF Model's abstract syntax. The other properties are inherited from superclasses of `Class`.

Thus, when a MOF generator transforms a metamodel, it can produce two kinds of XMI artifacts:

- An XMI document that contains *all* the properties of *all* of the elements of the metamodel, which are M2 elements. This document validates against "the" MOF DTD.

- A DTD for representing M1 instances of the metamodel's M2 elements.

It is important to understand the difference between these two artifacts. Unlike the XMI document, which validates against "the" MOF Model, the DTD does not contain all of the properties of the metamodel. There is some loss of information because the intent of the DTD is merely to describe a format for representing M1 instances of the metamodel's M2 elements. That format does not contain all of the metamodel's properties.

```
<!ELEMENT Model:Class (Model:ModelElement.name|
                       Model:ModelElement.annotation|
                       Model:ModelElement.container|
                       Model:ModelElement.constraints|
                       Model:Namespace.contents|
                       Model:GeneralizableElement.supertypes|
                       XMI.extension)*>
<!ATTLIST Model:Class
  name CDATA #IMPLIED
  annotation CDATA #IMPLIED
  isRoot (true|false) #REQUIRED
  isLeaf (true|false) #REQUIRED
  isAbstract (true|false) #REQUIRED
  visibility (public_vis|protected_vis|private_vis) #REQUIRED
  isSingleton (true|false) #REQUIRED
  container IDREFS #IMPLIED
  constraints IDREFS #IMPLIED
  contents IDREFS #IMPLIED
  supertypes IDREFS #IMPLIED
  %XMI.element.att; %XMI.link.att;>
```

Figure 5.26   A fragment of "the" MOF DTD (for MOF 1.4).

For example, consider our simple table-column data metamodel that contains an OCL invariant forbidding the name of a column to be the same as the name of its owning table (see Figures 5.6 and 5.7). The DTD for representing tables and columns does not contain this invariant; it merely defines the format for representing a table and column. An intelligent MOF tool reads the *metamodel* to ascertain the fact that this invariant exists. An important consequence is that the DTD cannot be reverse engineered to yield the original metamodel in all its detail.

The other MOF mappings we have mentioned can also be applied to "the" MOF model. Soon XMI for XML Schema will be applied to "the" MOF Model to produce "the" MOF XMI Schema. The OMG has also run "the" MOF Model through the MOF-CORBA mapping. The result is IDL for CORBA objects that represent M2 elements, that is, that represent the elements of metamodels. The OMG has standardized this IDL, which I refer to as *"the" MOF Model IDL*. The JMI specification applies its MOF-Java mapping to "the" MOF Model, and the resulting APIs are for Java objects that represent M2 elements. JMI standardizes these Java APIs and I call them *"the" MOF Model Java APIs*.

Figure 5.27 portrays the fact that, because "the" MOF Model is itself MOF-compliant, the MOF technology mappings can be applied to it just as they can be applied to any MOF-compliant metamodel.

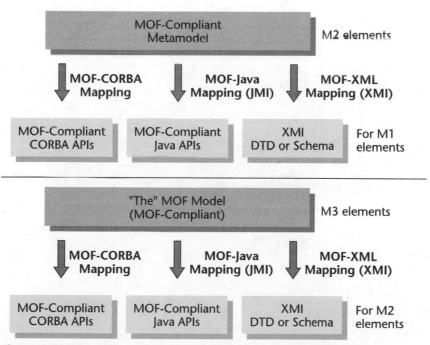

Figure 5.27 Applying standard MOF mappings to "the" MOF model.

The ability to represent M2 metamodels in a manner that is consistent with the representation of M1 models helps to streamline MOF metadata management. Generators and generic MOF code need to be able to read metamodels dynamically, so the representation of metamodels is a significant issue. Figure 5.28 illustrates that a MOF metadata tool manages M2 metamodels and "the" MOF Model (M3) similarly to the way it manages M1 models. This is a case where it is useful to ignore the difference between metalevels and view the absolute metalevels as arbitrary.

If you feel squeamish about the details of self-description, don't be concerned. It takes a little getting used to. You may have to read this section over a few times. The most important thing to grasp is that, just as it is important to be able to represent *models* as XML documents, CORBA objects, Java objects, and so on, it is also important to be able to represent *metamodels* as XML documents, CORBA objects, Java objects, and so on. MOF's self-describing nature makes it possible to use the same mechanisms to generate metamodel representations that are used to generate model representations.

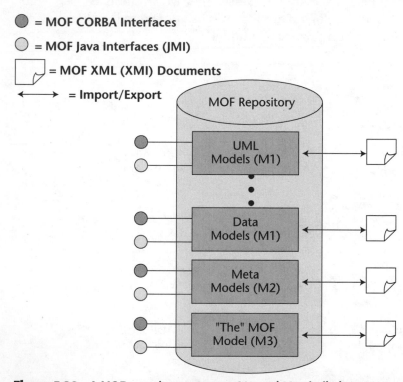

Figure 5.28 A MOF repository manages M2 and M3 similarly to M1.

Additional Applications

This section takes a look at some of the newer MOF-based technologies coming on line.

Human Usable Textual Notations

Consider a UML model created with a UML tool. You can't see all the properties of the model by looking at the model diagrams. Some of the properties aren't visible unless you drill down into property dialogs. Furthermore, on any given model diagram the modeler is likely to have suppressed some of the detail for the particular viewpoint that diagram is intended to present. A person who wants to ascertain all of the model's properties has to assemble the bits and pieces from an assortment of diagrams and dialogs.

Thus, it is often convenient to render all the properties of a model linearly into human-usable text. This provides a sure way to examine all the detailed properties of the model. A human-usable textual notation (HUTN) for a UML model might look something like Figure 5.29. This example is not the best that one could do in designing a HUTN for UML, but it should convey the general idea. Of course a UML model can be rendered textually via XMI, but XML is not really friendly to humans, especially for complex models.

```
Class ApartmentBuilding extends Building
{
    attribute address String;
    ...
}
Class Apartment
{
    ...
}
Association Building_Apartment
{
    Association End aptBuilding type ApartmentBuilding
        [aggregation_composite] 1..1
    Association End apt         type Apartment
        [isOrdered,isNavigable] 1..*
}

...
```

Figure 5.29 Human-usable textual notation.

It can also be convenient in some cases for a human being to write a model textually via a HUTN rather than create it graphically. To some extent, this is a matter of personal taste. Some people feel more comfortable defining models linearly in text, and some feel better anchored with a GUI approach. For the majority there are good uses for both, and it is ideal to be able to switch back and forth easily between the two ways of modeling.

The OMG issued an RFP for a HUTN for UML. Work on it was delayed for a while, but when work resumed, consciousness in the OMG about the principles of the MOF had risen considerably.

Thus, as we go to press, the OMG is finalizing a MOF-based approach to the HUTN problem.[16] Instead of designing a HUTN just for UML, the MOF-based approach defines a parameterized MOF-HUTN mapping so that, given a metamodel and some mapping parameters, a generator can produce a HUTN suitable for modeling in accordance with that metamodel. The UML HUTN will mostly likely be generated from the UML metamodel via the parameterized mapping, rather than being handcrafted. Textual notations for varied metamodels will therefore have consistency. MOF tools will be able to generate code for exporting models from repositories in HUTN form and for importing models expressed in HUTN form.

A vendor demonstrated a prototype of a MOF-based HUTN engine at an OMG meeting. For any given metamodel, it automates the production of XSL stylesheets that convert back and forth between the HUTN and XMI formats for that metamodel, and the HUTN and XMI formats are determined by the MOF-HUTN and MOF-XML mappings, respectively.

XMI's Reverse Mapping

There are, of course, XML DTDs and Schema that are not XMI-compliant and that various standards bodies or corporations have already adopted. We cannot ignore this reality.

Thus, the new XMI specification does more than extend XMI to cover XML Schema. It also defines a reverse mapping for transforming any arbitrary non–XMI XML DTD or Schema into a MOF metamodel. It even defines a way to produce a MOF model from a non–XMI XML document for which there is no DTD or Schema, although it is preferable to reverse engineer from a DTD or Schema.

As Figure 5.30 illustrates, you can start with a DTD or Schema; produce a MOF metamodel; and then use the MOF-IDL, MOF-Java, and MOF-XML forward mappings to produce MOF-compliant APIs as well as XMI DTDs and Schemas. In other words, it's possible to directly infer MOF-based APIs and XMI DTDs and Schemas from non–XMI XML DTDs and Schemas.

---

[16] [HUTN]

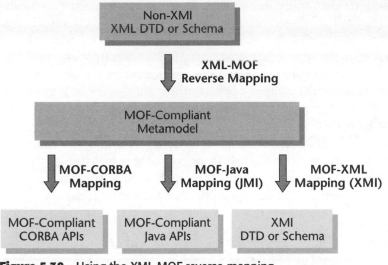

Figure 5.30 Using the XML-MOF reverse mapping.

This, in turn, makes it possible to automatically generate code that transforms a non–XMI XML document into MOF-compliant CORBA objects, Java objects, and/or XMI documents. Thus, the groundwork is in place for MOF tools to manage the metadata even though the original format description is not MOF-based.

As we've pointed out, a non–XMI XML DTD or Schema cannot express all the semantics that a MOF metamodel can. This has ramifications for the reverse mapping. For example, there is not enough information in a DTD or Schema to enable a reverse mapping engine to determine whether an association in the resulting MOF metamodel should use composite aggregation, since XML does not have a concept similar to composition. Thus, the reverse mapping always defaults to ordinary associations.

However, the reverse mapping is a parameterized mapping. The parameters can be used to fill in semantic information missing from the DTD or Schema. For example, the modeler can set a parameter to determine whether a particular association produced by the reverse mapping should be ordinary or use composite aggregation.

Beyond the standardized mapping parameters, there is further opportunity to semantically enhance the metamodel produced via the reverse mapping, by writing invariant rules in OCL that may have been documented only informally for the DTD or Schema. Therefore, typically a MOF metamodel produced by a reverse mapping tool should be enhanced by a modeler before running it through a compiler that executes any of the MOF forward mappings, assuming that sufficient documentation about the semantics of the original DTD or Schema is available.

Be aware, though, that there are certain kinds of enhancements to the reverse-engineered MOF metamodel that you can make that actually change the structure of the model. For example, since DTDs have no inheritance and Schemas only have single inheritance, there may be opportunities to use MOF multiple inheritance to streamline the metamodel produced via reverse engineering. Changes of this nature carry a price in that, once you make them, the abstract syntax of the MOF metamodel in its altered form cannot be directly inferred from the combination of the non–XMI DTD or Schema and the reverse mapping parameters. This limits the degree to which you can automatically generate code to transform non–XMI XML documents into MOF-compliant Java objects, CORBA objects, and XMI documents. Once you cross this line, you are going to need some hand coding to do that transformation.

Weaknesses

The MOF has some limitations that are worth pointing out. Most MDA experts already recognize these shortcomings, and there are plans in place to address most of them.

Lack of Coverage of Graphical Notation

MOF does not have a language for defining graphical notation. Thus, if you require a graphical notation optimized for a particular kind of model defined by a metamodel, there is no standard way to declare that notation and to associate notational constructs with the constructs defined by the metamodel's abstract syntax.

Consequently, standards-based MDA development environments that support new graphical notations by reading standardized notation descriptions are not possible. As we have discussed previously, UML profiling supports only a limited ability to define new graphical notations, so it does not fill this gap.

An MDA development environment could support the ability to define new graphical notations elegantly, but it would have to do so in a proprietary fashion given the lack of support by standards.

Lack of Support for Versioning

Good metadata repository tools that can scale to enterprise demands must support versioning of models. It should be possible to hold multiple versions of a model in a repository. In fact, it should be possible to traverse forward and backward over a series of versions of a model.

Metadata repository tools that have this kind of versioning exist. However, the lack of MOF support for versioning means they have to use proprietary mechanisms to support it.

Misalignment with UML

This is the flip side of the UML weakness discussed in Chapter 3. The misalignment of UML and MOF is also MOF's problem. The abstract syntax of UML and MOF should share a common core. UML 1.X and MOF 1.X come close to doing so, but close isn't good enough.

MOF-CORBA Mapping Problems

The MOF-IDL mapping is in need of upgrading. The interfaces produced by the generation rules are not efficient in distributed systems.

First, the mapping predates CORBA value types and thus does not make use of them. A related problem is that a class in a MOF metamodel that has N attributes is transformed into a CORBA interface that has accessor and mutator operations for each attribute, thus requiring N distributed calls to get or set all attribute values.[17] It is possible to work around the second problem by defining operations on the class in the MOF metamodel that access or set several attribute values, but a more generic solution is required.

The problem can be solved by applying something along the lines of the Value Object pattern, either in the MOF-CORBA mapping or by extending the MOF Reflective Interfaces. As explained previously, the Reflective Interfaces are fixed interfaces inherited by generated interfaces.

Another shortcoming of the mapping is that its support for parameterized transformation is limited. It would be beneficial if a knowledgeable human CORBA engineer could select from certain options that control how the transformation should be performed, so that the mapping was more flexible.

Interoperability Problems Due to Immaturity

The MOF-based standards are rather new. As a result, interoperability among conforming products is not as dependable as it should be. In theory, when a UML tool exports a UML model via XMI, another tool should be able to import it. However, in practice, there are problems because of the immaturity of the standards.

---

[17] The mapping does not use CORBA attributes because at the time that the mapping was defined CORBA attributes did not support user-defined exceptions.

Future Directions

This section describes current initiatives to deal with some of MOF's inadequacies.

Interoperability Testing

For perspective on the interoperability situation, it is useful to consider the history of the OMG's IIOP, which is the principal "on-the-wire" protocol for CORBA- and J2EE-based distributed systems.

Interoperability via IIOP was not a practical reality until the OMG organized a temporary laboratory to which different IIOP vendors sent engineers to run tests and iron out problems. Some problems were the result of bugs in code, and some were due to bugs or ambiguities in the IIOP specification. The engineers fixed the code bugs on-site, and the lab managers noted problems with the specification and referred them to the appropriate task forces for resolution. The OMG periodically sets up labs for further testing as IIOP evolves.

As of press time, the OMG was in the early stages of organizing such a testing process for XMI that will initially focus on the exchange of UML models via UML's concrete XMI-based syntax. A first round of such testing is necessary in order to achieve true interoperability. A round of interoperability testing for CWM's concrete XMI-based syntax has already occurred.

MOF 2.0

The OMG issued three MOF 2.0 RFPs in late in 2001, and MOF repository vendors are drafting several more. Collectively, the RFPs address most of the other weaknesses described in the previous section. The RFPs are synchronized with the UML 2.0 RFPs.

It will probably take until at least 2004 to complete all of the MOF 2.0 specifications and for implementations of them to appear and mature. Thus, the foreseeable future portends an increasingly comprehensive MOF that still will take a fair amount of time to fully develop.

MOF in the Computer Industry

This section discusses how MOF has penetrated the software industry. It considers MOF's presence in database technology and other enterprise software offered by big vendors.

It also looks at how MOF relates to the Resource Description Framework (RDF), which is the basis for the W3C's work on metadata for the Web dubbed the *Semantic Web*.

MOF and Enterprise Software

Without fanfare, IBM and Oracle are making CWM (which, of course, is MOF-based) an important factor in their data warehousing product lines. CWM has metamodels for relational database modeling, multidimensional database modeling, schema transformation, and more. The fact that the big database players are taking MOF seriously should serve as a wakeup call to other companies.

To understand the opportunity and the danger this situation presents, consider the role that data access standards have played in the industry. Second-tier software vendors and Global 1000 corporations can successfully write software that accesses the big data stores because of the existence of data access standards such as SQL and JDBC. Applications that don't support these standards are handicapped.

Enterprise software is becoming more and more metadata driven all the time. A lot of metadata will end up in IBM and Oracle databases, accessible via XMI and MOF APIs. There is a possibility that, within 2 to 3 years, applications that don't support MOF will be disadvantaged when they try to access the big metadata stores.

MOF is also wired into IBM's WebSphere software at a deep level. This fact isn't visible to the WebSphere user, since WebSphere uses MOF internally. IBM has defined metamodels for all of the different kinds of metadata that Web-Sphere uses at various abstraction levels and middleware layers. WebSphere represents this metadata in-memory as abstract syntax trees that are accessible via JMI APIs. Internally, WebSphere thus uses a consistent set of APIs to manipulate the different kinds of metadata.[18]

For example, when WebSphere transforms a Java object model into a relational data model, it reads an abstract syntax tree representing the object model and writes an abstract syntax tree representing the data model. APIs generated from a metamodel for Java represent the abstract syntax tree for the Java object model. APIs generated from a relational database metamodel represent the abstract syntax tree for the relational data model. The consistent use of APIs derived from metamodels for its internal manipulations endows Web-Sphere with efficiencies not otherwise achievable.

WebSphere uses XMI files for persisting metadata unless a conventional format is required for legacy reasons. The component that reads and writes XMI is driven by metamodels at runtime, so that WebSphere's developers don't have to write special parsers and writers for every kind of metadata.

Unisys also has a MOF engine that it is using internally in the development of new applications. This engine, too, is not necessarily visible to users of the applications. IBM and Unisys, to differing degrees, make their MOF technology available for license or purchasing.

---

[18] WebSphere actually uses a somewhat more advanced version of MOF and JMI based on MOF 2.0 proposals to the OMG.

Sun Microsystems is a relative latecomer, but there are now a number of MOF-oriented Java Standards Requests (JSRs) active in the Java Community Process (JCP), some of which I've mentioned already. Furthermore, at press time, Sun had recently released a beta version of a MOF repository that will be part of its Forte-NetBeans development environment.

MOF and the Resource Description Framework (RDF)

The W3C's Resource Description Framework supports the description of Web content, including "sitemaps, content ratings, stream channel definitions, search engine data collection (Web crawling), digital library collections, and distributed authoring, using XML as an interchange syntax."[19] However, the W3C actually defines RDF in abstract terms and positions the RDF XML Schema as an encoding of the abstract semantics.

While there is overlap between RDF and MOF, they have somewhat different design centers. RDF is being applied to metadata about resources on the Web, although it is not theoretically limited to the Web. MOF has been applied primarily to enterprise software tooling, although this is not a technical limitation.

One approach to integrating MOF and RDF would be to define a MOF metamodel of RDF. This would allow RDF to leverage the MOF API mappings to produce JMI and CORBA interfaces to RDF metadata. It would make it easier for RDF metadata to coexist in integrated or federated repositories that include the enterprise metadata being created via MOF. All of this would add value to RDF metadata. Note that an XMI encoding of RDF derived from the metamodel would be somewhat different from RDF's current XML encoding.

Another approach, which is not mutually exclusive with the first approach, is to define a MOF-RDF mapping. This would make it possible to express any MOF metadata as RDF metadata and thus would add value to MOF metadata.

As of the time of this writing, there have been initial contacts between teams working on MOF 2.0 and RDF regarding these integration possibilities.

What You Can Do Now

Stop hand-coding XML DTDs, XML Schemas, and Java APIs for representing and managing metadata. Consider hand-coded DTDs, Schemas, and APIs to be legacy artifacts that will have to be integrated with standards later, and so avoid creating more of them.

MOF-based metadata management tools are now available. There are even free tools available that will generate XMI DTDs and JMI interfaces from a metamodel. When you have identified metadata you need to manage, define a metamodel for it and generate the DTDs and APIs.

[19] [W3C RDF]

Even if you don't use a full-blown MOF repository right away, if the DTDs and APIs you use conform to the XMI and JMI standards, you will have a much easier time transitioning the metadata to a MOF repository than would otherwise be the case. Furthermore, if your development group is savvy about MOF, it will be at an advantage when you need to access MOF-based metadata in the corporate metadata stores of the future.

As MOF mappings to new technologies, such as WSDL, are defined, apply these same principles to using such technologies to represent and manage metadata.

Summary

MOF takes an approach to metadata integration that is distinctly different from earlier attempts to build integrated metadata repositories. The key difference is that, rather than trying to unify all modeling under one modeling language, MOF assumes that there must be different languages for different system aspects and different levels of abstraction. MOF is a key underpinning of MDA in that it gives architects a high degree of freedom to define diverse modeling languages, while still making it possible to manage diverse metadata in an integrated fashion.

MOF applies MDA principles to the production of metadata management software by focusing on metamodels. A MOF metamodel consists of a definition of the abstract syntax for a language along with some informal, textual elaboration of the language's semantics. An abstract syntax definition is a class model that uses UML-like class-modeling constructs. Hence, you can use UML tools to define an abstract syntax. Class models that define abstract syntax drive MOF-based metadata management tools.

A MOF technology mapping specifies how to translate any MOF-compliant abstract syntax into some concrete form that can be used to represent models that conform to the abstract syntax. There are three standardized mappings:

MOF-CORBA. Defines how to represent models as CORBA objects.

MOF-XML (XMI). Defines how to represent models as XML documents.

MOF-Java (JMI). Defines how to represent models as Java objects.

A mapping to WSDL is also in the pipeline.

CHAPTER 6

Extending and Creating Modeling Languages

This chapter begins by explaining UML's profiling mechanisms. It analyzes the trade-offs between extending UML via profiling and extending it via MOF. It also considers the advantages and disadvantages of leveraging UML when defining new modeling languages. It makes some observations on the differences between UML tools and MDA tools. Finally, it explains some of the differences between UML models and MOF models.

Extending UML via Profiles

In Chapter 2 we discussed the use of UML profiles. Here we take a closer look at UML profiles.

A Family of Languages[1]

UML's architects made a fundamental decision not to try to make UML all things to all people. Instead they equipped it with built-in extension mechanisms. The extension mechanisms make it possible, by means of a general-purpose UML tool, to define and use additional modeling constructs beyond those that the base UML defines.

[1] This phrase is reused with permission from Cook 2000.

A set of extensions essentially constitutes a dialect of UML, which, as explained earlier, is officially called a *profile*. Thus, UML is not one language but, instead, is a foundation for a family of UML-based languages. MDA makes heavy use of the extension mechanisms because of the need to support different system aspects and abstraction levels.

The extension mechanisms that UML provides are *stereotypes* and *tagged values*. A UML profile is a definition of a set of stereotypes and tagged values that extend elements of the UML metamodel.

Stereotypes

Figure 6.1 is a class model that is an expanded version of Figure 4.1. It uses a simple UML profile that I defined for the examples. The profile is for creating platform-independent models of distributed components.

The profile defines three stereotypes that appear in the model. These stereotypes are named `DCEntityContract`, `DCControllerContract`, and `UniqueId`.

UML notation denotes the assignment of a stereotype to a model element via what UML calls a *keyword*. Keywords are surrounded by guillemets, the French equivalent of English quotation marks. The name of the stereotype is the keyword. Thus, in our example stereotypes are denoted by <<DCEntity Contract>>, <<DCControllerContract>>, and <<UniqueId>>.[2]

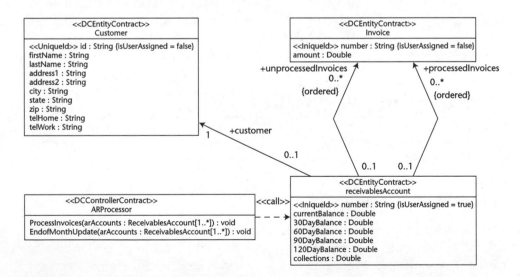

Figure 6.1   Stereotypes and tagged values.

---

[2] Although in UML notation the most common usage of keywords is to denote the stereotyping of a model element, keywords have other uses as well. For example, UML denotes an interface via the keyword interface, that is, with a class box that has the keyword <<interface>> at the top of the box. Interface is not a stereotype, but rather an element of the base UML.

The DCEntityContract stereotype is an extension of the UML meta-model's element Class. Thus, a DCEntityContract is a class that defines the contract of a distributed entity component. A DCControllerContract defines the contract of a distributed controller component. The base UML does not support making such distinctions.

The fact that the ReceivablesAccount, Customer, and Invoice classes are DCEntityContracts is expressed by placing <<DCEntityContract>> at the top of their respective class boxes, following UML notation rules. The stereotypes <<DCEntityContract>> and <<DCControllerContract>> make significant distinctions and are important input to generators, which are unlikely to treat the two identically.

For each of the DCEntityContract classes in our example, one attribute is stereotyped <<UniqueId>>, demonstrating that stereotypes can extend other UML metamodel elements besides Class. A UniqueId is an attribute whose values constitute unique identifiers for components that support the contract that the class defines. The fact that an attribute is a UniqueId is expressed by prepending the <<UniqueId>> keyword to the attribute declaration in the class box.

Figure 6.1's class model (partially) defines some contracts that components can support. As alluded to earlier, it is at a level of abstraction above component middleware such as EJB and .NET. A generator could refine this model into a middleware-specific UML model expressed in a middleware-specific profile, or it could directly produce artifacts for the chosen middleware. An EJB-specific generator, for example, would map a <<UniqueId>> stereotyped attribute to an EJB primary key class. Compilers targeting other middleware would map the <<UniqueId>> attribute differently.

Stereotypes can extend any kind of UML metamodel element. Our example profile has two stereotypes that extend the Class element and one that extends Attribute, but we could also define stereotypes that extend Association, Parameter, and so on. In fact, stereotypes are not limited to extending elements used for class modeling. They can also extend elements used for state modeling, activity modeling, and so forth.

It's also possible to define an icon for a stereotype, and to represent a stereotyped model element via the icon. Some people prefer denoting stereotypes via keywords and some by icons; it's largely a matter of personal taste, and UML's graphical notation permits either approach.

Tagged Values of Stereotypes

The definition of a stereotype can include the definition of tags. For example, the <<UniqueId>> stereotype of Attribute could define a tag that indicates whether the identifier's values are user-assigned or system-assigned. Other properties pertaining to unique identifiers that are not supported by the base UML language could be defined as tags of <<UniqueId>> as well.

Figure 6.1 illustrates a simple way to encode values of tags—that is, tagged values—in a model. I've defined a tag for <<UniqueId>> named isUser-Assigned whose values can be true or false. Our class model encodes concrete values of this defined tag—false for Customer and Invoice and true for ReceivablesAccount. The encoding is delimited by curly braces, and the syntax inside the curly braces is <tag name> "=" <tagged value>.

Standalone Tagged Values

You can also define tags that are not part of any stereotype definition. The modeler adds the values of such tags to instances of the UML model elements that the tags extend.

For example, let's define two tags that extend the UML metamodel's Operation element. The first tag, named isTx indicates whether an operation is transactional, that is, whether it is necessary to roll back any state changes the operation makes if it is not completed successfully. This is an appropriate specification for a model at this abstraction level, even though at this level we do not specify the mechanism used to ensure transactional integrity.

The second tag, named isIdempotent, indicates whether an operation is idempotent, that is, whether it is benign to execute the operation more than once.

If you're not familiar with the concept of idempotency, consider a clustered, distributed infrastructure that seeks to recover gracefully from system failure by failing over to another system that resumes processing. Such a system can make good use of an idempotency indicator on operations. In certain situations it can be very expensive for the infrastructure to keep track of whether an operation that was in progress when failure occurred ever finished executing and thus whether the infrastructure needs to reexecute the operation automatically when fail over recovery occurs.

If an operation is marked as idempotent, a smart infrastructure does not pay the price to ensure that it knows, upon fail over, whether the operation has actually executed or not—it simply invokes the operation, knowing that if it executes a second time, no harm is done. It is appropriate to specify idempotency at our platform-independent abstraction level because it is a characteristic of the fundamental logic of the operation irrespective of whether the implementation platform is EJB, .NET, and so on.

Figure 6.2 encodes concrete values of the isTx and isIdempotent tags as part of operation declarations. Note that it's permissible to encode more than one tagged value within the curly braces and that a comma delimits the two values.

The ProcessInvoices operation is idempotent because it only handles unprocessed invoices. If it executes when all invoices have already been processed, it detects that there are no unprocessed invoices and does nothing else. This rule holds regardless of the middleware implementation platform and thus is appropriately manifested in the platform-independent model.

<<DCControllerContract>>
ARProcessor
ProcessInvoices(arAccounts : ReceivablesAccounts[1..*]) : void {isTx = true, isIdempotent = true} EndOfMonthUpdate(arAccounts : ReceivablesAccounts[1..*]) : void {isTx = true, isIdempotent = false}

Figure 6.2   Tagged values not associated with a stereotype.

The `EndOfMonthUpdate` operation is not idempotent because each time the operation executes it moves current balances to 30 day balances, 30 days to 60, and so forth. Executing it an extra time would result in balances being advanced 30 days too far.

Most UML modeling tools provide additional means other than the curly braces notation to encode tagged values in models. Typically they provide dialogs or scripting tools for specifying the definitions of the tags, and dialogs for applying values of the tags to model elements. Some do not support the curly braces notation at all.

Can't We Do This at M1?

A common question at this point is: Why do we have to extend UML to model additional concepts such as idempotency and transaction support? Another way of phrasing this question, based on an understanding that our accounts receivable model is an M1 model, is: Why can't we use UML modeling constructs, such as subclassing, at the M1 level to model such additional concepts?

To understand why this is not an attractive option, let's try to go down that path. Suppose we define two classes, `IdempotentService` and `NonIdempotentService`. All operations of any class descended from `IdempotentService` in the inheritance hierarchy would be presumed to be idempotent, and operations of classes descended from `NonIdempotent Service` would be presumed to be nonidempotent. That would work to some extent, but would make it impossible to define a service that has both idempotent and nonidempotent operations, such as our accounts receivables service. Furthermore, idempotency would not be directly manifest. To determine whether an operation is idempotent you would have to up-cast over potentially several levels of the inheritance hierarchy.

Now, imagine further that we try to handle the specification of whether an operation is transactional strictly via M1 modeling without extending UML. Thus we define two classes, `TransactionalService` and `Non TransactionalService`, which determine their descendents' transaction support. This results in the same problems as trying to handle idempotency this way.

Moreover, the combination of handling both idempotency and transaction support this way has a multiplicative effect. A transactional, idempotent

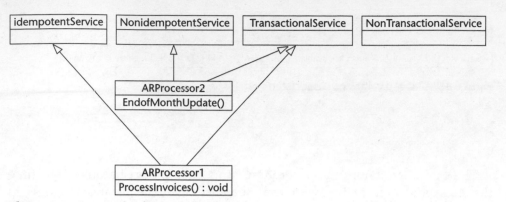

Figure 6.3   Less optimal, pure M1 approach.

operation, such as `ProcessInvoices`, would have to be a member of a class that descends from `TransactionalService` and `IdempotentService` (see Figure 6.3). A transactional, nonidempotent operation, such as `EndOf-MonthUpdate`, would have to be a member of a class that descends from `TransactionalService` and `NonIdempotentService`. Thus, the combination of the two distinctions makes the inheritance hierarchy fairly complex. Furthermore, any operation that is transactional can't be in the same class as one that isn't. Combine this with the fact that any operation that is idempotent can't be in the same class as one that isn't, and we have now boxed ourselves in quite a bit.

The problems of inheritance hierarchy complexity and lack of flexibility increase exponentially as we define additional classes meant to determine properties of member operations.

By contrast, new modeling-language constructs that directly indicate an operation's idempotency and transaction support, such as those in Figure 6.2, are free of these complications.

Defining a Profile Formally

We can define a UML profile with the same degree of precision with which we model a business application domain, such as accounts receivable. The OMG has laid out the basic technique, which is to create a formal UML model of the profile. The elements of such models are specific stereotypes, tags, and the UML metamodel elements that they extend. In UML parlance, a formal model of a UML profile is sometimes called a *virtual metamodel*.

For example, Figure 6.4 is part of a model that formally defines the stereotypes and tags of our simple profile for platform-independent distributed component modeling. A stereotype is represented as a class adorned by the keyword <<stereotype>>. The <<metaclass>> keyword adorns the UML metamodel elements being extended. The OMG standard does not dictate the coloring of the class boxes.

The model says that the stereotypes DCEntityContract and DCControllerContract extend the UML metamodel element Class and that the stereotype UniqueId extends the UML metamodel element Attribute. Tags associated with a stereotype are represented as attributes of the class representing the stereotype.

UML 1.x's graphical notation guide does not specify a way to model the definition of a standalone tagged value, that is, one that is not part of a stereotype definition. Our model uses a technique that the UML Profile for EJB specification uses,[3] which is to create a class that contains attributes representing all the tags that the profile defines for a particular element of the UML metamodel. Figure 6.4 uses this technique to model the fact that isTx and isIdempotent are tags for the UML metamodel element Operation.

Note that the declaration of the type of the tags as Boolean has no standard meaning in UML 1.4. All tags in UML are actually typed as strings.

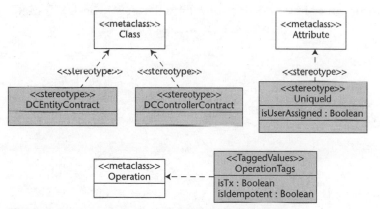

Figure 6.4 Formal class model of the sample profile.

[3] [JSR26]

```
------------------------------
--DCEntityContract Invariants
------------------------------

--At least one attribute is stereotyped <<UniqueId>>.

context DCEntityContract inv:
   self.feature->exists (isStereotyped ('UniqueId'))
```

Figure 6.5 Invariant for the sample profile.

A rigorous model of a profile includes invariant rules in the class model. For example, our profile requires that all <<DCEntityContract>>-stereotyped classes have at least one <<UniqueId>>-stereotyped attribute. (More than one <<UniqueId>>-stereotyped attribute is permitted, in which case the attribute values are concatenated to constitute an identifier.) This rule can be written as a formal invariant as in Figure 6.5.

Note that the isStereotyped operation is not part of the OCL specification but is defined as part of the UML Profile for CORBA specification, using OCL's ability to specify convenience operations.[4]

Figure 6.6 is a fragment of the UML metamodel that highlights the fact that, when the above OCL expression references feature, it is traversing an association in the metamodel. This illustrates the point that the UML metamodel is the context for a profile's constraints. Therefore, an architect or engineer who defines a UML profile must have fairly strong knowledge of the UML metamodel, or at least of the part of the metamodel being extended.

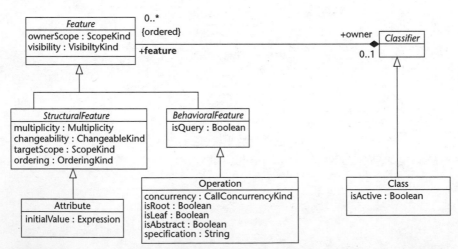

Figure 6.6 The fragment of the UML metamodel extended by the sample profile.

[4] [UML4CORBA] section 2.2.3.2.

```
----------------------
--UniqueId Invariants
----------------------
--The owning class is stereotyped <<DCEntityContract>>.

context UniqueId inv:
   self.owner.isStereotyped ('DCEntityContract')
```

Figure 6.7   Additional invariant for the sample profile.

Our simple profile has another important constraint: An attribute can only be stereotyped <<UniqueId>> if its owning class is stereotyped <<DCEntity Contract>> (see Figure 6.7).

One other thing that a formal definition of a profile must do is to declare the subset of the UML metamodel that is its scope of concern. It does this by specifying the packages of the UML metamodel that the profile imports. For example, the scope of concern of our sample profile is the set of packages that supports class modeling.

Extending UML via MOF

Profiling is not the only way to extend UML. In this section we examine an alternate approach using MOF and consider the trade-offs between that approach and profiling.

Anatomy of a Heavyweight UML Metamodel Extension

The UML metamodel is defined via MOF, and so you can extend it via MOF. UML extensions that use the full power of MOF are sometimes called *heavyweight extensions*. As we have seen, MOF offers metamodelers most of the familiar UML class-modeling constructs.

Figure 6.8 takes the heavyweight approach to defining the UML extensions that we defined via profiling in our previous example.

- It defines DCEntityContract and DCControllerContract as full-blown subclasses of the UML metamodel element Class instead of making them merely stereotypes of Class.

- It defines UniqueId as a subclass of Attribute rather than as a stereotype of it.

- It defines a subclass of Operation called EnterpriseOperation, which has isTx and isIdempotent as attributes.

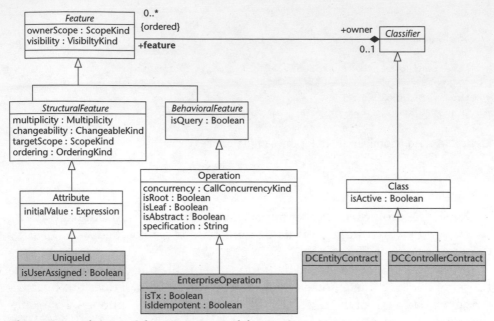

Figure 6.8   A heavyweight UML metamodel extension.

Our sample heavyweight extension, to be complete, needs to include invariants. The invariants are almost identical to the ones declared for the sample profile, so I don't repeat them here.

Profiles versus Heavyweight Extensions

When faced with a need to extend UML, an architect has to decide whether to do so via a profile or a heavyweight extension. Thus, it is important to understand the trade-offs between the two approaches.

The main advantage of the profile approach is that a modeler who wishes to use extensions defined by a profile can do so with generic UML tools. Consider the profile defined by Figures 6.4 and 6.5. Generic UML tools can be configured to support these extensions. A modeler who wishes to use the extensions does not have to depend on vendors to revise their tools, as would be the case with a heavyweight extension. In fact, Figures 6.1 and 6.2, which use the profile, were created with a generic UML tool. The quality of support for profiling varies widely among UML tools, but the major ones all support it. A good profiling tool can enforce the semantics of the profile so that, when a model declares that it is supposed to conform to a specific profile, the tool can detect when that conformance is violated.

The main disadvantage of the profile approach is that it restricts the architect of the extension from using the full semantic power of object-oriented class modeling that MOF offers. For example, we have already mentioned the weak typing of tags. In addition, you can't declare new associations among UML metamodel elements and can't declare them among stereotypes either. Such restrictions can be serious, especially for complex extensions. Creators of heavyweight extensions are free to use MOF's rich set of modeling mechanisms. MOF tools can use the greater semantic depth to intelligently manage the new kind of metadata. But taking advantage of the greater semantic expression usually makes it impossible to use the extensions when modeling with generic UML tools.

UML 2.0 will offer more power to profilers than UML 1.X. However, profiles will still not have the full power of heavyweight extensions, so there will still be a trade-off between usability by generic UML tools and semantic power.

Creating New Modeling Languages

As stated, MDA does not require you to use UML for modeling. You can use other languages, as long as you supply a MOF metamodel for each of the languages. In many cases UML will be the language for specifying some, but not all, of the aspects of a system.

Tight Domain Focus

Some kinds of models are fundamentally different from UML models because their modeling constructs don't fit easily into any of the UML modeling paradigms. When creating a MOF metamodel to define the abstract syntax of such modeling constructs, it often does not make sense to try to extend the UML metamodel.

For example, Figure 6.9 is a simple metamodel supporting graphs such as the graph in Figure 6.10. Such graphs are not UML models. A graph metamodel defined as a heavyweight UML extension would carry the baggage of the UML metamodel and thus would have a large footprint.

On the other hand, the metamodel depicted in Figure 6.9 tightly focuses on the graph domain. Hence, the model that Figure 6.10 expresses has a much smaller footprint in a MOF repository or XMI document than it would if the metamodel were derived from the UML metamodel.

A specialized graph-modeling tool that knows about these kinds of graphs would be able to support the special graph notation of Figure 6.10.

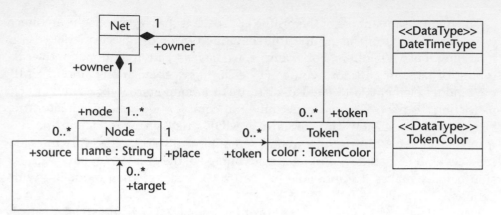

Figure 6.9 Simple metamodel for graph modeling.

Adapted, with permission, from [XMI], figure 5-1, p. 5-2.

The Metamodel + Profile Strategy

There may be a requirement in some cases to use a generic UML tool to draw our graphs. In that case, a UML profile for graph modeling could supplement the graph metamodel. Such a profile could support rendering the graph of Figure 6.10 as in Figure 6.11, for example. This rendering is not as ideal as the rendering using the graph-specific notation, but it satisfactorily expresses the semantics. The formal definition of the profile would have to:

- Select a very small subset of the UML metamodel as its scope

- Highly constrain the use and interpretation of the UML constructs included in its scope

- Define the <<Node>> stereotype and the tagged value used to describe a Node's tokens

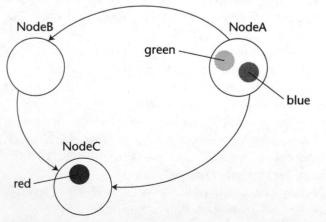

Figure 6.10 Sample graph expressed via non-UML notation.

Adapted, with permission, from [XMI], figure 5-3, p. 5-4.

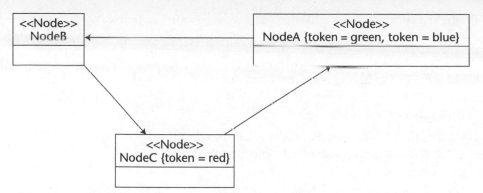

Figure 6.11   Sample graph expressed via a UML profile.

Our profile is rather crude. It's possible to do a more elegant job that would better mimic the special graph notation of Figure 6.10, but it still would fall short of completely reproducing that notation.

Given the "Metamodel + Profile" strategy, there are two tactics for representing Figure 6.11 as MOF metadata:

Render it as a UML model.   Using this tactic, the APIs that represent the model in a MOF repository will be those generated from the UML metamodel. When the model is encoded in an XMI document, the document will conform to the XML DTD and Schema generated from the UML metamodel. The advantage of this approach is that a UML tool that knows how to render UML models as MOF metadata can render the graph model accordingly without having to add any new functionality or configuration scripts that know about the graph profile or metamodel. The UML metamodel defines the abstract syntax of the stereotype and tagged value constructs. The MOF technology mappings translate the abstract syntax into concrete representations—for example, DTD elements and Java interfaces—for representing a stereotype such as <<Node>> and a tagged value such as red in XML documents and as Java objects.

Render it as a graph model.   Using this tactic, the APIs that represent the model in a MOF repository will be those generated from the graph metamodel. When the model is encoded in an XMI document, the document will conform to the XML DTD and Schema generated from the graph metamodel. The advantages of this approach are that the metadata footprint is small and the semantic information is more precisely aligned with the graph domain concepts. In order to use this tactic, the generic UML tool would have to have the configuration knowledge that allows it to do metamodel-specific rendering of the metadata. Such configuration knowledge would be part of a modeling framework for the graph domain that plugs in to the generic tool.

There are some notable instances of the "Metamodel + Profile" strategy in the software standards arena. In each case, the metamodel is not an extension of UML:

UML Profile for EJB.   The OMG has adopted a MOF metamodel of Java and EJB[5] to complement the UML Profile for EJB[6] that the Java Community Process is working on.

UML for EAI.   This specification, mentioned earlier, actually defines both a MOF metamodel and a UML profile for modeling enterprise application integration.[7]

UML Profile for CORBA.   The OMG has defined a MOF metamodel of CORBA[8] and a UML Profile for CORBA[9] as well.

Heavyweight + Lightweight Extension Strategy

There is an important variant of the "Metamodel + Profile" strategy, in which the metamodel is a heavyweight UML extension. I call this the "Heavyweight + Lightweight Extension" strategy since a profile is, in effect, a lightweight UML extension.

For example, we might define a metamodel for database-modeling constructs that extends the UML class-modeling constructs, but also define a UML profile so that modelers can use generic UML tools to model databases.

UML Tools versus MDA Tools

As we've discussed, the primary motivation for creating UML profiles is to create specialized languages that generic UML tools can handle. It is to UML's credit that it has a profiling mechanism, so that UML modelers are not saddled with a rigid, one-size-fits-all language. It allows us to use UML-based languages for various aspects of a system. It is easier to combine languages that have a common basis than ones that are completely disparate.

However, the limitations of UML profiles are still significant. The degree of freedom to define new syntax and semantics is considerably less than that available for MOF metamodeling. While you can use UML tools to *define* a new MOF metamodel, you run into problems, as we have seen, trying to use UML tools to create models of the kind defined by the metamodel. For example, we

---

[5] [UML4EDOC], Chapter 5
[6] [JSR26]
[7] [UML4EAI]
[8] [CCM]
[9] [UML4CORBA]

can use a UML tool to define our graph metamodel, but not to support the special graph notation illustrated in Figure 6.10. To use the UML tool to draw graphs, you must define a UML profile and accept the limitations profiling imposes. You face this trade-off regardless of whether your MOF metamodel is an extension of the UML metamodel.

We can envision MDA tools on the horizon that provide much more freedom and eliminate the distinction between metamodels and profiles. With such tools you simply define the abstract syntax for your domain and define graphical concrete syntaxes. You also supply generators that interpret the syntaxes and that, via transformations, generate other models, code, or executables. Thus, the trade-off between profiling and metamodeling ceases to be a consideration. However, commercial availability of such technology based on standards is probably several years away.

UML Modeling versus MOF Metamodeling

MOF class models are, strictly speaking, intended to be models of modeling constructs, while UML models are supposed to be models of real-world entities and processes such as customers and accounts. In other words, MOF metamodels are M2 things and UML models are M1 things.

However, MOF and UML class modeling are so similar that you can use UML tools to create MOF metamodels if you follow a few basic rules.

The UML Profile for MOF[10], which was adopted by the OMG while this book was being written, spells out the rules in full detail for using UML to specify MOF metamodels. I cover only the basic principles.

UML Constructs that MOF Does Not Support

There are some UML class-modeling constructs that MOF does not support. Thus, if you want to create a class model that is a valid MOF metamodel and that, therefore, can be fed to a MOF-based generator, you need to avoid using these constructs. Here are the basic rules:

- Don't use association classes.
- Don't use qualifiers.
- Don't use *n*-ary associations (that is, use only binary associations).
- Don't use dependencies.

In UML an *association class* is an association that is a full-blown class and thus can have class properties such as attributes. MOF does not support association classes. Figure 6.12 illustrates that you can decompose an association

---

[10] [UML4EDOC], Chapter 6.

class that relates any two classes A and B by modeling a class that has separate associations with A and B, respectively. Some MOF generators do this decomposition logic automatically and thus accept association classes. But if you want to guarantee that your model will be acceptable to a MOF generator, avoid association classes.

Qualifiers are also known as *qualified associations*. They are not widely used by UML modelers, but some do use them quite heavily. They are a bit complex, so explaining what they are is beyond the scope of this book. If you are accustomed to using them, suffice it to say that, since a qualifier is essentially an attribute of an association, one way to work around this limitation is to use an approach similar to association class decomposition, that is, modeling the association as a class with the qualifier as an attribute of the class.

A binary association is an association between two classes. An *n-ary association* is an association among more than two classes. Most UML tools support only binary associations, as is the case with MOF. If you use *n*-ary associations, you'll have to decompose them into binary associations, usually by modeling the *n*-ary association itself as a class, as illustrated by Figure 6.13.

In UML a *dependency* indicates a semantic dependence of one model element on another but, unlike an association, it does not mandate that the system maintain links between instances of the elements at runtime. MOF does not support modeling dependencies, and there is no workaround. If you use them, the best outcome is that a MOF-based generator will ignore them. The worst case is that it will reject them.

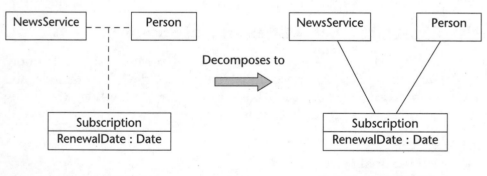

Figure 6.12 Decomposing association classes.

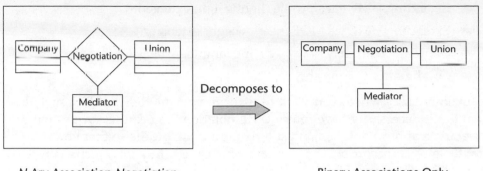

N-Ary Association *Negotiation*,
Associating Three Classes

Binary Associations Only

Figure 6.13:   Decomposing an *n*-ary association.

What You Can Do Now

It pays to think carefully about what your language requirements are. What are the system aspects that the languages need to address? When considering any particular domain, ask yourself what kinds of people—what Alan Cooper would call *personas*[11]—will be modeling the domain. Is UML notation appropriate for them? With what kinds of tools might you need to exchange models? If they are UML tools, you probably need to be able to import and export models via XML that conforms to the UML XMI DTD or Schema, and that means you will need a UML profile for the domain even if you use a non-UML notation.

Coming up with a basic language strategy is an important first step in transitioning to MDA.

Summary

MDA does not require that you use the base UML for all your language needs. UML profiling and MOF give you many options to support the modeling of a particular aspect of a system:

[11] [COOP 1999]

- Extending UML via a profile (lightweight extension)
- Extending UML via MOF (heavyweight extension)
- Defining an entirely new modeling language via MOF
- Combinations of the above

Even in cases where you want to manage your models as UML metadata, you don't necessarily have to use UML notation. You can use your own proprietary graphical notation, but still define a UML profile so that you can render the models according to a standard concrete UML syntax, such as the UML XMI DTD. That way, UML tools can import the models. For example, an EAI tool might use its own specialized graphical notation, yet it could export and import XMI renditions of EAI models where the XMI conforms to the UML Profile for EAI.

MOF doesn't support all of UML's class-modeling constructs. This must be taken into account when creating metamodels.

Building Compilable
Class Models

As of this writing, MDA mappings don't actually define how to compile UML class models, which are M1 things. They define how to compile *MOF* class models, that is, MOF metamodels, which are M2 things. As mentioned in earlier chapters, the OMG and Java Community Process have already applied these mappings to several standardized metamodels to produce standard APIs and information formats, including Java APIs, CORBA APIs, XML DTDs, and XML Schemas. Mappings of various UML profiles will emerge soon. These mappings will define how to compile M1 models, but will leverage certain principles of the MOF mappings for mapping class models.

It is thus worth examining these basic mapping principles. Drawing on these principles, this chapter lays out a set of guidelines for building class models that the new breed of generators that conform to these mapping standards can compile efficiently. Developers can use these guidelines to help ensure that the APIs and information formats generated from their class models are of high quality and that the implementations of the generated APIs and formats that tools produce are optimal.

The Scope of the Guidelines

In this section we establish the scope to which the modeling guidelines apply.

Class Modeling versus Behavioral Modeling

So far, all standardized MDA mappings take class models as input. The OMG has not yet standardized mappings that take behavioral models—that is, state models, interaction models, activity models, and action semantics—as input. There are commercial generators that process behavioral models, but the generation algorithms are not standardized.

It is only a matter of time before the OMG and other standards initiatives, such as ebXML and RosettaNet, standardize mappings for UML behavioral models. But in this chapter, as in this book, we focus on class models.

Level of Abstraction

As we have already seen, MOF metamodels are platform-independent, meaning they are independent of:

- Information-formatting technologies such as XML DTD and XML Schema
- 3GLs and 4GLs such as Java, C++, C#, and Visual Basic
- Distributed component middleware, such as J2EE, CORBA, and .NET
- Messaging middleware such as WebSphere MQ Integrator and MSMQ

The sample profile defined in Chapter 6 is also platform-independent in the same sense. This particular level of abstraction is a recurring theme because, as mentioned earlier, it is one level above today's typical development environments and thus is important for raising the development abstraction level.

For this reason, the MDA mappings that have been standardized so far are oriented to supporting generators that process models that are platform-independent models in this sense. Thus, this chapter's discussion of the mappings' basic principles assumes this abstraction level. You can apply some of the principles to models that are at lower levels of abstraction, but that is not the focus of these guidelines.

In this chapter, when I refer to a platform-independent model (PIM), I actually mean a PIM that is a *class* model.

What the Standard MDA Mappings Produce

Let's review what generators based on the standard MDA mappings produce.

The outputs standardized by MDA mappings are APIs and information formats expressed in the languages of the target technologies, including Java, XML, and CORBA IDL. The standards don't specify the exact code that *implements* the generated APIs and formats. As we've seen, however, they specify the semantics of the APIs and formats produced sufficiently to support interoperability between implementations of the APIs and formats.

For example, the JCP's Java Metadata Interface (JMI) specification defines how to generate Java APIs from a class model and specifies the semantics of those interfaces, but does not specify the exact code that implements the interfaces. For interoperability purposes, standardizing the syntax and semantics of APIs is sufficient. Specifying the derivation of implementation code would tie implementers' hands too much.

The OMG's XML Metadata Interchange (XMI) standard specifies how to derive an XML-based information format—that is, an XML DTD or Schema—from a MOF class model and how to produce XML documents that conform to the DTD or Schema. It does not specify the exact code that actually produces and manages the XML documents, although it specifies the semantics of such code so that different code bases conforming to the specification can interoperate.

UML versus MOF

Although MOF is close to being a subset of UML, this chapter points out a number of cases where MOF and UML are slightly out of phase with each other. This complicates matters when trying to leverage MOF technology for constructing M1 models and processing them with generators. It forces us to have to explain the differences and modelers to have to understand them.

UML 2.0 should address these differences. As mentioned in Chapter 3, the UML 2.0 Infrastructure RFP specifically mandates that UML 2.0 correct the misalignment between MOF and UML.

There are cases where it's useful to employ a generator that implements the MOF technology mappings to transform an M1 model, since there are generators available that can perform these transformations. In such cases the M1 model must adhere to the restrictions imposed on MOF metamodelers (Chapter 6 covered these restrictions). Furthermore, there are some special issues that arise with M1 class models that are covered later in this chapter.

Purposes of the Guidelines

As I mentioned, independently of whether your PIM is a UML model or a MOF metamodel, MDA mappings will follow some basic principles. Our guidelines flow from these principles and have three general goals:

- Ensure that the generator does not reject the model.
- Ensure that APIs and information formats that the generator produces are of the highest possible quality.
- For generators that produce implementations of the generated APIs and information formats, ensure that the implementations are optimal.

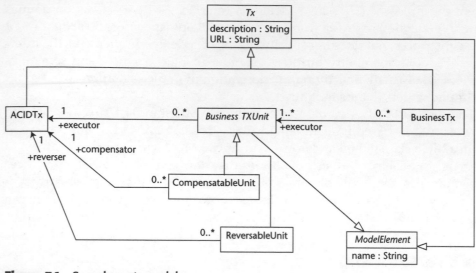

Figure 7.1   Sample metamodel.

Some of this section's examples use the sample metamodel whose abstract syntax is shown in Figure 7.1. Appendix A contains informal definitions of the classes of metadata that the metamodel defines.

Don't Define Accessor and Mutator Operations for Attributes

When you define an attribute of a class, don't also define routine accessor and mutator (that is, get and set) operations for the attribute in your class definition. MDA mappings that generate APIs from a class definition expand attributes into accessor and mutator operations automatically. The generated APIs also include an operation for every operation declared in the class. Therefore, if you define accessor and mutator operations in the class, they will produce redundant operations in the generated APIs.

Figure 7.2 illustrates the basic rule for mapping an attribute when generating an API for the owning class. It also shows the specific JMI application of the general rule, which makes it clear that declaration of accessor and mutator operations in the class model would be redundant.

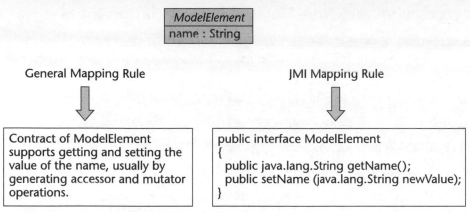

Figure 7.2   API generation rule for class attributes.

The standard algorithms for generating CORBA IDL-based APIs, defined in the MOF specification, also adhere to this fundamental rule. Note that the general principle is that the contract of the class must support getting and setting the value of the attribute by some means. The general rule does not actually *require* that this be accomplished via a pair of operations. A mapping to CORBA IDL could be defined such that each UML or MOF class attribute generates a CORBA attribute. However, the architects of the standardized MOF-IDL mapping decided to generate a pair of operations because at the time the mapping was defined CORBA attributes did not support user-defined exceptions.

Note that this basic mapping rule does not necessarily hold for class models that are at a middleware-specific level of abstraction. For example, an EJB-specific class model that directly specifies Java interfaces and classes using the UML Profile for EJB[1] must explicitly define every operation, including simple accessors and mutators that have been generated from a PIM. As stated, however, the MDA mappings we are discussing are for PIMs.

Use Association End Navigability Judiciously

UML modelers often are not concerned with being precise about whether the ends of associations in their models are navigable. However, generators treat navigable ends quite differently from non-navigable ones.

[1] [JSR26]

Navigable versus Non-Navigable Association Ends

When defining an association between two classes, A and B, there are four possible choices the modeler can make as to the navigability of the association ends.

- The A end is navigable and the B end is not.
- The A end is not navigable and the B end is.
- Both the A and B ends are navigable.
- Neither the A nor the B end is navigable.

The choice the modeler makes significantly affects the content of APIs and information formats generated from the class model. Many modelers don't bother to specify navigability of association ends, accepting whatever default values the modeling tool provides. While this attitude may be acceptable for informal modeling, it is impractical if the goal is to build a compilable model.

Navigability and Contracts

To begin to understand why this is so, consider Figure 7.3. The association between BusinessTxUnit and ACIDTx is navigable on the ACIDTx end, as denoted by the open-headed arrow. It's not navigable on the BusinessTxUnit end. The ACIDTx end is named executor. The association as specified says that for any instance of BusinessTxUnit there is exactly one instance of ACIDTx that plays the role of being that BusinessTxUnit's executor.

The navigability on the ACIDTx end affects the contract of the class on the *opposite* end of the association, namely the contract of BusinessTxUnit. MDA API generators treat the navigable end as a property of the opposite class. The effect of this treatment is evident in the interface generated for BusinessTxUnit by JMI, which has accessor and mutator operations for getting and setting the value of the BusinessTxUnit's executor ACIDTx, as Figure 7.3 demonstrates.

Now, consider Figure 7.4, which focuses on the class opposite a *non-navigable* association end. In our sample association, ACIDTx is the class opposite the non-navigable end of the association. The standard API mappings do not consider a non-navigable end to be a property of the opposite class. The result in our example is that the contract of an ACIDTx does not support getting and setting the values of the BusinessTxUnits for which it is the executor.

Thus, a modeler should define an association end as navigable only when it is truly necessary. Since a navigable association end enlarges the size of the API generated for the opposite class, overuse of navigability causes generators to produce unnecessarily large and complex APIs.

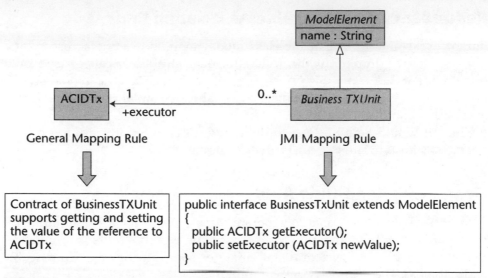

Figure 7.3 API generation rule for navigable association ends.

Note that in our example the only generated APIs we show are those that define the contracts of the two associated classes, that is, the APIs for `BusinessTxUnit` and `ACIDTx`. It's important to understand that making the `BusinessTxUnit` end of our sample association non-navigable does not mean that the generated APIs don't support determining which `BusinessTxUnit` instances are linked to a particular `ACIDTx` instance. There are additional APIs that are generated for the association itself that support this kind of querying, which we'll look at shortly.

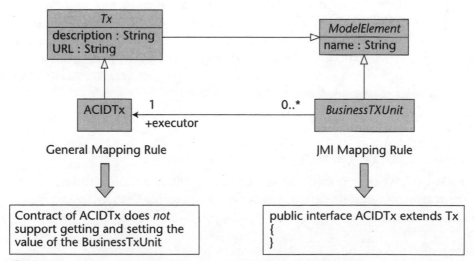

Figure 7.4 API generation rule for non-navigable association ends.

Redundancy and Navigable Association Ends

Earlier, we pointed out that the class model shouldn't define accessors and mutators that are implied by the declaration of an attribute because they would be redundant. We apply this principle similarly here: The class model should not define accessors and mutators that are already implied by the navigable association ends.

Thus, it would be a mistake to define getExecutor and setExecutor operations for BusinessTxUnit in our class model.

Generating Read-Only APIs

It's not necessarily desirable to generate accessor *and* mutator operations for every single attribute and navigable association end. It's quite common that the requirements of a system dictate that, for some attributes and navigable ends, accessors be generated but not mutators.

UML 1.X does not really provide a means to control whether mutators are generated. It does have a property for attributes and association ends called changeability. The description of the semantics of this property is somewhat inconsistent in the UML specification, but it's often interpreted to indicate whether the value of the property is allowed to change once an instance of the class has been initialized. This is quite different from indicating whether the intent is to provide a mechanism that supports a client's setting the value.

Most likely UML 2.0 will clear up this confusion and provide two separate indicators for the two different concerns. In the meantime, MOF, unlike UML, *does* have an indicator for attributes and association ends, whose intent clearly is to indicate whether the contract supports the ability of a client to set the value. This indicator is a Boolean property named isChangeable.

The UML profile for MOF chooses to interpret the ambiguous UML property as meaning the same thing as the MOF's isChangeable. The UML property, though, is not Boolean. Its type is ChangeableKind, an enumeration that has three possible values: changeable, frozen, or addOnly. The UML Profile for MOF interprets these values as follows:

changeable.   Equivalent to MOF isChangeable = true. (This is the default value.)

frozen.   Equivalent to MOF isChangeable = false.

addOnly.   Not supported. (MOF-based generators should probably reject models that designate attributes or navigable association ends as addOnly.)

Unfortunately, some UML tools don't support the UML changeability property. MOF-based generators work around this deficiency by providing UML tool add-ins that define a tagged value corresponding to the MOF isChangeable property. The add-ins allow modelers to specify, for each attribute and navigable association end, whether isChangeable is true or false. True is the default value.

When a generator sees that isChangeable is false for an attribute or navigable end, it infers that, for the contract of the affected class, it should not generate a mechanism that clients can use to set the value. If the mapping to the target API language adheres to the typical pattern of generating an accessor operation and a mutator operation, the mutator operation is omitted. Readers familiar with CORBA IDL will thus note that declaring isChangeable = false is similar to a CORBA attribute being declared readonly, in that CORBA language mappings do not generate mutator operations for readonly attributes.

The value of isChangeable for an attribute or navigable association end has no effect on information format generation. Information formats such as XML DTDs are not APIs, and thus the question of whether to generate a mutator API is moot.

The general principle to take away from this detail about MOF is that you should check how the particular generator you're using supports the ability to declare that a mutator should not be generated. Use this capability when warranted. Generator vendors should be sure not to neglect the ability to suppress mutator generation.

Navigability and Information Formats

MDA generators that produce information formats also treat navigable and non-navigable association ends differently, following principles similar to those that API generators use. Figure 7.5 again illustrates the rule that, when a generator produces an information format definition for a class, it considers navigable association ends opposite the class to be properties of the class. It also shows how an XMI generator applies the general rule to our sample association in order to produce an XML DTD.

I show only a fragment of the generated XMI DTD code for BusinessTxUnit. The fragment shows that the executor ACIDTx is defined as a property of BusinessTxUnit because in the class model executor is a navigable association opposite BusinessTxUnit. From this example it should be clear that overuse of navigability causes generators to produce unnecessarily bloated information formats.

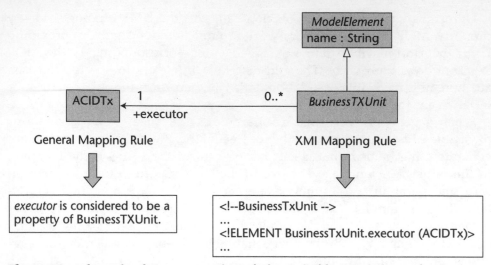

Figure 7.5 Information format generation rule for navigable association ends.

Avoiding Name Clashes

Since generators treat a navigable association end as a property of the opposite class, it's important not to give the same name to two ends opposite the same class. Failure to observe this rule leads to name clashes in generated APIs and information formats.

Figure 7.6 shows the potential for this kind of name clash and how to avoid it. Also keep in mind that if the name of a class attribute is the same as the name of one of the class's opposite navigable association ends, that too results in a name clash.

Navigability and Modularity

It's a common UML and MOF modeling practice to use packages to organize model elements into manageable groupings. It's important to the architecture of such systems to keep tight control over the dependencies among packages. If a model with mismanaged dependencies is submitted to an MDA generator, the problematical dependencies will be carried through to generated artifacts such as Java APIs and XML DTDs.

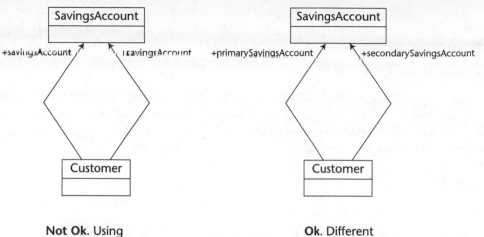

Not Ok. Using same association end name means two properties of Customer have the same name.

Ok. Different association end names distinguish the two properties of Customer.

Figure 7.6 Navigable end name clashing.

For example, the architecture of a financial accounting system may dictate that the general ledger system be independent of the accounts payable and accounts receivable systems. The accounts payable and receivable systems know about the general ledger system because they have to post debits and credits to the ledger. However, the general ledger system is specifically constructed to be independent of the other systems so that it can be deployed with or without those systems and so that new satellite systems, such as inventory and construction job costing, can be added on to the system as a whole without necessitating changes to the general ledger code.

Figure 7.7 illustrates this point. The dashed arrowheaded line uses UML notation to indicate the intent that the AccountsPayable package be dependent on the GeneralLedger package and not vice versa. You can define an association between an element in the GeneralLedger package and an element in the AccountsPayable package without violating this intent as long as the association end for the element in the AccountsPayable package is non-navigable.

Figure 7.7(a) shows an association that does not violate the independence of the GeneralLedger package. The APAcct's end of the association is non-navigable, so the contract of GLAcct is not affected by the association.

The association defined in Figure 7.7(b) does violate the independence of the GeneralLedger package because the end opposite of GLAcct is navigable. Generators that produce APIs infer that the contract of a GLAcct includes a means for clients to get and set the APAcct instances to which a GLAcct is linked.

The class diagram defining the association in Figure 7.7(c) is ambiguous because of an ambiguity in UML notation. When an association line has arrows at neither end, it can mean that neither of the ends is navigable or that both of the ends are navigable. There is no way to ascertain which of these two possibilities is actually the case simply by looking at the diagram. You have to use the UML tool's drill-down dialogs or context menus to examine the detailed properties of the association in order to see whether the ends are navigable.

If neither end of the association in Figure 7.7(c) is navigable, then the independence of the GeneralLedger package is not violated. If both ends are navigable, then the navigability of the end opposite GLAcct violates this independence even though the navigability of the end opposite APAcct is not a problem.

Note that the ambiguity of the notation in Figure 7.7(c) does not confuse generators because they don't read class diagrams; instead, they read the actual properties of the model that the UML tool stores. The ambiguity only affects human modelers.

Although we've considered the impact of navigability on modularity from the point of view of the contracts of generated APIs, the picture is very similar when we look at it from the viewpoint of the properties of generated information formats such as XML DTDs. The association defined in Figure 7.7(a) adds a property of type GLAcct to the format element corresponding to APAcct, which is acceptable. However Figure 7.7(b)'s association adds a property of type APAcct to the GLAcct format element, thus violating the GeneralLedger package's independence.

A MOF Complication

MOF 1.X does not consider an association end to be navigable in the sense in which we've discussed it in this section unless a MOF construct called a *reference* is declared on the opposite class. A reference declaration in a class refers to a navigable association end opposite the class. This anomaly will almost certainly be fixed in MOF 2.0.

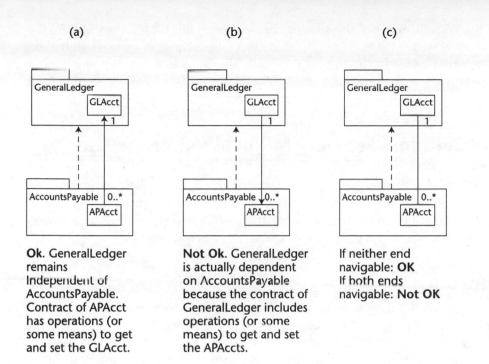

(a)

Ok. GeneralLedger remains Independent of AccountsPayable. Contract of APAcct has operations (or some means) to get and set the GLAcct.

(b)

Not Ok. GeneralLedger is actually dependent on AccountsPayable because the contract of GeneralLedger includes operations (or some means) to get and set the APAccts.

(c)

If neither end navigable: **OK**
If both ends navigable: **Not OK**

Figure 7.7 Navigability implies dependency.

Thus, with MOF 1.X there are actually three possibilities with respect to an association end:

It is non-navigable. In this case even the association API (which we look at later) does not have a means for accessing and changing links at run-time.

It is navigable but there is no reference. In this case, the association API has means for accessing and changing links, but the opposite class does not.

It is navigable and there is a reference. In this case both the association API and the opposite class have means for accessing and changing links.

In MOF 2.0 there most likely will only be two possibilities—navigable and non-navigable.

This complication is the reason that some of the OMG's standard MOF metamodels often declare a navigable association end *and* a derived attribute of the same name in the opposite class. UML denotes a derived attribute by prepending a "/" character to the attribute name. The UML Profile for MOF uses derived attributes to declare references.

Use Care in Specifying Multivalued Properties

A multivalued attribute or association end has a multiplicity whose upper bound is greater than one. UML and MOF provide the modeler with some choices about the characteristics of such multivalued properties. It is important to understand the implications of the various options.

Ordering

UML and MOF allow you to specify whether the contents of a multivalued attribute or multivalued association end are ordered. MDA generators use ordering information when generating APIs.

For example, if a multivalued attribute or multivalued navigable association end is marked as ordered, then the JMI mapping dictates that generated Java APIs use the Java `List` interface; if the multivalued attribute or end is not ordered, the generated APIs use the Java `Collection` interface.

UML tools are uneven in their support for the specification of ordering. Generators usually supply tool add-ins to fill in the gaps. The default is usually unordered, so if you don't override the default, a JMI-compliant generator will assume that you don't need the `List` interface. This can be a real problem if you need the `List` APIs to allow you to deal with ordering.

The bottom line: Don't blindly accept the tool defaults for ordering. Think carefully about each of your multivalued attributes and association ends, and make the correct specification regarding ordering.

Uniqueness

When a model defines a multivalued attribute, association end, or parameter, the question arises as to whether the modeler's intention is to allow duplicate values in the collection or whether, to the contrary, each member of the collection must be unique. UML 1.X does not provide a means to express this distinction, while MOF does via its `isUnique` property.[2] Consequently, the UML tool add-ins packaged with MDA generators usually provide a means for the modeler to indicate uniqueness as a tagged value, where the default is not unique.

---

[2] At press time the current versions of MOF and UML required that multivalued association ends have no duplicates. This will probably change in MOF and UML 2.0.

Uniqueness does not always affect how generators produce APIs and information formats. However, it does affect the behavior of the generated implementations of the APIs and formats, which should enforce all specified uniqueness constraints.

Here again the fact that tool add-ins usually supply defaults can lull you into neglecting to think about uniqueness when you model a multivalued element. The defaults are not always what you want. Be deliberate about specifying uniqueness or non-uniqueness.

Use Aggregation . . . Properly

Often times modelers avoid using aggregation when they define associations. There are a number of reasons for this. One is that the UML specification and many books about UML refrain from nailing down precise semantics for aggregation. This reluctance to define the semantics stems partially from a lack of agreement in the UML community as to the meaning of aggregation.

However, MDA generators follow very specific rules about aggregation semantics. When a generator maps an association, the syntax (signatures) of the generated APIs are the same regardless of whether the association is an aggregation. However, the semantics of the APIs—that is, the behavior that they are supposed to execute—differ according to the association's aggregation properties. These semantics are part of the MOF standard, and MOF-based generators must implement them in order to ensure interoperability among MOF-compliant products. As mentioned earlier, standards for applying transformations to UML-based PIMs that will emerge over the next few years will build on the groundwork laid by the MOF mappings.

Aggregation Properties of Association Ends

Aggregation is usually thought of as a whole-part relationship. An association end has a property named `aggregation` that can have one of three values: `none`, `shared`, or `composite`. If the property is `none`, then the end is not an aggregate; that is, it's not the "whole" in a whole-part association. If the property value is `shared`, then the end is a whole, but is considered a "weak" aggregate. If the property value is `composite`, then the end is a "strong" aggregate. The UML graphical notation uses a white diamond to denote that an end is a shared aggregate and a black diamond to denote that it is a composite aggregate.[3]

It's illegal for more than one end of an association to be an aggregate; that is, the aggregation property value may be `shared` or `composite` at most for one of the ends of an association. This means that only one end can be the "whole."

---

[3] There is a possibility that, in UML 2.0, the aggregation property will be specified on the other end of the association, that is, on the part rather than the whole.

Composite Aggregation

Figure 7.8 illustrates the properties of composite aggregation. In terms of our example, the semantics of the association are that, if an instance b1 of B is linked to an instance a1 of A via the association, then when a1 is destroyed b1 no longer has the context required to give it meaning, and thus must also be destroyed.

The association between an apartment building and an apartment is a good example of composite aggregation from everyday life. Destruction of the apartment building implies destruction of all of the apartments that the building contains.

In terms of our example, the definition of composite aggregation also requires that any instance of B can be owned at most by one instance of A; that is, ownership cannot be shared.

Some modelers mistakenly assume that the multiplicity of the composite aggregate end of an association must be 1..1 and thus often don't bother to specify it. However, it can also be 0..1.

- An instance of B can be owned by only 1 instance of A.
- Multiplicity on the A end can be 0..1 or 1..1, so it must be specified !!
    - 0..1 means that a B can exist without being linked to an A.
        - But if a B *is* linked to an A, then if that A is destroyed that B must be destroyed as well.
- Multiplicity of B is unconstrained.
- A.k.a "black diamond".

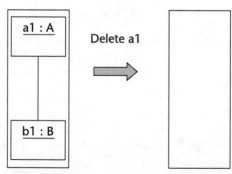

Delete a1

Figure 7.8 Composite (strong) aggregation semantics.

A multiplicity of 0..1 on a composite aggregate end means, in terms of our example, that an instance b1 of B may exist independently of any instances of A that is, it may be created and live on without being linked to an A. However, if an instance b1 of B *is* linked to some instance a1 of A, then if a1 is destroyed, b1 must be destroyed too, regardless of whether the link between b1 and a1 was established when b1 was created or not until some time afterward.

A good example of a 0..1 multiplicity on a composite aggregate end from the world of computing is the association of a database transaction with a two-phase commit transaction. We can model this association as shown in Figure 7.9. A database transaction can execute on its own without being part of a larger two-phase commit transaction. However, if it is one of the transactions managed by a two-phase commit transaction, then it's not independent. Note that Figure 7.9 models run-time transactions, unlike our previous transaction example shown in Figure 7.1, which models transaction metadata.

The behavior of implementations of generated APIs is affected by the principles of composite aggregation. In terms of Figure 7.8, a generated destroy operation on a1 should automatically destroy b1. Thus, the generator can enforce the semantics of aggregation when appropriate without the programmer having to write the procedural 3GL code to do so. This is what raising the level of abstraction is about.

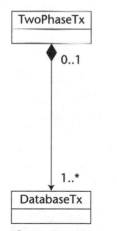

Figure 7.9 A composite aggregate end with 0..1 multiplicity.

Composite aggregation also affects how XMI streams an instance of a class. It renders composed instances as nested XML elements; that is, it serializes all the properties of composed instances within the serialization of the composite instance. For example, an XMI rendering of instance a1 of Figure 7.8 would contain a complete rendering of all of the properties of the composed instance b1. On the other hand, XMI renders noncomposed instances as XML references. If in Figure 7.8 the association were just an ordinary association rather than a composition, XMI rendering of instance a1 would contain only a reference to an XMI b1 element, whose properties would be rendered elsewhere.

Most class models of more than trivial complexity are likely to have composite aggregation semantics in a number of places, whether or not the modeler identifies them. Failure to identify these aggregations is a failure to fully exploit the power of MDA generators.

Shared Aggregation

Shared aggregation is a controversial subject. Early versions of the MOF attempted to define its semantics, and subsequent versions backed off. Some people suggest that we can do without shared aggregation.

The basic idea of shared aggregation is that ownership is shared rather than exclusive. In Figure 7.10 the E end of the association is a shared aggregate of F. This permits a situation, shown in the figure, where an instance f1 of F can be owned by more than one instance of E. One possible interpretation of shared aggregation is that, when one of the owners is destroyed, f1 may continue to exist; however, when the last owner is destroyed, f1 must be destroyed. However, there are other interpretations. There is no consensus in the industry about the semantics of shared aggregation.

Some UML tools default to shared aggregation when the modeler selects aggregation. Modelers often don't take the time to change the default to composite because they aren't considering the important difference in semantics between shared and composite. Here again, this practice may be all right for informal modeling. But MDA generators treat shared and composite aggregation very differently. In fact, because shared aggregation is not precisely specified by MOF, as of this writing MDA generators don't treat shared aggregation any differently from an ordinary association with no aggregation.

Therefore, if composition semantics are what you're after, make sure you specify that is what you mean rather than just falling back on shared as the default form of aggregation. In my opinion, it would be best for tools to treat composition as the default kind of aggregation.

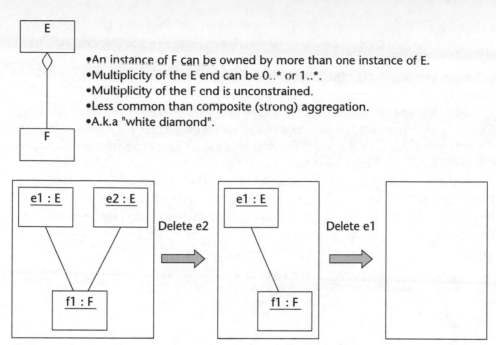

•An instance of F can be owned by more than one instance of E.
•Multiplicity of the E end can be 0..* or 1..*.
•Multiplicity of the F end is unconstrained.
•Less common than composite (strong) aggregation.
•A.k.a "white diamond".

Figure 7.10 Possible semantics of shared (weak) aggregation.

Use Abstract Classes

Here I use the terms *abstract* and *concrete* in a different sense than I've tended to use them so far. In UML and MOF, an abstract class is one that cannot be directly instantiated. Only nonabstract (also called concrete) subclasses of the abstract class may be instantiated. This is very similar to the meaning of abstract in Java. Unfortunately, there is some overloading of terminology here with our emphasis on levels of abstraction.

Nevertheless, if you take the time to think about which classes in your PIM are abstract in the UML-Java sense, and to specify them as such, MDA generators will reward you for your efforts. Specifically, they won't generate factory operations for abstract classes. Thus, they will produce APIs with smaller footprints than would be the case if every class were concrete, and those APIs will be more correct because it's probably not a good idea to provide a client with a means to directly create an instance of an abstract class.

Figure 7.11 and Figure 7.12 illustrate the point. Figure 7.11 demonstrates that, because `ACIDTx` is concrete, generators produce factory operations for it. In Figure 7.12 we see that, because `Tx` is abstract (as denoted by the italicized name, in keeping with UML notation), generators don't produce factory operations for it.

Note that the standardized API generation rules for producing Java and CORBA APIs produce an instance management interface for each class in the model, in addition to the interface that represents instances of the class.[4] Generated instance management interfaces descend from certain MOF Reflective Interfaces that, among other things, allow a client to obtain a list of all instances of the class. The factory operations generated for a concrete class from the model are part of the instance management interface generated for that class.

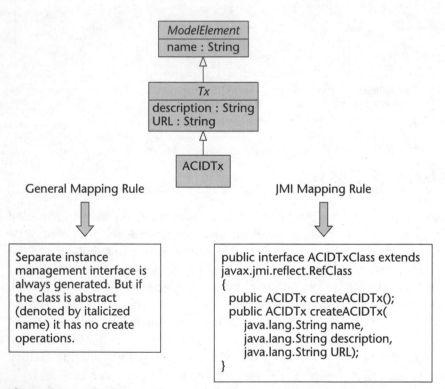

General Mapping Rule

JMI Mapping Rule

Separate instance management interface is always generated. But if the class is abstract (denoted by italicized name) it has no create operations.

```
public interface ACIDTxClass extends
javax.jmi.reflect.RefClass
{
    public ACIDTx createACIDTx();
    public ACIDTx createACIDTx(
        java.lang.String name,
        java.lang.String description,
        java.lang.String URL);
}
```

Figure 7.11 Mapping nonabstract classes.

[4] The MOF and JMI specifications refer to generated instance management interfaces as *class proxies*, which I find to be a confusing term.

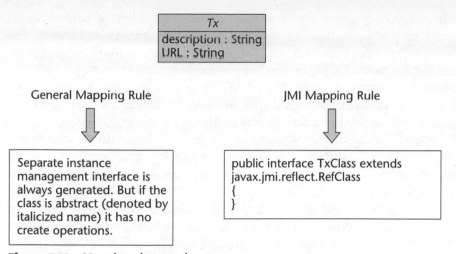

Figure 7.12   Mapping abstract classes.

Distinguish "Interesting" versus "Uninteresting" Operations

I've emphasized the fact that a PIM should not contain operations that will be produced by the generator when transforming the model into lower-level APIs. These are the operations that are implied by the PIM's *structural features*, that is, by the definitions of attributes and associations. They include not only accessor and mutator operations, but also the other operations we have seen that generators produce, such as factory operations and operations defined in the Reflective Interfaces that are the ancestors for all the generated APIs.

A more concrete (that is, less abstract) model, such as an EJB-specific model, must define these operations; however, since more abstract information in the PIM determines them mechanically, I refer to such operations as *uninteresting operations*.

An *interesting operation* is one that is not implied by the structural features of the class model. For example, an operation that performs an end-of-month accounts receivable rollover cannot be inferred from the attributes and associations of a PIM. The PIM must define such operations. Therefore, they are interesting to the modeler constructing a PIM.

A generator transforms an interesting operation definition in a PIM into an operation in the target API technology. Early MDA generators did not produce implementations of such operations. They simply generated the correct signature with "empty curly braces" and left it to the programmer to write the implementation code. However, as I've mentioned, new generators are coming on line that parse OCL pre- and post-conditions for operations and produce code that enforces the conditions. This does not necessarily implement all the intended semantics of the operation, but it is very useful and cuts down on the amount of code the programmer has to fill in.

Furthermore, some post-conditions, while formally considered assertions, can actually be used to infer the state changes that the implementation must execute. Figure 7.13 is a set of post-conditions for the end-of-month receivables rollover operation that we saw in Chapter 4. The OCL uses the @pre suffix to indicate the change in state that must occur during the course of execution of the operation. Implementation generators can use such post-conditions to generate the code that actually makes the state change. The post-conditions do not prescribe the technique used to make the state changes, only that the changes must occur.

```
--------------------------------------------------
--ARProcessor::EndOfMonthUpdate post-conditions
--------------------------------------------------
--For all of the ARaccounts the following holds:
   --The Collections value is its previous value plus the previous
   --  120DayBalance and
   --The 120DayBalance is the previous 90DayBalance and
   --The 90DayBalance is the previous 60DayBalance and
   --The 60DayBalance is the previous 30DayBalance and
   --The 30DayBalance is the previous currentBalance
   --The currentBalance is 0.

context ARProcessor::EndOfMonthUpdate (arAccounts : Set
(ReceivablesAccount)) post:

   arAccounts->forAll
   (
      currentBalance = 0 and
      30DayBalance =  currentBalance@pre and
      60DayBalance =  30DayBalance@pre and
      90DayBalance =  60DayBalance@pre and
      120DayBalance = 90DayBalance@pre and
      Collections = collections@pre + 120DayBalance@pre
   )
```

Figure 7.13   Post-conditions that specify state changes.

There are already generators on the market that go much further in producing implementations of interesting operations. They act upon behavioral models such as state machine and activity models that describe the internals of operations. There are also a number of action-modeling languages that have been used for some time as input to code generators. The new UML Action Semantics specification that we mentioned earlier is standardizing the semantics for action modeling. However, as yet there are no *standardized* mappings of these behavioral models to targets such as Java.

Note that MDA generators ignore operations defined in a PIM when producing information formats. For example, XMI ignores them because its purpose is to generate a DTD that defines the representation of instances. As we have seen, a DTD generated from an M2 metamodel describes the format for representing M1 instances of the M2 metamodel elements. Similarly a DTD generated from an M1 model describes the format for representing M0 instances of the M1 model elements. Operations defined in the model are irrelevant to this purpose.

Strive for Computational Completeness

A model that is slated to be submitted to a generator should be computationally complete. A PIM abstracts away quite a bit that would be visible in more concrete models and code. So what does computationally complete mean in this context?

Syntactic Completeness

There is a certain kind of completeness that is required in order for a model to be accepted by a generator. I call this *syntactic completeness*. There are a few categories of common omissions that compromise syntactic completeness. Here are some guidelines for avoiding these pitfalls:

Specify the type of all attributes and operation parameters.   Some tools let you enter an attribute or a parameter without specifying its type so that you can fill it in later. However, generators need to know these types. Furthermore, the types themselves need to be defined somewhere in the model; if they're not, then the generator will consider them to be unresolved references, just as a Java compiler treats a reference to an undeclared variable.

Specify the multiplicities of both ends of all associations.   As mentioned, many modelers believe that they don't have to specify the multiplicity of the composite aggregate end of an association. Many also believe they need not specify the multiplicity of the non-navigable end of an association. Both of these beliefs are fallacious. Generators use and require all the multiplicity information.

Specify the names of all associations and association ends.   Many modelers don't bother to name the non-navigable ends of an association nor to name the association itself. It's often a good idea to suppress these names from class diagrams because they produce clutter that makes the diagrams harder to understand and often don't provide information that is useful for human beings inspecting the diagrams. However, it's a mistake not to assign names at all because MDA generators use the names when they produce APIs.

As alluded to earlier, generators produce APIs for the associations themselves. The association APIs are distinct from the APIs of the classes that participate in the associations. The APIs for associations use the association names and the names of both navigable and non-navigable association ends.

Figure 7.14 illustrates, via highlighting, how a generator uses association and non-navigable end names when it applies the JMI mapping rules to an association. In the example, `BusinessTxUnit_ACIDTx` is the name of the association, and `businessTxUnit` is the name of the non-navigable association end.

Don't leave unused model elements "dangling."   One of the biggest causes of syntactic incompleteness is the existence in the model of partially defined elements that go undetected by the modeler because they do not appear on any model diagram. Modeling tools generally allow a model element to be deleted from a particular diagram without being deleted from the model. This is a must feature for a serious modeling tool because it is vital to be able to suppress selected elements from specific model diagrams in order to present different views of the model and to avoid clutter.

This important feature has a cost, however. It is common for a modeler to create a model element, start to fill in its properties, then quickly change her mind and decide that the element should not be in the model at all. It is easy to make the mistake of deleting the element from the diagram without deleting it from the model.

The model element—frequently an association—is then left "dangling" in the model, not visible in any of the class diagrams. Most UML tools provide browsers for the model information that make it possible to edit and delete elements that are not shown by any diagram.

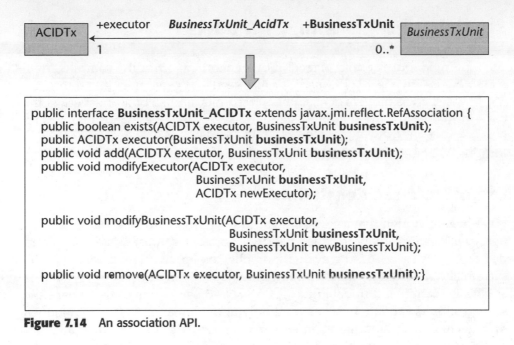

Figure 7.14 An association API.

Semantic Completeness

There is another kind of completeness that a generator can't determine, but that affects the quality of the implementation code that the generator produces. A *semantically complete* model makes full use of the semantic constructs that the modeling language and generator support.

We gave the example earlier of composite aggregation. If you don't use it in places where it should be used, the generator will not flag it as a problem. But the behavior of the generated implementation will not include the enforcement of composition semantics.

Similarly, if you fail to indicate where read-only APIs should be generated, which multivalued attributes and association ends are ordered, and which classes are abstract, the generator won't complain. But you won't be taking advantage of the generator's full power.

Design by Contract (DBC) raises semantic completeness issues. A generator does not judge whether the modeler has done a complete job of specifying invariant rules for classes and pre- and post-conditions for operations, but we are increasingly seeing generators that transform assertions written in OCL into code that validates the assertions. If you don't specify the assertions in OCL, then you don't get this benefit.

Special Concerns with M1 Models

As I pointed out, at this stage MDA generators officially compile MOF metamodels—that is, M2 PIMs. We've also seen that generators that transform M1 PIMs, such as models of customers, accounts, and so on, can leverage the basic principles of the mapping standards. However, be aware that certain issues arise in transforming M1 models that are less likely to arise when transforming M2 models.

Use of Deferred Constraints

MOF has the notion that a constraint, such as an invariant rule, has an *evaluation policy*. An evaluation policy has two possible values, immediate and deferred. An immediate evaluation policy on an invariant means that the system should validate the constraint automatically at key junctures, such as at object creation and update time. A deferred evaluation policy means the system should validate the constraint only upon demand. APIs generated via MOF technology mappings all inherit an operation, refVerify, that allows a client of any metadata object[5] to demand validation of its constraints. The operation has a parameter that allows the client to request validation of the constraints for any metadata owned via composite aggregation as well.

It makes sense for M2 metamodels to use deferred constraints rather liberally because it's often necessary to store incomplete models that are works in progress and thus not fully well formed. Thus, from a practical standpoint, incomplete M1 metadata needs to be storable.

However, deferred constraints are suspect in M1 models because it seldom makes sense to store M0 data that is not well formed. M0 data are things like accounts receivables records, medical records, and so on. Dirty data at the M0 level is generally a serious liability.

Need for Lower-Level Models

When a generator transforms a PIM to more concrete artifacts, its output might be difficult to manage. For example, a complex PIM yields a significantly larger set of Java-specific APIs when transformed by a generator, due to the production of uninteresting operations and other kinds of pattern replication.

Thus, as we've mentioned before, UML models of the generator's output—that is, platform-specific models—help to make the output more intellectually manageable. This is more important for M1 models because they tend to be an

---

[5] A metadata object is an object—such as a Java object or a CORBA object—that represents metadata. A short term for metadata object is *metaobject*, which is why MOF is the *Meta Object* Facility.

order of magnitude more complex than metamodels and because the implementations of M1 models typically stray more from cookbook patterns because of the complications of accessing legacy systems.

What You Can Do Now

As you build platform-independent models going forward, adhere to the principles described in this chapter. PIMs that don't follow the guidelines should be considered legacy, and you should not be creating more legacy artifacts. Even if you are not going to run your PIMs through generators just yet, the investment you make in building these models will pay richer dividends in the long run if MDA tools can use them without extensive retrofitting.

Summary

The guidelines in this chapter pertain to constructing M1 and M2 platform-independent class models. The guidelines are:

- Don't define operations implied by the structural features—that is, the attributes and associations—of the model.
- Carefully consider the ramifications of association end navigability.
- Don't blindly accept a tool's defaults for detailed properties of multi-valued attributes, including ordering and whether to allow duplicate values.
- Use composite aggregation where indicated and avoid shared aggregation until the semantics of the later are nailed down better.
- Use abstract classes where indicated.
- Make your models syntactically and semantically complete.

While these principles apply to both M1 and M2 PIMs, there are special considerations when modeling at the M1 level:

- Deferred constraints make less sense than for M2 models.
- The greater complexity of M1 models makes platform-specific models of generator output more compelling.

CHAPTER 8

Modeling at Different Abstraction Levels

This chapter suggests some approaches to sorting out the kinds of models that a model driven development process requires and the basic relationships and mappings among those kinds of models. It should give you a sense of why we model at different abstraction levels and of the kinds of issues that arise when we do so. It doesn't go so far as to define a full-blown, model driven development process, although the ideas hopefully make some contribution to defining such a process or to specializing existing ones such as the Unified Process[1] and Catalysis.[2]

The chapter starts out by identifying the various kinds of models we find at different abstraction levels and the different kinds of IT personnel that create and use the models. It then walks through a set of interrelated examples that exemplify the different kinds of models. It shows how the models relate to one another and to generated code, exploring mapping issues in some depth.

The chapter also contains a section covering different approaches to synchronizing models and code. This section analyzes the impact of round-trip engineering on a model driven development process and investigates how MDA can help automate the synchronization of the various tiers in enterprise systems.

A brief section touches upon using physical models to automate deployment.

[1] [JBR 1999]
[2] [DSZWIL 1999]

A Basic Model Taxonomy

Figure 8.1 depicts a basic taxonomy of different kinds of models. You needn't consider it definitive. Some development processes classify models somewhat differently or use different terms. I present this taxonomy because the discussion that follows requires some vocabulary to refer to various kinds of models. The taxonomy makes several distinctions:

Business versus system models.   A business model describes aspects of the business, irrespective of whether those aspects are slated to be automated. A system model describes aspects of a computer system that automate elements of the business. Thus, the scope of a system model may be smaller than the scope of a corresponding business model. For non-enterprise systems the more general term *domain model* is more appropriate than business model.

Logical versus physical models.   A logical model describes the logic of a system via class and behavioral models. A physical model describes physical artifacts and resources used during development and runtime, including model files, source code files, executable files, archive files, and processors.

Requirements versus computational models.   A requirements model describes the logical system rather than the business but does so in a computation-independent fashion, meaning that, as much as possible, it doesn't take technical factors into account. A computational model describes the logical system as well, but takes technical factors into account. Computational models provide more complete fuel for generators.

Platform-independent versus platform-specific models.   As already explained, the distinction between a platform-independent model (PIM) and a platform-specific model (PSM) depends on the specification of a reference set of platform technologies of which PIMs are independent. For the context of this book I've specified that PIMs are independent of information-formatting technologies, 3GLs, 4GLs, distributed component middleware, and message-oriented middleware. PIMs and PSMs are computational models. A PIM takes some technical factors into account, while a PSM derived from a PIM takes additional technical factors specific to the platform into consideration.

So far this book has dealt exclusively with computational models because they are what distinguish MDA from an approach in which models are strictly design artifacts. In this chapter, I look at some of the other kinds of models, but still maintain the primary focus on computational models.

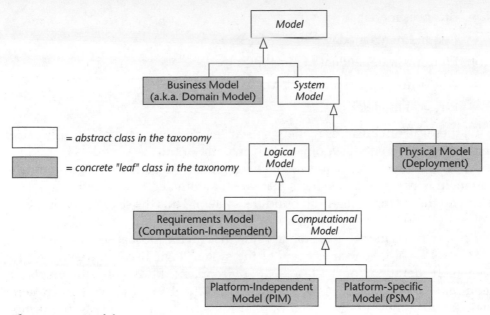

Figure 8.1   Model taxonomy.

By providing this taxonomy I don't mean to insist that all development organizations use all of these kinds of models for all projects. There are costs to maintaining a large number of models and keeping them synchronized with each other. Tools can reduce those costs by automating some of the synchronization, but they don't eliminate all of the costs.

Iterative Development

A requirements model is more abstract than a PIM, which is more abstract than a PSM. People often assume that you complete the more abstract models before moving on to define more concrete ones.

However, that is not actually the case, because a scalable model driven development process necessitates revising artifacts at all levels of abstraction throughout the process. Thus, in terms of common development process parlance, model driven development is an *iterative* process, which is the opposite of a *waterfall* process. The waterfall analogy depicts a process composed of sequential steps, in which the completion of one step of the process triggers the next step.

How the Models Fit Together

The model types in Figure 8.1 whose boxes are shaded represent concrete "leaf" types in the taxonomy. These are the models that we actually create, which are:

- Business models
- Requirements models
- Platform-independent models (PIMs)
- Platform-specific models (PSMs)
- Physical models

Of these, all but business models are system models, each looking at the system from a different viewpoint. The viewpoint of business models is the furthest removed from the computing environment. As stated, business models can include parts of the business that aren't automated but that still are interesting to those who design and build the system. Thus the scope of their viewpoint is the broadest.

Requirements models describe the system from the most abstract viewpoint. PIMs provide a less abstract view of the system logic because they factor in some considerations of the technical environment. PIMs are refinements of requirements models. PSMs provide an even less abstract view of the system logic because they are described in platform-specific terms. PSMs are refinements of PIMs. Physical models don't deal with system logic and, therefore, provide a very different view of the system.

Ideally, tools let you look at the system from any one of these viewpoints. Each viewpoint addresses a particular set of stakeholders in the development process. Let's examine who these stakeholders are.

MDA Personas

As alluded to earlier, Alan Cooper's Interactive Design approach[3] to designing end-user, computer-based devices promotes defining *personas* to describe archetypal users of the device in question. If we consider MDA a device that people use to develop software systems, we can define MDA personas, that is, the archetypal people involved in the process.

Cooper advocates giving the personas human names like "Mary" rather than role names such as "middleware engineer." In ongoing projects people gradually learn the names, and their brevity and human orientation has positive effects on discourse within design and development teams. However, I find it awkward to use human names for the personas in this section because it requires the reader, who will not be engaged with the names for weeks or months, to remember what role is assigned to each name. Thus, I break Cooper's rule by supplying role names here rather than human names.

[3] [COOP 1999]

The following role definitions aren't authoritative, because I haven't provided a definitive model driven development process. I offer them as a contribution to these larger tasks.

Business Analyst

The business analyst understands the company's business processes and the information that the processes use. He has experience in using flowcharts and tables to define business processes. He doesn't have any programming experience.

He creates business models. He can be trained to use business process modeling tools as long as they aren't oriented toward technical computer people. For example, it wouldn't be appropriate to ask him to define mathematically formal invariants and pre- and post-conditions, although he could be trained to state such assertions in his native spoken language. He is learning how to create UML models that use a limited subset of UML's capabilities.

Requirements Analyst

The requirements analyst has a technical background. She programmed for a while, but moved into modeling, which she prefers. She knows UML and can practice Design by Contract in a mathematically precise fashion.

She creates requirements models for business components and applications, working with business analysts to identify the aspects of the business models that need to be automated. Coordination with business analysts extends throughout the life cycle of the development and deployment of a system, in order to ensure that requirements models stay current and in synch with business models.

Application Engineer

The application engineer develops business components and applications.

He creates and maintains PIMs from which generators produce PSMs and code. He might enhance the generated PSMs and code manually, depending on the policies of his development organization. (Later in this chapter, I examine the different kinds of policies governing such enhancements.)

He works with requirements analysts to make sure that PIMs and requirements models stay current and in synch.

Middleware Engineer

The middleware engineer is a programmer who knows EJB, CORBA, and message-oriented middleware. She is familiar with UML.

She works with the application engineers to ensure that their applications perform well in specific middleware environments.

Quality Assurance Engineer

The quality assurance engineer is an experienced programmer and is learning UML. She is responsible for testing the output of the application and middleware engineers. She works with them when she finds a problem or something that seems questionable.

She uses the testing harnesses generated from the PIM to test the system and might enhance them manually. PSMs also help her manage the testing process.

Deployment Engineer

The deployment engineer is responsible for system deployment. He has some programming background, but that is not his strong suit. He is very knowledgeable about networks.

He enhances skeletal deployment models generated from the PIM and feeds them to a deployment automation tool. The tools can generate instrumentation that yields reports that profile the performance of the system's runtime artifacts as well as their resource consumption. He often works with quality assurance and middleware engineers to analyze the reports, and sometimes works with application engineers as well.

Network Administrator

The network administrator manages the corporate network. She can write scripts such as network logon scripts, but has little if any programming background. She sometimes works with deployment and quality assurance engineers to pinpoint performance issues and has learned how to read deployment models.

Architect

As pointed out in Chapter 2, one of the ways that MDA extends enterprise architecture is to include modeling frameworks—that is, implementations of specialized modeling languages and mappings—in the enterprise infrastructure. The analysts and engineers that take part in the development of business components and applications use that infrastructure.

The architect defines and maintains the model driven enterprise architecture, specifying how various modeling frameworks and other infrastructure elements fit together. He oversees the work of the various analysts and engineers to ensure that they adhere to the architecture and to gather feedback from them in order to improve the architecture.

Infrastructure Engineer

The infrastructure engineer develops and maintains the infrastructure software used during the development of business components and applications. The infrastructure includes system services, which may sit on top of third-party middleware. It also includes modeling frameworks, some of which he develops and some of which the company purchases from third parties.

The infrastructure engineer sometimes works with middleware engineers, who help him optimize generators. He also seeks to ensure that the infrastructure is meeting the needs of the application engineers by meeting with them regularly.

The modeling frameworks for which he is responsible include those used by business and requirements analysts, so he meets with them periodically as well.

Persona Synopsis

As I've said previously, not all development groups will use all of the different kinds of models. Furthermore, a person may assume more than one persona. Thus, real departments may look quite different than this neat persona categorization would suggest.

Introduction to the Examples

The primary audience for this chapter's examples consists of architects and infrastructure engineers. The sample models and accompanying explanations delve into the issues that those tasked with creating, purchasing, and integrating modeling frameworks need to take into consideration. Application, middleware, quality assurance, and deployment engineers should also find the material interesting in that it provides a glimpse of what application development is like with MDA.

The sample models use Herzum-Sims concepts, focusing mainly on the enterprise tier of business components and how to deal with that tier at different levels of abstraction. The examples are mostly class models. However, the concepts presented via the examples aren't really specific to the enterprise tier nor to class models. You can extrapolate the principles to other tiers of business components, to behavioral models, and to EAI and B2Bi models.

The model addresses the domain of currency options. The context for the business model is a company that does a great deal of international business. The company is not in the options brokerage business but, rather, uses options purchasing and selling as a way to hedge the currency exchange rate risk it incurs in the normal course of its international business. If you're not familiar with the basics of hedging currency risk via options trading, read Appendix B, which will help you understand the examples.

Although the examples include business and requirements models, the bulk of the discussion is about PIMs and PSMs because, as stated earlier, a salient characteristic that separates MDA from previous modeling methodologies is that it uses models as development artifacts. PIMs and PSMs, being computational models, are best suited for that purpose.

Business Models

A business model describes a business domain, such as the currency options domain. As explained previously, it may describe aspects of the business that are not subject to automation, in addition to aspects that are.

Figure 8.2 is a fragment of a business model. It's a UML activity model that describes the business process of hedging against the risk of currency exchange rate fluctuations during the life of a contract, where the terms of future payments are denominated in a foreign currency.

The business model is without regard to which parts of the business process are subject to automation. For example, some of the decisions, such as deciding whether a certain level of exchange rate risk is acceptable, might be less amenable to automation than deciding whether an option is currently "out of the money" or "in the money," which can be determined by a straight mathematical calculation.

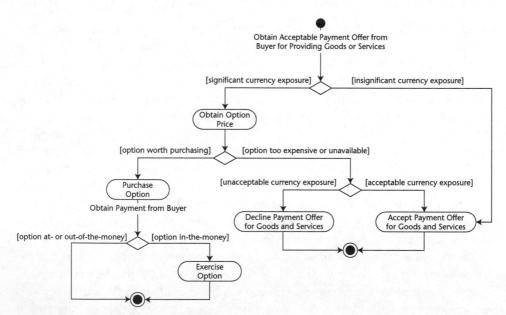

Figure 8.2   Part of a business model.

The model uses UML's activity metamodel and notation, without extensions.

A business model does not consist only of activity models, and not all activity models are parts of business models. A business model can also have class models, interaction models, collaboration models, and use case models. Hubert's Convergent Architecture uses CRC cards (Class, Responsibilities, and Collaborators),[4] which are not UML-based.

Figure 8.3 is a business use case model that complements the activity model. The use case model uses a profile of UML's use case metamodel. The profile defines the stereotype <<business use case>> of the UML metamodel element UseCase and the stereotype <<business actor>> of the UML metamodel's Actor element. The stereotype labels aren't visible because icons are defined for these stereotypes, and the icons indicate that the elements carry the stereotype. A business use case is distinguished from an ordinary use case by a diagonal line in the icon. A business actor is distinguished from an ordinary actor by a diagonal line as well.

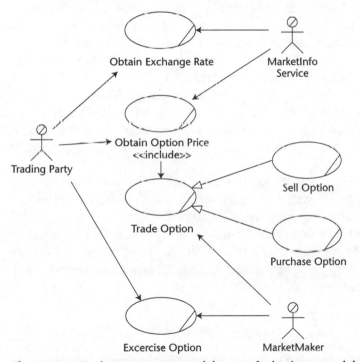

Figure 8.3 Business use case model—part of a business model.

---

[4] [HUBE 2002]

Requirements Models

In an ideal world a requirements analyst would simply submit requirements models to generators that would produce the required systems. In practice, you have to refine a requirements model into a computational model (that is, a PIM) that a generator can process.

Requirements models can use general-purpose UML constructs for activity, class, interaction, collaboration, and use case modeling. Specialized languages more specific to requirements modeling can be useful as well.

Keep in mind that the following example of a requirements model is restricted to coverage of the enterprise tier of the system, and is fragmentary even at that.

Figure 8.4 is a class model of the information that the options system must manage. It's an idealized model of the information because it's independent of technical design decisions; in other words, it's computation-independent.

For example, CurrencyOption is partitioned into sets of subclasses, Put-Call and American-European. This stipulates that a currency option can be an American put, a European put, an American call, or a European call. But since Put, Call, American, and European have no attributes of their own, during technical design they might be collapsed into two enumerated types, where one has the allowable values put and call, and the other has the values american and european. Alternately, they might be collapsed into two Boolean types isPut and isAmerican. The same kinds of technical design decisions might be applied to the Sale and Purchase subclasses of Trade. The point is that, in a requirements model, such technical design decisions do not surface.[5]

Figure 8.5 shows the invariants for the information model. Note that it's possible—and desirable—to state invariants formally in requirements models.

The European invariant captures the essence of the characteristic of European options that distinguishes them from American options. This invariant constitutes the entire distinction, which has nothing to do with the continent in which the option is created but, rather, has to do with whether the option can be exercised before the expiration date.

---

[5] I am indebted to Haim Kilov for some of these ideas about requirements models. Kilov also expresses dependency relationships in such information models [KR 1994 and KILOV 1999]. He applies similar techniques to information models that are parts of business models.

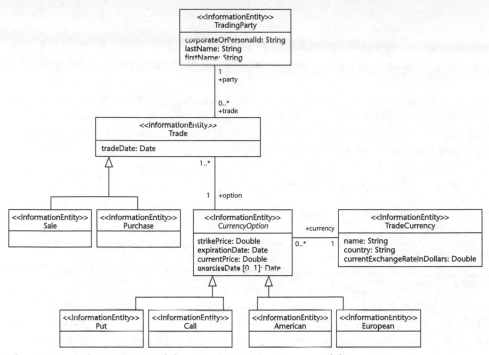

Figure 8.4   Information model—part of a requirements model.

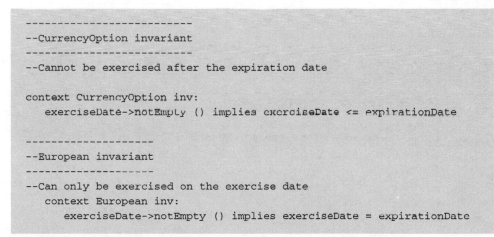

```
--------------------------
--CurrencyOption invariant
--------------------------
--Cannot be exercised after the expiration date

context CurrencyOption inv:
   exerciseDate->notEmpty () implies exerciseDate <= expirationDate


--------------------
--European invariant
--------------------
--Can only be exercised on the exercise date
   context European inv:
      exerciseDate->notEmpty () implies exerciseDate = expirationDate
```

Figure 8.5   Invariants for information model—part of requirements model.

Note that our requirements model has no composite aggregations, but composite aggregations are appropriate for requirements models because they can express semantics that are independent of technological factors. It just so happens that in this fragment there are no composition semantics.

Note also that the requirements model doesn't specify navigability of association ends. When I created this model, I simply accepted the tool default, which makes both ends navigable. I regard navigability as a technical design issue.

Figure 8.6 is also a part of our sample requirements model. It provides a structural view of the operations that the trading desk performs.

It's advisable to specify the pre- and post-conditions for the controller's operations, although here I show only one of them, which we'll use shortly:

```
--The option must not already have been exercised.

context TradingDesk::ExerciseOption(option : CurrencyOption) pre:
    exerciseDate->isEmpty ()
```

Figure 8.4 and Figure 8.6 use a simple, nonstandard profile that I defined for requirements models. It employs the stereotypes <<InformationEntity>> and <<Controller>> to distinguish information-oriented classes from control- or process-oriented ones. The <<create>> stereotype of Dependency is a general-purpose stereotype that UML 1.X defines. It indicates that the TradingDesk creates instances of Trade. <<use>> is a standard UML keyword that labels a dependency as a usage. In the UML metamodel, Usage is a subclass of Dependency. In this case, the usage dependency says that the TradingDesk uses instances of CurrencyOption.

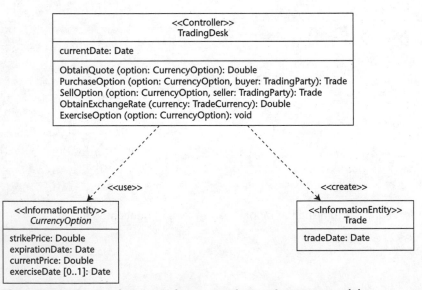

Figure 8.6 Structural process view—part of a requirements model.

Thus, the requirements model uses a mix of profiles. Some are standardized and some are proprietary, although it's preferable to use standardized languages as much as possible.

Requirements models can also include use case models, collaboration models, activity models, and so on. As noted earlier, some formal development processes center around use cases, some around collaboration models, and some around class models.

Platform-Independent Models (PIMs)

Here's a summary of the main points covered earlier about PIMs:

- A more accurate definition of PIM, given how I use the term, would be "platform-independent computational model," since a requirements model is platform independent as well.

- Platform independence is a relative term. When asserting that a language or a model is platform-independent, you must specify the platform technologies of which it is independent.

- For the examples in this book, platform-independent means independent of information formatting technologies, 3GLs, 4GLs, distributed component middleware, and messaging middleware. Models that are platform-independent in this sense are a rung above the predominant abstraction level that programmers work at today.

We now examine fragments of a PIM that refines the sample requirements model for the currency option hedging system. An application engineer might refine the requirements model manually, although it might be possible to define a mapping that a tool could use to help automate the refinement. Like the requirements model that it refines, the PIM focuses on the enterprise tier.

The PIM (Figure 8.7) reflects a technical design decision to implement `Trade`, `TradingParty`, `CurrencyOption`, and `TradingDesk` as distributed components, and to implement `Currency` as a nondistributed object that is passed by value. However, the model is noncommittal as to the distributed component platform—such as EJB or .NET—that implements and hosts the components, and thus it satisfies our criteria for platform independence.

The model uses an expanded version of the sample profile defined in Chapter 6 for describing distributed components at a platform-independent abstraction level.[6] Figure 8.7 employs the profile to model the contracts of distributed entity components, refining the requirements information model of Figure 8.4. This model fragment reflects a number of technical design decisions that did not surface in the requirements information model:

[6] Jack Greenfield, Oliver Sims, and Mike Rosen contributed to developing elements of this profile.

- It collapses the separate subclasses for distinguishing put versus call, American versus European, and trade versus purchase into the enumerated types `OptionKind`, `ExerciseKind`, and `TradeKind`, respectively.

- It defines unique identifier attributes for the entities via the `<<UniqueId>>` stereotype defined in Chapter 6.

- It specifies that the collection of trades ascribed to a trading party is an ordered collection. It does so via the standard UML `{ordered}` property.

- It manifests decisions about association end navigability.

- It designates some attributes and navigable association ends as read-only via the `{isChangeable = false}` tagged value.

Our platform-independent distributed component profile, and the model that uses that profile, make certain assumptions about the underlying implementation technology. Specifically, they assume the notion of remotely accessible entity and controller components that have certain characteristics. At this level of abstraction, these assumptions are not severe enough to bind the models to specific implementation technology, but they do impose constraints on the choice of implementation.

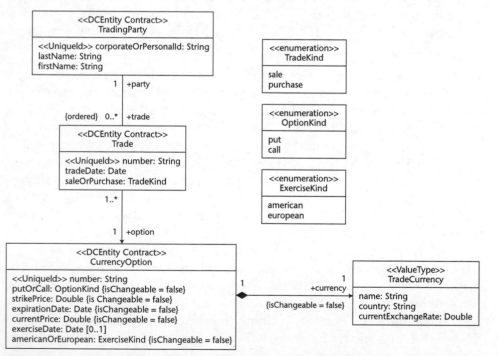

Figure 8.7: Platform-independent model of the entity contracts.

It's possible to map the profile to EJB, as we shall see, or to other distributed component technologies, such as the component technology embodied by COM+ that has been incorporated into .NET, or to transaction-processing systems such as IBM's CICS.

Figure 8.8 shows the invariants for Figure 8.7's CurrencyOption contract. They are derived from the requirements model's invariants for the Currency Option and European classes. Since the design decision to create the ExerciseKind enumerated type eliminated the requirements model's European class, the European invariant shows up in the PIM as a somewhat differently expressed invariant of CurrencyOption.

Figure 8.9 models the currency option distributed component, which supports the CurrencyOption contract and is realized by <<focus>> and <<auxiliary>> classes. The <<focus>> and <<auxiliary>> stereotypes are standard stereotypes defined by UML 1.X that support a Herzum-Sims component pattern.[7] The <<EntityDC>> and <<Realize DCContract>> stereotypes are part of our sample profile. <<EntityDC>> extends the UML metamodel's Subsystem element, which is a kind of package. <<RealizeDCContract>> extends the standard UML 1.X stereotype <<realize>>. It's legal for a profile to define a stereotype that extends another stereotype.

```
--------------------------
--CurrencyOption invariants
--------------------------


--Cannot be exercised after the expiration date

context CurrencyOption inv:
    exerciseDate->notEmpty () implies exerciseDate <= expirationDate


--A European option can only be exercised on the expiration date.

context CurrencyOption inv:
  (americanOrEuropean = ExerciseKind::#european and
   exerciseDate->notEmpty () )
     implies exerciseDate = expirationDate
```

Figure 8.8 Invariants for the entity PIM.

[7] [HS 2000]

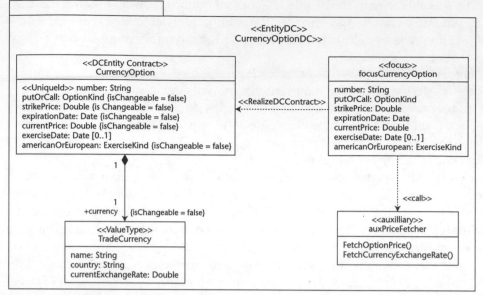

Figure 8.9 PIM for a distributed entity component.

The mapping of the PIM down to a PSM in the next section looks only at the refinement of the `CurrencyOptionDC` entity component, but Figure 8.10 should give you an idea of what a controller component looks like in the PIM. The `TradingDeskDC` is a refinement of the `TradingDesk` controller in the requirements model fragment of Figure 8.6.

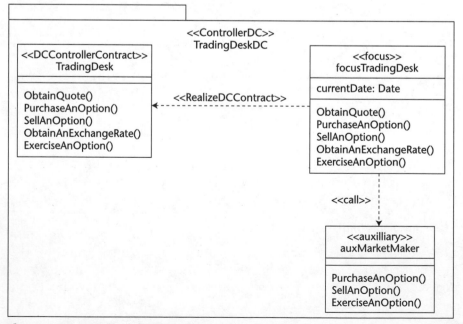

Figure 8.10 PIM for a distributed controller component.

There are a number of properties that we could specify regarding the various operations in the `TradingDeskDC` controller component that Figure 8.10 doesn't show due to space limitations. These include identifying operations that are queries—that is, operations that don't effect any state changes, which UML's standard `{query}` property expresses. We could also use some of the tags we defined in Chapter 6 to specify which operations are idempotent (query operations are by definition idempotent) and which are transactional.

Platform-Specific Models (PSMs)

Given the definition of platform independence within the context of these examples, a platform-specific model is a computational model that is specific to some information-formatting technology, programming language, distributed component middleware, or messaging middleware. The PSM that we look at in this section is specific to EJB.

An EJB-Specific Model

The EJB-specific PSM refines the currency option PIM. The PSM results from applying an EJB technology mapping to the PIM. Like the PIM that it refines, the PSM addresses the enterprise tier only.

The PSM (see Figure 8.11) uses the UML Profile for EJB currently being defined by the Java Community Process.[8] All the stereotypes in the PSM whose names start with "EJB" are part of this profile. The profile supports modeling components at an EJB-specific level of abstraction. It defines additional stereotypes that the sample PSM doesn't use, as well as a number of tags. All of the stereotypes that the PSM uses whose names don't have the "EJB" prefix are UML 1.X standards.

Figure 8.11's EJB entity bean component `ejbCurrencyOption` is a refinement of the PIM's `CurrencyOption` entity component of Figure 8.9. Following the UML Profile for EJB's rules, the PSM models the bean as a stereotyped subsystem, which, again, is a kind of package. The PIM's `TradingDeskDC` controller component maps to an EJB session component in the PSM, although I don't show that here.

The mapping that produces the PSM replicates the J2EE Blueprints Value Object pattern described in Chapter 2, which supports efficient data exchange in distributed systems. It generates a value object named `voCurrency Option`. It produces operations for the value object by transforming attributes in the PIM's `CurrencyOption` entity contract into get and set operations. On the other hand, the EJB remote interface `ejbCurrencyOption` has only one get and one set operation. These operations get and set a value object.

---

[8] [JSR26]

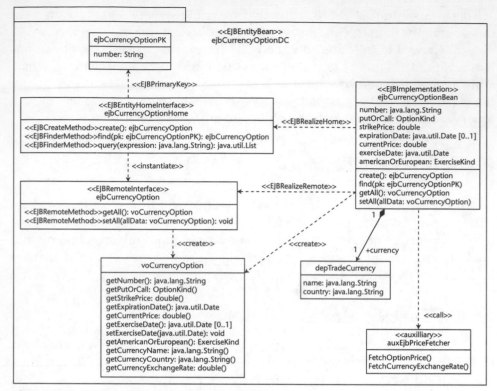

Figure 8.11 EJB-specific component model (PSM).

If the remote interface had gets and sets for each of the PIM's individual attributes, then a client needing to get or set a number of attributes would have to make a number of network calls instead of just one.

The mapping also produces an EJB home interface and primary key class, based on the declaration of the unique identifier attribute in the PIM's CurrencyOption entity contract. Space does not allow Figure 8.11 to show the complete signature of the create operation in the home interface, which has parameters for each of the attributes of the PIM's CurrencyOption contract.

Java Plus Semantics

The PSM is at *the same abstraction level* as the Java interfaces and classes it describes. For example, the Java declarative code corresponding to the PSM's ejbCurrencyOption interface is as follows:[9]

---

[9] The PSM fragment doesn't show the fact that ejbCurrencyOption extends javax. ejb.EJBObject because the <<EJBRemoteInterface>> stereotype implies it, but a complete rendition of the PSM would show it.

```
interface ejbCurrencyOption extends javax.ejb.EJBObject
{
    voCurrencyOption getAll ( );
    void setAll (voCurrencyOption allData);
}
```

The PSM has the same interface and class declarations that the Java code has, including all member fields and methods whose types are the same as in the Java code. However, since UML is more semantically expressive than Java interface and class declarations, the PSM can add valuable semantic content to such declarations.

For instance, consider the declaration of the getExerciseDate operation in the voCurrencyOption value object. The 0..1 multiplicity specification says that it's permissible semantically for getExerciseDate to return a null value. The return values of voCurrencyOption's other operations default to a multiplicity of 1..1. The distinction between a multiplicity of 0..1 and 1..1 can't be expressed by an operation declaration in a Java interface or class. This is a classic example of the greater semantic depth of the PSM.

The PSM could also specify invariant rules and pre- and post-conditions for operations, some of which would be directly traceable to constraints in the PIM, and some of which would not be. For example, the generator could translate the PIM's invariant rules about exercise dates into invariants for voCurrency Option. On the other hand, the PSM could have pre- and post-conditions for the operations of ejbCurrencyOptionHome, which have no analog in the PIM since the PIM has no home interface.

Tracing between Abstraction Levels

It's possible to formally capture the relationships between elements in the PSM and elements in the PIM. For example, Figure 8.12 models the fact that the ejbCurrencyOptionPK class (PK = primary key) for the currency option EJB component is traced back to the number attribute in the PIM's Currency Option class, which is the unique identifier attribute for the class. This figure uses the standard UML stereotype <<trace>> of UML's Abstraction element. Abstraction is a subclass of Dependency.

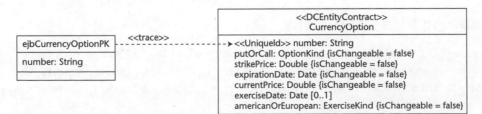

Figure 8.12 Formal relationship between elements at different abstraction levels.

You can also use this kind of formal specification of tracings to capture the relationship between a PIM element and a requirements model element or between a requirements model element and a business model element.

There are some other points worth noting about Figure 8.12:

- The direction of the dependency arrow is correct because in UML a dependency arrow points from the dependent element to the element upon which it depends. However, many find this counterintuitive when depicting mappings. Consequently, in informal PowerPoint style diagrams I direct mapping arrows to point in the direction of refinement, that is, from the more abstract element to the more concrete ones.

- The official UML 1.X specification permits you to specify a dependency, such as a trace dependency, between any two model elements. Unfortunately many UML tools only allow you to specify dependencies among classes and packages.

Limitations of Declarative Models

Neither our PIM nor the PSM contains enough information for a generator to produce a complete implementation. For example, in most enterprises not all of the entity components' attribute values are stored in databases. Some are abstractions of information in legacy applications that have to be extracted and inserted via specialized calls to the legacy systems.

This kind of inconsistency in enterprise systems makes it challenging from a practical standpoint to generate a complete implementation from a declarative model, a limitation I mentioned earlier. Later in this chapter and in Chapter 10, I discuss ways of dealing with this limitation.

Parameterizing a PIM-PSM Mapping

I've mentioned several times that parameterized mappings are important to MDA. Application and middleware engineers use mapping parameters to fine-tune the output of generators. This section examines mapping parameterization in detail.

Mapping PIM Collections

Consider Figure 8.13, which zeroes in on a subset of the PIM's entity contracts. Earlier, we pointed out that, via the standard UML {ordered} property, the PIM specifies that the collection of trades ascribed to a trading party is an ordered collection.

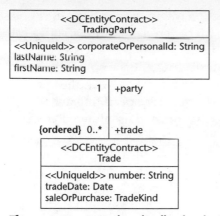

Figure 8.13   An ordered collection in the PIM.

The `trade` end of the association between `TradingParty` and `Trade` is navigable. (As explained in Chapter 7, an arrow on neither end of an association means either that both ends are navigable or that neither end is navigable. Here I mean for both ends to be navigable.) Therefore, the mapping to EJB treats `trade` as a property of `TradingParty`.

The value object generated for the EJB trading party component in the PSM thus has a `getTrade` operation, as illustrated by Figure 8.14. A get operation is sufficient to support setting the values because, once the collection is returned via the get operation, the client can use the interface on the collection to set values. The `getTrade` operation's return type should be one of the Java collection interface types.[10] The question is, which Java collection type should the operation return?

Figure 8.14   Question—What is `getTrade`'s return type?

---

[10] A Java array is an unlikely choice for representing the collection since the collection's size is unbounded.

Figure 8.15 shows the standard Java collection interfaces we have to choose from. The interfaces in the shaded boxes are for ordered collections, so we can eliminate the others. Of the remaining candidates, SortedSet is for collections that are not permitted to have duplicates because it is a subtype of Set, while List and SortedMap are for collections that may have duplicates.

Let's assume that our PIM profile defines a tag for specifying whether a multivalued collection specified by an association end is allowed to have duplicates. We can fashion our tag after MOF's isUnique property, so that a tagged value of {isUnique = true} means duplicate values are not allowed. (As mentioned in Chapter 7, UML 1.X restricts collections represented by multivalued association ends from having duplicates. In practice, however, some profiles ignore this technicality because it's too limiting. UML 2 will probably remove the restriction altogether.)

If duplicates aren't allowed in the collection, then it's clear from Figure 8.15 that the only choice for the Java collection type is SortedSet, and the question as to what type the PSM's getTrade operation should return is settled.

However, suppose for the sake of argument that we apply an {isUnique = false} tagged value to the PIM, as shown in Figure 8.16. Maybe we want to allow duplicates because information will flow into the system from multiple sources whose data overlaps to some extent, and it's optimal not to make the system screen for duplicates as each entry comes in. This is the kind of technical consideration that a requirements model doesn't take into account, but that may appropriately surface at the PIM level.

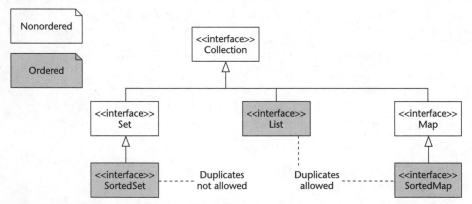

Figure 8.15 The Java collection interfaces.

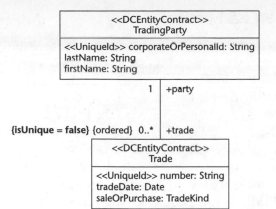

Figure 8.16   Specifying that the collection may contain duplicates.

If duplicates are allowed, then the question as to what Java collection type the getTrade operation in the PSM should return isn't settled. As evident from Figure 8.15, List and SortedMap are both candidates. There are several approaches to dealing with this variability:

Same Always.   Always generate a List or always generate a SortedMap.

Engineer Overrides.   One of the two collection interfaces is the default, which an engineer can override globally or on a case-by-case basis.

Abstract It.   Determine whether the choice between the two collection types is based on a platform-independent concept that would be meaningful to express in the PIM. If so, enhance the PIM profile to make it possible to express the distinction in PIMs in a platform-independent fashion.

JMI's Approach

JMI uses the "Same Always" approach, generating a List in all cases. However, JMI is meant to be applicable to M2 models—that is, to metamodels—rather than to M1 models such as our PIM. So we don't necessarily want to accept all of the JMI rules for our mapping.

Defining a Parameterization Language

The "Engineer Overrides" approach requires defining a language to enable the engineer to make the specification. A UML profile engineered for such a purpose could define a tag for indicating the desired collection type. An engineer could apply a conforming tagged value to a PIM.

Figure 8.17 demonstrates applying such a tagged value to the PIM's trade association end in order to select the List interface. Accordingly, the PSM's getTrade operation returns a List (Figure 8.18).

Note that if the PIM *contains* a Java-specific tagged value, it isn't really a PIM. Thus, it's important for tools to make it easy to filter out platform-specific mapping parameters applied to a PIM. Then we could say that the platform-specific tagged values are *associated with* the PIM rather than being part of the PIM. More generally, a proper MDA environment should allow the modeler to easily filter out all elements expressed in terms of a particular language and, just as readily, to bring them back. If a tool has this general capability, the modeler should be able to command it to filter out all elements expressed in terms of the profile for parameterizing the Java mapping. Such a profile would probably contain more than just the one tag I've defined.

In sum, the tagged value technique supports the "Engineer Overrides" approach to settling the List vs. SortedMap question. It does so by creating a language that is specific to the PIM-Java mapping. Mappings to other platforms could not reuse this language.

Searching for an Abstraction

On the other hand, the "Abstract It" approach, if possible in this situation, would define a platform-independent construct that could be used to drive not only the PIM-Java mapping, but mappings to other platforms as well.

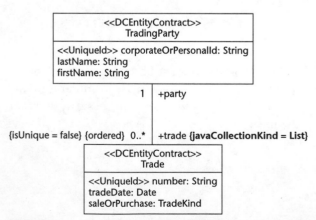

Figure 8.17   Applying Java mapping parameters to a PIM.

voTradingParty
getTrade(): **java.util.List** getNumber(): java.lang.String getFirstName(): java.lang.String setFirstName(fName: java.lang.String): void getLastName(): java.lang.String setLast Name(lName: java.lang.String): void

Figure 8.18 `getTrade` returns `List`.

To decide whether the "Abstract It" approach is viable in this particular case, we must determine whether there is a platform-independent semantic distinction between `List` and `SortedMap`. The essence of the difference between the two is that a `List` is an ordered collection of objects, whereas a `SortedMap` is an ordered collection of keys that map to objects. In Figure 8.15, we see that Java makes a similar distinction for unordered collections, where there is a choice between `Map`, which is a collection of object keys, and `List` and `Set`, which are collections of objects.

We can express this basic distinction between a collection of objects and a collection of object keys in a platform-independent fashion because the same distinction shows up in other implementation technologies. In fact, this distinction even applies meaningfully to the case where an association end is single valued, since there is still a question as to whether the link is maintained by an object reference or as a key that maps to an object. Thus, we could expand our PIM profile to include the definition of a new tag on association ends[11] that we call `isKeyed` (Figure 8.19).

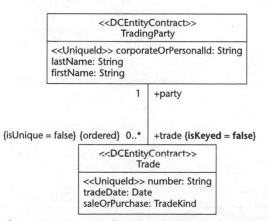

Figure 8.19 Extending the platform-independent profile.

---

[11] We might want to restrict the tag to apply to navigable association ends only.

We have thus abstracted the List vs. SortedMap distinction into a more fundamental semantic distinction that we can express at a higher level of abstraction than Java. For example, by setting the value of isKeyed to false in our PIM, we imply that the Java collection interface is List, since we've already specified that the collection is ordered and may contain duplicates.

Table 8.1 is a truth table that shows the Java collection interfaces implied by different combinations of values of the standard ordered/unordered property and of the isUnique and isKeyed tags.

Note that Java does not offer variants of the Map and SortedMap interfaces that are constrained not to contain duplicate keys. Thus, if the PIM says that a keyed collection with unique key values is required, the standard JDK implementation of Map will not suffice, and the generator that produces the implementation of Map will have to fill in this gap. Similarly, if the PIM says that a keyed, ordered collection with unique key values is required, the generator can't simply reuse the standard JDK implementation of SortedMap.

Table 8.1 Truth Table for PIM-Java Collections Mapping

UNIQUE	ORDERED	KEYED	JAVA INTERFACE	COMMENT
false	false	false	Collection	
false	false	true	Map	
false	true	false	List	
false	true	true	SortedMap	
true	false	false	Set	
true	false	true	Map	The implementation code generator must override the standard JDK implementation of Map to disallow duplicate keys.
true	true	false	SortedSet	
true	true	true	SortedMap	The implementation code generator must override the standard JDK implementation of SortedMap to disallow duplicate keys.

Consider also that the ability to easily filter out values of the tags we've defined as part of our profile—isUnique and isKeyed—would be useful even though they are platform-independent. A PIM without those values is more abstract than one with them. There may be a need to reuse the more abstract PIM in different settings where the values of the tags might differ. That is why modeling tools should, in general, make it possible to filter models by language. We can conceive of these two tagged values as a small language that expresses technical design properties of association ends, that is, that deals with one particular aspect of system design. One could argue that the ordered/unordered property also should be part of the language supporting that aspect, but it's part of the base UML 1.X.

From an MDA perspective, the "Abstract It" approach of abstracting the semantics to the PIM is superior to tagging the PIM with platform-specific mapping parameters. A PIM that contains an isKeyed tagged value is still a PIM, and the tagged value can be useful when mapping to platforms other than Java. A value of the isKeyed tag is not a mapping parameter. It's part of the PIM.

Nevertheless, at this time, when the industry is still in the early stages of applying MDA to enterprise development, it isn't likely that an attempt to abstract everything to the PIM level will succeed. There are other examples of variability in how the PIM should be transformed to EJB, and we might not be able to abstract them all. A development group should thus be wary of trusting that our bit of PIM language engineering takes into account all possibilities and may still need to provide a PIM-Java mapping profile that gives engineers an override capability as a fallback.

"Same Always" is the best approach in an ideal world because it abstracts away the technical issue completely, letting the mapping to EJB deal with it. For example, a mapping for a distributed environment might dictate universal use of keys rather than object references, rendering even a platform-independent isKeyed tag unnecessary. As model driven enterprise architecture matures, PIMs and generators will abstract away more and more technical issues.

Analogously, in the early days of C compilers, programmers wrote directives in the C code telling the compiler to place certain variables in machine registers. As C compilers improved this practice faded out.

Parameterizing a PSM-Code Mapping

The general approaches to parameterizing the PIM-PSM mapping that we've examined are relevant to other kinds of mappings, such as requirements-PIM or PSM-code. Here we look at the latter case.

Selecting Implementations

Suppose some approach has been used to settle the List vs. SortedMap question in favor of List for our PSM's getTrade operation. A generator that produces Java implementation code must consider how to implement the List interface. Java provides two classes that implement List (see Figure 8.20). One is ArrayList and the other is LinkedList.

Approaches to handling this variability are similar in many respects to the approaches for deciding whether to use the List or SortedMap interface:

Same Always.   Always generate ArrayList or always generate LinkedList.

Engineer Overrides.   One of the two implementation classes is the default, which an engineer can override via a tagged value.

Tag the PIM.   Associate the tagged value with the PIM instead of with the PSM. This way, the engineer doesn't have to enhance the PSM, which simplifies the synchronization of the PIM and PSM. (We talk more about this advantage later in this chapter in our discussion of round-trip engineering.)

Abstract It.   Determine whether the choice between ArrayList and LinkedList is based on a concept that would be meaningful to express in a platform-independent fashion in the PIM. If so, enhance the PIM profile to make it possible to express the distinction in PIMs in a platform-independent fashion.

The "Engineer Overrides" approach requires the definition of a tag. Figure 8.21 demonstrates applying a value of such a tag to the PSM.

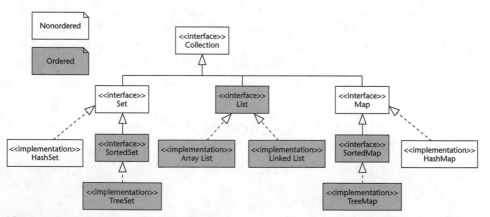

Figure 8.20   The Java collection classes.

voTradingParty
getTrade(): java.util.List {**impl = ArrayList**} getNumber(): java.lang.String getFirstName(): java.lang.String setFirstName(fName: java.lang.String): void getLastName(): java.lang.String setLast Name(lName: java.lang.String): void

Figure 8.21   Parameterizing the PSM—Java code mapping.

The "Tag the PIM" approach requires associating the tagged value with the PIM, as shown in Figure 8.22.

The "Abstract It" approach is possible only if we can identify platform-independent semantics that characterize the distinction between `ArrayList` and `LinkedList`. Usually. `LinkedList` provides better performance with queues and when element insertion and removal occurs frequently.[12] Thus, we might enhance our platform-independent profile by defining an `isQueue` tag value. Figure 8.23 demonstrates applying a value of this tag to the PIM.

We could also define another platform-independent property that indicates that the collection should be optimized for frequent insertion and removal.

<<DCEntityContract>> TradingParty
<<UniqueId>> corporateOrPersonalId: String lastName: String firstName: String

1   +party

{isUnique = false} {ordered} 0..*   +trade {isKeyed = false} {**impl = arrayList**}

<<DCEntityContract>> Trade
<<UniqueId>> number: String tradeDate: Date saleOrPurchase: TradeKind

Figure 8.22   Applying code generation parameters to the PIM.

[12] [JCOL]

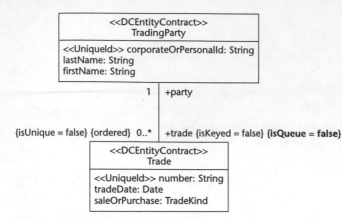

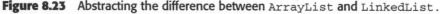

Figure 8.23 Abstracting the difference between `ArrayList` and `LinkedList`.

Elements That Are Less Traceable to the PIM

"Tag the PIM" and "Abstract It" both have the advantage of not entailing intervention by an engineer at the PSM level, which, as I have mentioned, simplifies PIM-PSM synchronization. However, both rely on the fact that the element of the PSM that we are deciding how to implement is directly traceable to an element in the PIM. The PSM's `getTrade` operation that returns a `List` (as in Figure 8.21) is traceable to the `trade` association end in the PIM (which is shown in Figures 8.22 and 8.23), and thus it's clear that `trade` is the PIM element that we need to tag. However, we are not always so fortunate.

Figure 8.24 focuses on the PSM's `ejbCurrencyOptionHome` interface for the currency option entity bean that was generated from the PIM. The `query` operation returns a collection of currency option beans. What determines the collection interface that is the type of the return value? There is no obvious parallel element in the PIM for that operation. So it's not clear which element in the PIM we would tag were we to use the "Tag the PIM" or "Abstract It" approaches.

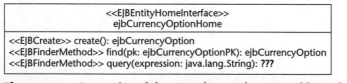

Figure 8.24 Properties of the PSM that are less traceable to the PIM.

In this situation, it's more challenging to figure out how to infer the collection type from the PIM. We could define tags for the <<EntityDC>> stereotype at the PIM level that make it possible to express whether a query operation should be generated for a component and, if so, what the collection properties of the return value should be, as shown in Figure 8.25. Or, more ideally, we could decide that there is one fixed pattern for how to generate the home, and thus suppress the issue totally at the PIM level.

Benefits of Read-Only PSMs

It's worth pointing out that if code generation proceeds directly from the PIM, it's still useful to generate a PSM, even though in such cases the PSM is a read-only artifact. There are two principal benefits the PSM provides regardless of whether engineers are allowed to modify it.

One benefit is that a UML-based PSM can help human beings visually grasp the platform-specific architecture that was generated from the PIM. This can be helpful to an application engineer during debugging. A tool that is smart about PIM-PSM-code synchronization can amplify this benefit substantially.

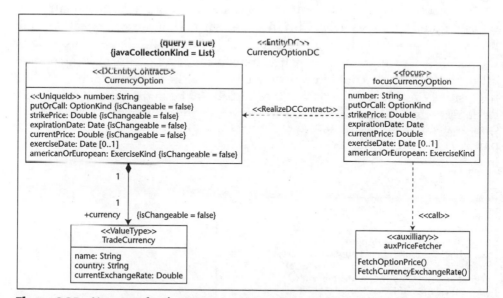

Figure 8.25   New tags for the PIM <<EntityDC>> stereotype.

The other benefit is that, as we have seen, a declarative UML-based PSM is at the same level of abstraction, yet semantically richer than the corresponding Java declarative code. The additional semantic information provides further help during debugging and quality assurance testing. For example, pre- and post-conditions at the PSM level are especially useful for testing and debugging because each operation they constrain corresponds to one identically structured operation in the Java code.

Also, if the generator produces only part of the implementation, the PSM constitutes a specification for programmers who complete the implementation manually. It's easier for a programmer to translate platform-specific specifications into code than to translate platform-independent specifications.

PIM Typing Issues

Our sample PIM and PSM avoid some issues that are particularly important for M1 models.

Consider the <<DCEntityContract>> class in our PIM, in which the StrikePrice and CurrentPrice attributes are typed as Double and represent money amounts (Figure 8.26 reproduces this class). Suppose we wanted to generate CORBA IDL from the PIM. It's likely that we would want the type of the corresponding CORBA attributes to be one of the IDL-based currency types defined in the CORBA Currency standard. This raises a question as to how a generator producing CORBA-specific APIs would know to use one of the CORBA Currency types when it transformed the platform-independent attribute. It certainly couldn't rely on the name of the attribute to indicate this necessity. What should the type of these attributes be in the PIM? If we simply declare them as of type Double and leave it at that, the generator could not infer that the value represents money.

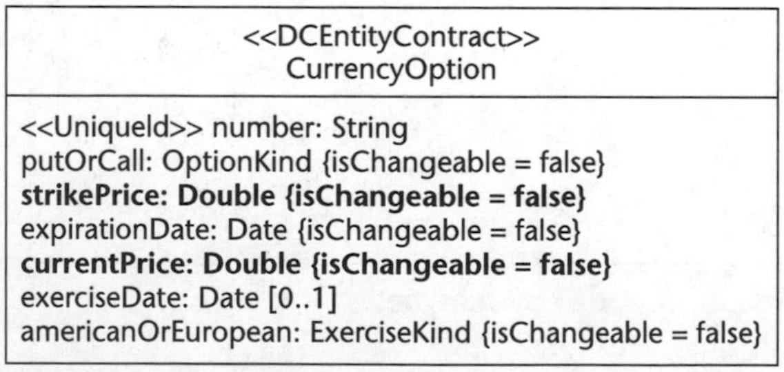

<<DCEntityContract>>
CurrencyOption

<<UniqueId>> number: String
putOrCall: OptionKind {isChangeable = false}
strikePrice: Double {isChangeable = false}
expirationDate: Date {isChangeable = false}
currentPrice: Double {isChangeable = false}
exerciseDate: Date [0..1]
americanOrEuropean: ExerciseKind {isChangeable = false}

Figure 8.26 Monetary amounts.

This scenario focuses on the CORBA platform and the money domain, but the pattern of this problem occurs with other platforms and domains as well. Microsoft COM Automation, for example, has a CY (formerly CURRENCY) intrinsic type for declaring monetary amount types in Microsoft IDL. Thus, when a generator produces MIDL, the same kind of issue arises. The OMG and Microsoft have also defined types for additional domains via their respective IDLs.

There are two basic approaches to solving this problem, which is similar to the problem we analyzed about deciding which Java collection types to use. For convenience, we express the approaches in terms of CORBA and money but, again, you can apply them to other technologies and domains:

Engineer Overrides.   Make the parameterization of the mapping to CORBA sufficiently flexible as to allow an engineer to specify the type that an attribute or parameter should assume when it's refined for CORBA. A UML profile to support this aspect of system description would allow CORBA engineers to specify the CORBA types where required. If the engineer does not apply a tagged value to specify the type, then the default type that the mapping dictates prevails.

Abstract It.   Define an M1 money PIM that defines platform-independent money types, and define mappings from the platform-independent types to the more concrete CORBA Currency types. PIMs could then use the platform-independent money types, while generators that transform M1 PIMs could use the mappings.

The "Engineer Overrides" approach provides a lesser degree of automation than the "Abstract It" approach because in the first approach you might have to engage an engineer knowledgeable about the CORBA Currency types to specify the currency aspects of every business-oriented system. Later on, you would have to bring someone in again, perhaps not the same person, when the PIM has to be retargeted to some other lower-level technology such as Microsoft IDL-based systems.

The "Abstract It" approach, on the other hand, encapsulates all of this specialized knowledge in the platform-independent types and their mappings. This approach requires more work up front, so most likely it only provides an acceptable return on investment if the knowledge thus encapsulated is used to produce multiple systems.

Money is just one of many such domains encountered in M1 models. Time and dates are additional examples. From a practical standpoint, the "Engineer Overrides" approach may have to be available as a fallback for some time because it's difficult for "Abstract It" to cover 100 percent of all domains perfectly, especially while PIM languages for enterprise systems are immature.

"Engineer Overrides" is not well supported by all of the standardized mappings yet, let alone the more ambitious "Abstract It" approach. However, regardless of progress on the standardization front, MDA tools and plug-in modeling frameworks need to support at least the "Engineer Overrides" approach in order to be usable in a real enterprise environment.

Multiple Parameterizations

You might want to associate more than one set of mapping parameters with a model. This section explains why.

Multiple Parameter Sets in the PIM

If there are mappings of our platform-independent, component-modeling profile to several platforms, we may need a PIM-PSM mapping parameterization language for each mapping. This would allow a PIM, such as our example, to be associated with several sets of parameter values, each of which parameterizes the mapping to a specific platform

For instance, in addition to defining a language for parameterizing the mapping to EJB, we might define one that parameterizes the mapping to .NET. An EJB generator would ignore any .NET mapping properties associated with the PIM and might not even know anything about them. As we've said, a good tool should allow easy filtering of such values by language, so that in one simple operation the tool can make all information associated with a specific language—such as a language for parameterizing a .NET mapping—visible or invisible.

Furthermore, we might want to have multiple sets of EJB mapping parameter values. Each of these sets would use the same parameterization language, but would have different values of the parameters to be used in different builds of the system, targeted to different EJB-based environments. Therefore, tools should support the filtering of distinct value sets expressed in the same language.

Figure 8.27 illustrates what our PIM can contain and the mapping parameters with which it can be associated:

- Property values corresponding to the base UML constructs such as class names, attributes, operations, invariants, Boolean values specifying whether a class is abstract or concrete, and so on.

- Property values corresponding to the platform-independent profile for modeling distributed components, such as instances of the <<UniqueId>> stereotype and values of the isKeyed tag.

- Optionally, one or more sets of platform-specific mapping parameter values. Each set of mapping parameter values corresponds to a profile that parameterizes the mapping to some platform.

Figure 8.27 makes it clear that platform-specific mapping parameters are associated with the PIM and are not part of it.

As MDA for enterprise systems matures, increasing use of the "Same Always" and "Abstract It" approaches will gradually obviate the need for tagging PIMs with platform-specific mapping parameters. Support for associating multiple platform-specific parameterizations with the PIM is a tactical necessity in the meantime.

Multiple Parameter Sets in the PSM

In environments where engineers are allowed to modify PSMs, it sometimes makes sense for a PSM to contain multiple sets of code generation parameterization values, each set targeted to a different runtime environment for the same technology platform.

For example, you might need code generation to be different for a single-host environment than for an environment in which the logical host is widely distributed. Therefore, even though both scenarios employ the same code generation parameterization language, they require different values of the parameters. (Of course this kind of variability could also be handled by runtime configuration rather than being statically bound at generation time.)

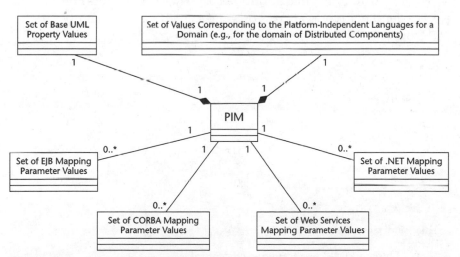

Figure 8.27   Associating mapping parameters with a PIM.

Language Definition Strategies

In Chapter 6, we investigated several language-definition strategies:

Profile.   Define a UML profile.

Heavyweight Extension.   Define a "heavyweight" UML metamodel extension via MOF.

New Metamodel.   Define a new metamodel.

Heavyweight + Lightweight.   Define a "heavyweight" UML metamodel extension via MOF and define a profile.

Metamodel + Profile.   Define a new metamodel plus a UML profile.

A PIM-Java mapping parameterization language is supposed to work with generic UML tools, so we need a UML profile. Thus, we can eliminate the "Heavyweight Extension" and "New Metamodel" strategies in this case.

The simplest strategy is to just define a UML profile (the "Profile" strategy) as shown in Figure 8.28. (Note that the enumeration declaration is informal, since all tags are typed as strings.)

However, it may also be useful to define a heavyweight extension of the UML metamodel via MOF, as shown in Figure 8.29 (the "Heavyweight + Lightweight" strategy) because that would make it possible to render the constructs as MOF metadata whose abstract syntax and concrete representations reflect the construct more directly. Let's examine the differences in the metadata for models that use heavyweight versus lightweight extensions.

The operation in a JMI interface for retrieving a model element's tagged values from a repository is `getTaggedValue`. That is the operation that has to be used to get the `javaCollectionKind` tagged value. That operation is generated from the standard UML metamodel's abstract syntax.

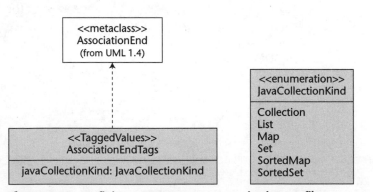

Figure 8.28   Defining a PIM-Java parameterization profile.

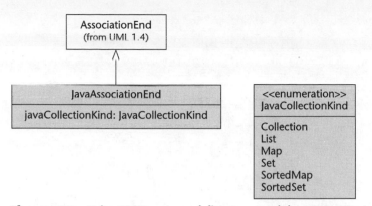

Figure 8.29   Using MOF metamodeling to extend the UML metamodel.

On the other hand, the expanded metamodel of Figure 8.29 would yield a JMI operation named `getJavaCollectionKind`. Thus, the semantics of the value are more manifest using this strategy. A modeling framework for a UML tool could render the `javaCollectionKind` parameter as a tagged value when the metadata needs to be in plain UML format, but could render it in the more manifest manner for the benefit of tools that can enforce the more direct syntax and semantics.

Similarly, an XMI document that encodes the model based on the standard UML XMI DTD would render a tagged value such as `{javaCollection Kind = List}` as a document element named `TaggedValue`. An XMI document based on the extended metamodel would encode the `List` value in a document element named `javaCollectionKind`.

However, our heavyweight extension has a downside. The class `Java AssociationEnd` is a contrived element. Logically it's not our intention to define a new kind of association end. Our intention is to define a parameter for mapping platform-independent association ends to Java, where they surface as get and set operations.

Furthermore, by putting `javaCollectionKind` in a subclass of the UML metamodel element `AssociationEnd`, we tie it to the UML metamodel, when in fact it might be useful in other contexts. For example, suppose we were using the simple graph metamodel of Chapter 6, which allows us to express models of graphs in which nodes have multiple tokens. Suppose further that we wanted to define a mapping that specifies how to implement a graph model in Java. We might want to use the `javaCollectionKind` construct to parameterize the mapping so that an engineer could decide the kind of Java collection to use for representing a node's multiple tokens.

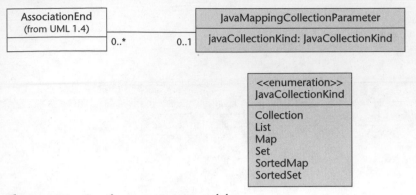

Figure 8.30　Creating a new metamodel.

Figure 8.30 therefore adopts the "Metamodel + Profile" strategy by defining a new metamodel (in addition to the profile) that is independent of the UML metamodel. When a tool needs to use the metamodel with UML, the metamodel's JavaMappingCollectionParameter class is temporarily associated with the UML metamodel's AssociationEnd element. This association is part of what an MDA tool would remove if commanded to filter out elements expressed in terms of the Java mapping parameterization language. With this strategy, our Java mapping parameter is orthogonal to the UML metamodel and more widely reusable as a consequence.

The javaCollectionKind mapping parameter is Java-specific, of course. However, the language-definition strategy considerations are very similar when creating new platform-independent constructs such as the isKeyed construct we defined earlier. You can choose from among the language-definition strategies when defining a group of such constructs.

Component Descriptors

The sample models in this chapter don't deal with a number of properties of the enterprise tier component that modern distributed component technologies usually put in a declarative component descriptor. Such descriptors are separate from the 3GL component-implementation code.

The common thread that unites component descriptor properties is that they concern the implementation rather than the basic business contract. Even though they have to do with implementation, it's possible to model them at the PIM level if we define suitable language constructs. Remember, our profile is for PIMs and thus is middleware-independent, but not entirely independent of all technical considerations.

The isTx tag defined in the profile example in Chapter 6 is an example of a construct addressing descriptor properties. Other properties of a component descriptor include flags that indicate whether:

- The component is reentrant.

- The component manages its own persistence or delegates that responsibility to the infrastructure.

- The component's unique identifiers are generated by the application or by the infrastructure.

- Controller components are stateful.

Component descriptors also include security properties.

Note that the Boolean isTx transaction property in our profile is simpler than the corresponding property in EJB, which can have several possible values:

- TX_NOT_SUPPORTED

- TX_BEAN_MANAGED

- TX_REQUIRED

- TX_SUPPORTS

- TX_REQUIRES_NEW

- TX_MANDATORY

Our profile narrows the choices, so that a true value of isTx maps to TX_REQUIRED, and a false value maps to TX_NOT_SUPPORTED. This kind of choice narrowing results when infrastructure engineers decide to constrain the implementations because they know their applications well enough to understand that the efficiencies they gain from consistency outweigh the lesser degree of flexibility. Historically, successful transaction-processing technologies, such as IBM's IMS, actually keep the transaction properties quite simple.

Other principles laid out so far about mapping to specific platform technologies also pertain to component descriptor properties. The only difference is that the platform-specific artifacts that generators produce from a PIM's component descriptor are not exclusively 3GL code artifacts. They include XML documents or descriptors in other kinds of formats. Nevertheless, the various PIM mapping approaches that I outlined earlier still apply.

In the following discussion about synchronizing models and code, I'll use the term "code" broadly to include other platform-specific artifacts such as XML-based component descriptors, except where I explicitly say "3GL code."

Synchronizing Models and Code

There are wide differences of opinion in the MDA community about whether to allow engineers to enhance relatively low-level artifacts that a generator produces from a more abstract model. For example, should programmers be allowed to modify Java code generated from a PIM? If so, how much freedom should they have and what are the ramifications of different degrees of freedom?

The "Forward Engineering Only" Approach

One camp feels strongly that the degree of freedom should be zero. The "Forward Engineering Only" approach permits no changes to code generated from a PIM. As a PIM changes during the iterative development process, synchronization ripples in one direction only (see Figure 8.31). Figure 8.32 illustrates that the development workflow is quite straightforward.

Real-time and embedded system applications of MDA have worked successfully with purely forward engineering for a number of years. Some of these systems consist of millions of lines of complex generated code.

For most kinds of systems it's impossible to generate complete implementations from purely declarative models. The "Forward Engineering Only" approach thus moves beyond declarative modeling, using behavioral models such as state machines and activity models. It also employs action languages that are precursors to Action Semantics for UML.

The action languages are critical for realizing the goal of practicing MDA with pure forward engineering. They express, in a platform-independent fashion, *how* to implement an operation. As I've mentioned previously, declarative semantics specify only an operation's contract, that is, *what* kinds of results are correct.

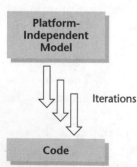

Figure 8.31 "Forward Engineering Only"—synchronization ripples in one direction.

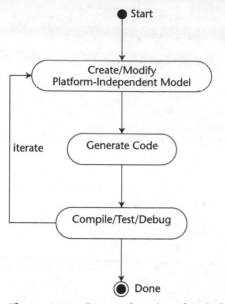

Figure 8.32   "Forward Engineering Only"—development workflow.

For example, suppose we define an operation that takes a positive floating point number as input and returns the square root of the number as output. We can specify all this via declarative pre- and post-conditions. However, pre- and post-conditions are insufficient to designate a specific numerical algorithm that we want the implementation to use to calculate the square root. Yet it's possible to express the desired algorithm without committing to a specific 3GL, by placing action statements in the operation definition. This is the primary role that action statements play.[13]

Action statements can also express fine-grained code generation logic that you can place in models. Figure 8.33 is an example of an action statement that generates specific Java code, fine-tuning a more general mapping of distributed component PIMs to EJB. The statement reads properties of the model. It generates code that implements the get logic for the `currentPrice` attribute of a `CurrencyOption` object by invoking a Web service via a dispatcher running in the implementation environment. Since UML Action Semantics has no concrete syntax other than XMI, I've invented a plausible one for this example. The expression references the PIM fragment shown in Figure 8.34.

---

[13] [MTAL 1998] is an excellent and brief summary of the ideas behind action languages.

```
Context CurrencyOption::currentPrice::get
   "WebServiceDispatcher.find(\"Options Price Info\").execute("+
      ("self.currency.country+","+
         self.putOrCall = OptionKind::#put ? "put" : "call"+","+
         self.americanOrEuropean = ExerciseKind::#american? "1" : "2"+","+
         self.expirationDate+")"
```

Figure 8.33   A code generation action statement embedded in an M1 class model.

For an American put option for the currency of the "UK" that expires on May 1, 2003, the code that the expression in Figure 8.33 generates would be:

```
WebServiceDispatcher.find("Options Price Info").execute
   ("UK","put",1,"05/01/2003")
```

Another way that some MDA tools support "Forward Engineering Only" is by allowing you to place 3GL code into an operation specification in a model, which the generator carries forward into the body of the operation in the code that it produces from the model.

If we were to use "Forward Engineering Only" for developing our options system example from earlier in this chapter, we would use the above techniques to put the entire specification of the system in the PIM and generate a complete implementation from the PIM, including Java code, testing harnesses, deployment scripts, and so on. The languages used to express the PIM would have to be very well developed in order to make this work.

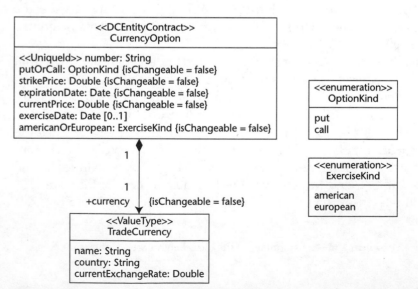

Figure 8.34   PIM fragment referenced by the code generation action statement.

The "Forward Engineering Only" approach has been proven to be tractable in the production of complex real-time and embedded systems. I comment on its applicability to enterprise systems shortly.

Partial Round-Trip Engineering

Partial Round-Trip Engineering allows engineers to enhance generated artifacts. However, enhancements must be additive. They may not overwrite or delete anything generated from the higher-level model. Furthermore, the engineer can't add anything that could be defined at the higher level of abstraction.

For example, a programmer may add some Java code to an operation implementation that was generated from a PIM. Later, when the PIM is enhanced and the code is regenerated, the generator doesn't overwrite the additions as long as the programmer has played by the rules. (Note that, for the moment, we aren't considering the role of PSMs. We factor PSMs into the discussion later.)

With "Partial Round-Trip Engineering," synchronization also ripples in one direction only, as shown in Figure 8.31. However, the development workflow is more complicated, as Figure 8.35 demonstrates. Furthermore, as we discussed, the development tool has to be intelligent enough to avoid overwriting programmer enhancements.

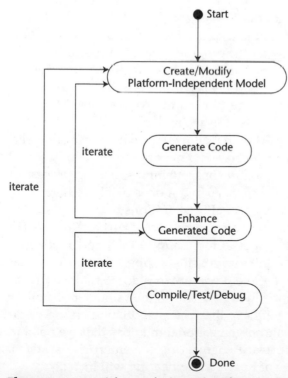

Figure 8.35 Partial Round-Trip Engineering.

There is precedence for "Partial Round-Trip Engineering" in GUI and meta-data repository development tools. Some environments for developing GUIs allow you to make a model of a WYSIWYG dialog or Web page and then generate code, such as Java or HTML, that has certain areas reserved for programmer additions. The programmer is not supposed to change anything that lies outside these reserved areas nor add things that define at the code level what can be defined at the WYSIWYG level. For instance, you're not supposed to define a new button directly in the code.

MOF metadata management tools also allow programmers to make additions to generated code, and they preserve those additions when the higher-level model is enhanced and the code is regenerated.

Some tools of this nature mark the boundaries between areas where additions are and are not permitted by generating markers in the code disguised to the compiler as comments, as in the following Java example:

```
//+Programmers add validation code here


//+End programmer-inserted validation code
```

The //+ is the delimiter that marks the boundary. The programmer may not make any additions outside the boundary. The generated code typically has several of these addition blocks. The fact that the delimiter starts with // means that a standard Java compiler doesn't reject it.

This technique for marking the boundaries is a bit unsafe unless the tool is quite sophisticated because it's easy for the programmer to inadvertently stray outside the boundary. Another safer technique that has emerged constrains the programmer to make all additions in entirely separate classes to which hooks are provided. The separate classes reside in separate source files. There are several metadata repository tools that use this technique.

"Partial Round-Trip Engineering" does not allow iterative reverse engineering. It doesn't preclude that some reverse engineering from a lower-level legacy system might be done on a one-time basis to jump-start the process of creating a higher-level model (see Figure 8.36), but it does preclude iteratively reverse engineering the lower-level system after alterations to it.

There is much successful development history with "Partial Round-Trip Engineering," even though most of it is in the realm of GUI and repository development. However, some of this approach's supporters concede that purely forward engineering is ideal if the pieces are in place to make it practical. Such is the case today for embedded and real-time systems, but not for enterprise systems. We do not as yet have the specialized languages, generators, implementation experience, and organizational memory that we need in order to go over completely to forward engineering for enterprise systems. Nevertheless, over time the degree of forward engineering will increase.

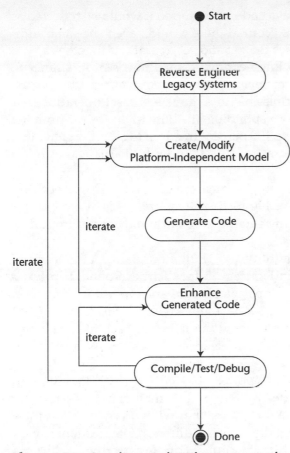

Figure 8.36   One-time, noniterative reverse engineering.

Full Round-Trip Engineering

The opposite pole from "Forward Engineering Only" is *Full Round-Trip Engineering*. In this approach, it's permissible to define something at the lower level of abstraction that is reflected back to the upper level, and to do so on an iterative basis.

This approach would, for example, allow a programmer to define a get/set operation pair in Java, resulting in an attribute being automatically added to a platform-independent model with which the Java code is synchronized. In our currency option example, the getExerciseDate and setExerciseDate operations in the Java voCurrencyOption class (Figure 8.11) correspond to the exerciseDate read-write attribute in the PIM's CurrencyOption class (Figure 8.9). "Full Round-Trip Engineering" would make it possible to define the get/set operation pair in the Java code, whereupon it would be reflected as a read-write attribute in the PIM. Of course, there would have to be some additional metadata in the code that ties the get and set operations together.

This kind of "Full Round-Trip Engineering" also allows a programmer to remove something from the lower level, with the removal reflected to the upper level. For example, it's permissible to remove a get/set operation pair from the Java code, causing the corresponding attribute to disappear from the PIM. The programmer doesn't have 100 percent freedom to alter the generated artifacts, but has considerably more freedom than with "Partial Round-Trip Engineering."

With "Full Round-Trip Engineering," synchronization can ripple both up and down the abstraction ladder, as Figure 8.37 illustrates. This puts a heavier burden on the tool than merely being smart enough to avoid overwriting additions to generated artifacts.

The development process workflow for "Full Round-Trip Engineering" looks like the workflow shown in Figure 8.35 for "Partial Round-Trip Engineering." However, this similarity doesn't capture an important difference. With "Full Round-Trip Engineering," a developer who wishes to can spend more time manipulating the code and less time iterating back to the higher-level model because the two-way synchronization allows her to do much of the development via hand-coding.

"Full Round-Trip Engineering" supporters argue that it will take time to wean programmers from 3GL code. Therefore, they maintain, this degree of freedom needs to be provided for a transitional period in order for MDA to be accepted and introduced incrementally. This is a different, or additional, justification from the justification for "Partial Round-Trip Engineering," which, as stated previously, is that we don't have the tools to generate complete enterprise systems yet.

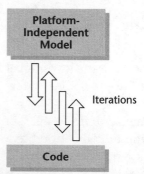

Figure 8.37 Synchronization rippling in both directions.

Round-Tripping and Tools

I'm skeptical about "Full Round-Trip Engineering" between code and PIMs. I would have to see scalable tools doing this before I change my mind, and I haven't seen any yet.

There are tools billed as supporting "Full Round-Trip Engineering" that actually don't support it in the sense in which I've described it. These tools provide two-way synchronization between a model and code that are at the *same* level of abstraction. Java editions of such tools, for example, support creating Java-specific models and synchronization between such models and Java code. Thus, the model is just a visualization of the code.

Some of these tools have devoted followings among some developers. They offer productivity gains over straight hand-coding, but they don't lift the level of abstraction in a fundamental sense. This limits the extent to which they can increase productivity. More seriously, they don't provide a buffer against platform volatility because the entire development process involves creating artifacts that are hard-wired to the chosen implementation technology such as Java.

On the other hand, tools that support "Forward Engineering Only" and "Partial Round-Trip Engineering" between PIMs and code are well established, even though "Forward Engineering Only" tools tend to be oriented toward real-time and embedded systems.

Round-Tripping and Architectural Enforcement

Earlier I stated that a crucial contribution that MDA makes to enterprise architecture is the ability to enforce an architecture. The "Forward-Engineering-Only" approach has the greatest capacity to enforce architectural styles that an architecture dictates. The more freedom engineers have to avoid the generator, the more difficult it is to ensure the quality of service of the software they produce and of other parts of the system they might affect.

Even if a programmer keeps his enhancements within boundary lines in the generated code, there are certain things he might do within those boundaries that negatively affect the system as a whole. For example, some distributed component architectures forbid the component programmer from spinning off threads—only the infrastructure is allowed to do so. The infrastructure's optimization logic decides when it is best to start a thread. If the programmer violates this rule, the 3GL compiler won't detect it, and subtle problems can result.

Round-trip engineering, whether partial or full, makes it more difficult to enforce these kinds of architectural styles.

Inter-Tier Synchronization

The concept of round-trip engineering is also applicable to synchronization among models at the same level of abstraction. For example, in multitiered distributed systems it's useful to be able to synchronize among platform-independent models of the system's various tiers. I described a taxonomy of tiers in Chapter 1 (refer to Figure 1.12). Figure 8.38 depicts platform-independent models for each tier of a system, where the system is a business component or application.

Now, suppose we make a change to the enterprise tier PIM. Since the resource tier maps the enterprise tier to external resources such as databases and packaged applications, the change very probably requires changes to the resource tier PIM. The workspace and user tier PIMs may also need to reflect the change.

Suppose, for example, that we delete an attribute from an enterprise tier entity. It's possible to infer, at least to some extent, the effect on resource tier mappings and workspace tier interactions that use the attribute. A good tool could automatically flag the elements in the resource and workspace PIMs that use the attribute and offer the option of removing references to it if removal is straightforward. In some cases where removal is complicated, such as if an interaction uses the value of the attribute to make a branching decision, the best the tool can probably do is to flag the interaction as requiring updating, although this is still a big help.

Now, consider what happens when we alter an interaction in the workspace tier. The workspace tier encapsulates the common patterns of interactions with the enterprise tier that clients in the user tier can reuse, including Web clients, fat clients, wireless handhelds, telephone keypads, or online B2B collaboration partners. Synchronization, therefore, ripples forward from the workspace tier to the user tier. The modification to an interaction requires changes to the user tier for all clients that use that interaction, but doesn't affect the enterprise and resource tiers.

A tool could offer to generate a simple default interaction when a new enterprise tier entity is defined. However, in complex systems such defaults don't cover all of the required interactions. Experience has also indicated that it's more difficult to generate default clients for the user tier based on the interactions in the workspace tier.

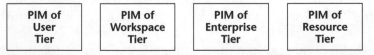

Figure 8.38 Platform-independent models of a system's distribution tiers.

Note that the workspace tier's abstraction of interactions with particular clients is of a different character than the PIM's abstraction of the workspace tier that suppresses concerns of specific middleware, programming languages, and information-formatting technologies. The PIM's abstraction does not exist at runtime. On the other hand, the system does maintain the separation of the workspace tier from the user tier at runtime. The PIM of a component's workspace tier abstracts away the various platforms over which the workspace tier can be implemented, whereas the workspace tier as a whole abstracts away the various kinds of clients that use the workspace tier interactions at runtime.

A related point is that it does make sense to have a PIM of a user tier client. At first glance this might seem strange because a user tier client is specific to a particular kind of client such as a Web client. But when we decide that we need to create a user tier Web client, we could still describe that client in a way that is specific to the Web but that doesn't commit us to using specific Web technology, such as Java or Microsoft. This is the role of a user tier PIM.

Figure 8.39 summarizes the ripple direction for forward engineering among tiers. These directions are based on the architectural separation of concerns that tiers enforce, which I explained earlier.

Strict maintenance of the tiers' separation of concerns prohibits using "Full Round-Trip Engineering's" two-way synchronization. For example, since the workspace tier is supposed to be an insulation layer keeping out concerns of specific kinds of clients, changes to clients in the user tier should not automatically cause changes to the workspace tier. Of course, an engineer may think of a system change in terms of a change to the client tier and then reason that the workspace tier requires a corresponding change. The forward engineering directions that Figure 8.39 depicts don't prohibit such reasoning, but do militate against trying to *automate* that reasoning.

However, "Partial Round-Trip Engineering" doesn't violate the separation. A tool that automatically ripples a change in a workspace tier PIM through to a user tier PIM could allow an engineer to enhance the tool's output within certain boundaries and be smart enough not to overwrite the enhancements when synchronization executes again.

Code for the different tiers needs to be synchronized as well. Figure 8.40 illustrates that the synchronization directions that derive from the tiers' separation of concerns apply to code synchronization.

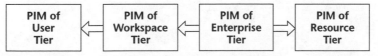

Figure 8.39 Inter-tier forward engineering directions.

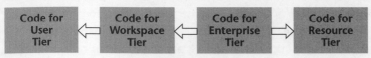

Figure 8.40   Inter-tier code synchronization.

In the Figure 8.40 scenario, if the code is generated via purely forward engineering from the various platform-independent models, then synchronization of the code among the tiers falls out automatically from synchronization among the tiers at the PIM level.

However, if round-tripping between PIMs and code is being practiced—that is, if programmers are making enhancements to code generated from PIMs—then inter-tier code synchronization is not straightforward.

Figure 8.41 illustrates this more complex scenario in an environment where round-tripping between PIMs and code is only partial. (The fact that round-tripping is partial is evident from the unidirectional synchronization arrows between PIMs and code). Tools can provide help with impact analysis by maintaining traces between elements generated from other elements so that an engineer can highlight a code or model element and ask to see all the trace dependencies involving that element.

For example, highlighting an operation in an enterprise tier component PIM would highlight, at both the PIM and code levels, workspace tier interactions that invoke the operation as well as elements in user tier clients that are dependent on the workspace interactions.

The tool could also support some automatic synchronization. For instance, if the type of a parameter in the PIM operation needs to change, the change would ripple forward in both dimensions, that is, from the enterprise tier PIM to the workspace and user tier PIMs, and from the PIMs to the code. But since this affects three PIMs and three code modules (follow the arrows in Figure 8.41), and since in our scenario engineers work on code modules directly, it can be difficult to manage. You can't allow an automated synchronization to ripple into a code module that someone is currently editing. Furthermore, if we use "Full-Round-Trip Engineering" between PIMs and code, the complexity goes up another order of magnitude.

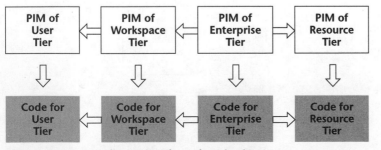

Figure 8.41   Two-dimensional synchronization.

The Impact of PSMs

Figure 8.42 further increases the complexity of our previous scenario by imposing platform-specific models, such as EJB specific models, between PIMs and code on the vertical dimension. As mentioned earlier, if these intermediate models are read-only—that is, if they merely provide a convenient view of the platform-specific implementation embodied in the code—then they don't complicate the development process.

However, if they are read-write PSMs—that is, if engineers are allowed to enhance them—then they make the development process less tractable, especially when different members of teams are working in parallel at different points along the dimensional axes. It's complicated enough with only "Partial Round-Engineering" and worse with "Full Round-Trip Engineering."

With "Partial Round-Trip Engineering," the tool has to provide a way to define boundaries in the PSM within which engineers may make enhancements. The tool must be smart enough to prevent those enhancements from being overwritten when the PIM is updated and the PSM regenerated.

With "Full Round-Trip Engineering," the tool not only has to be able to reflect upward the changes a programmer makes to code, but also has to reflect upward changes an engineer makes to the PSM.

Let's examine why "Full Round-Trip Engineering" complicates the read-write PSM scenario more than "Partial Round-Trip Engineering."

Suppose a programmer makes a legal enhancement to the generated code for the enterprise tier. Following Figure 8.42's synchronization directions, which assume only "Partial Round-Trip Engineering" in the vertical dimension, the enhancement potentially affects the code for the user, workspace, and resource tiers.

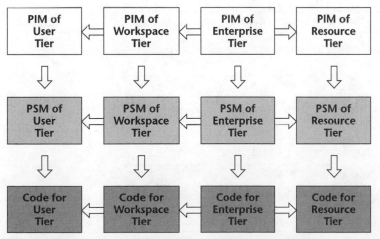

Figure 8.42   PSMs and "Partial Round-Trip Engineering."

With "Full Round-Trip Engineering," as depicted by Figure 8.43, a change to the enterprise tier code potentially affects all of the other elements. For example, the change to the enterprise tier code can ripple to the enterprise tier PSM and from there to the PSMs for the other tiers. In turn, the change rippled to the enterprise tier PSM can ripple to the enterprise tier PIM, which can ripple to the PIMs for other tiers. The more that an engineer's changes cause ripple effects on models or code that someone else might be editing, the more difficult it becomes to manage the development process.

Furthermore, the ripple path we just traced collides with other ripple paths from the same original source point. For example, the change to the enterprise tier code also ripples to the resource tier code and from there can ripple to the resource tier PSM and PIM, which we also arrived at via the other ripple path.

Thus, read-write PSMs and round-trip engineering contribute to a complexity explosion that even good MDA tools will be hard-pressed to manage. This is another important reason why I think MDA will move toward "Forward Engineering Only," and why I also think it will move toward restricting PSMs to being read-only. Additionally, it explains why, when using round-tripping as a compromise for a transitional period, partial rather than full round-tripping should prevail.

As "Forward Engineering Only" development processes advance and MDA tools that enable debugging in terms of a PIM's abstractions come online, the need for PSMs—even read-only PSMs—will tend to decrease, much as the need for 3GL compilers to save intermediate assembly code decreased when 3GL source-level debuggers matured.

Again, this discussion of round-trip engineering doesn't apply to tools that do round-tripping between PSMs and code only, which aren't full-blown MDA tools.

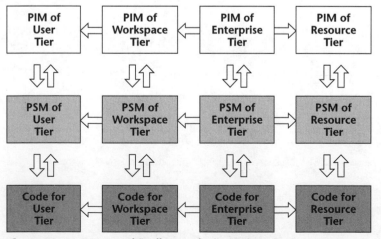

Figure 8.43 PSMs and "Full Round-Trip Engineering."

Dimensional Flexibility

Although I've concentrated on PIMs, PSMs, and code on the vertical dimension and distribution tiers on the horizontal dimension, an MDA tool that aspires to handle two-dimensional synchronization should ideally be agnostic as to what the actual points along these dimensions are.

As discussed, platform independence is a relative rather than absolute concept. Originally, for example, CORBA was conceived of as platform independent because it's independent of operating systems and programming languages. However, in the context of our examples, CORBA is a platform. Remember that our general definition of platform independence is independence from some *specified* platform or platforms. Thus, if an MDA tool were to lock itself into a particular notion of what the specified platforms are, it would be vulnerable to technology volatility.

It's perfectly viable—and often necessary—for a modeling *framework* that plugs into an MDA tool to presume a particular kind of platform independence. But the core of an MDA tool should ultimately not care how the modeling framework defines platform independence.

Moreover, a modeling framework may perform some limited synchronization between PIMs and more abstract models, such as requirements models (although this complicates synchronization). Thus, the number of points in the vertical dimension shouldn't be fixed.

Neither should an MDA environment make assumptions about the points along the horizontal dimension. This book uses a four-tier model of distributed systems. However, as mentioned previously, there are credible distributed computing practitioners who use five or six tiers. Furthermore, the points could represent something entirely different from tiers. However, a modeling framework that plugs into such an environment can make assumptions about the number and nature of the horizontal points and about the directions in which synchronization ripples.

Figure 8.44 depicts the viewpoint of an MDA environment that is independent of any assumptions about the nature of the two dimensions.

Synchronization Synopsis

I've argued that MDA should move toward "Forward Engineering Only" for two primary reasons:

- It has the greatest power to enforce an enterprise architecture.
- It's the simplest, most tractable approach to helping multiperson engineering teams be more productive.

I've also contended that read-write PSMs should be phased out as soon as it's practical to do without them.

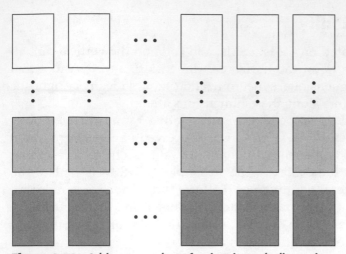

Figure 8.44   Arbitrary number of points in each dimension.

There will no doubt be some who challenge these views. The marketplace will be the ultimate arbiter.

I've also suggested the appropriate directions in which synchronization among tiers should ripple. The important idea to take away from that discussion is not necessarily the specific directions I chose but, rather, the fact that deciding what those directions are is an essential part of defining your mod-eldriven enterprise architecture.

Physical Models and Deployment Automation

A physical deployment model describes physical artifacts and resources used during development and runtime. From an MDA perspective, deployment models can drive automated deployment tools. MDA standards haven't addressed deployment automation yet, and thus this subject pushes MDA's envelope. But deployment is one of the most labor-intensive activities in complex enterprise systems, and therefore MDA will have to deal with it eventually. Here, I provide but a brief overview.

With a physical deployment model, a deployment engineer can specify that the runtime artifacts of an enterprise tier component should be packaged in an EJB EAR file with a particular name, which is to be deployed on a particular server at a specific network address. He can further stipulate that the executable file within the EAR should be launched in the same process address space as a particular instance of an EJB container running on that server. An automated deployment tool could read the model and carry out the deployment.

Deployment automation tools that can read such specifications exist today. However, the deployment metadata that drives them is generally not standardized and certainly isn't MOF-compliant. Thus, these tools tend to be disconnected islands in the overall enterprise system.

Using UML and/or some other MOF-compliant languages to describe deployment makes it possible to incorporate deployment automation into the MDA effort to automate more of the development process. For example, a generator that reads a component PIM and implements a mapping to EJB could generate a skeletal deployment model, since it knows certain outlines of the deployment requirements, such as that the EJB-specific artifacts need to be packaged in EAR files and that the executable needs to be co-located with a container process.

Furthermore, using MOF-compliant languages means that deployment metadata can be managed by MOF-based tools along with other metadata for the system.

What You Can Do Now

As part of defining your model driven enterprise architecture, lay out a basic approach to modeling at different levels of abstraction. Start defining your own MDA personas.

Tools that claim to be MDA tools are becoming available. Use the understanding you've gained from this chapter to guide you in evaluating such tools. Assess the approach they take toward modeling at different levels of abstraction. Do they promote round-trip engineering? If they promote "Full Round-Trip Engineering," do they do so between models and code that are at the same level of abstraction? Do they hard-wire assumptions about the number of distribution tiers?

The process of finding answers to these questions will tell you a lot about the tools and how well they fit your architectural strategy.

Summary

The basic kinds of models that I've discussed are:

- Business models
- Requirements models
- Platform-independent models (PIMs)
- Platform-specific models (PSMs)
- Physical deployment models

This model taxonomy is not definitive and can be mapped onto other model taxonomies, such as the ones that the Unified Process and Catalysis define.

I've focused mostly on PIMs, PSMs, and the mappings among PIMs, PSMs, and code. Although I explain the general principles of parameterized mappings in terms of a limited example, you can apply those principles broadly to PIMs, PSMs, and code that address multiple distribution tiers, EAI, and B2B integration.

There are three basic approaches to synchronizing PIMs, PSMs, and code:

- Forward Engineering Only
- Partial Round-Trip Engineering (round-trip engineering without iterative reverse engineering)
- Full Round-Trip Engineering (round-trip engineering with iterative reverse engineering)

MDA will evolve toward "Forward Engineering Only" because it has the greatest power to enforce an enterprise architecture and because it's the easiest to manage when developing complex systems. "Partial Round-Trip Engineering" may be necessary for a transitional period when applying MDA to enterprise systems.

"Full Round-Trip Engineering" between PIMs and code complicates the development process to a degree that may be excessive. This is not to be confused with full round-tripping between models and code at the same abstraction level, which does not truly accomplish the raising of the level of abstraction that MDA seeks.

Read-write PSMs also complicate the development process. The combination of "Full Round-Trip Engineering" and read-write PSMs may be too complex even for good MDA tools to manage, especially in team development environments.

An important new area for MDA is using physical deployment models to automate the deployment process.

Advanced Topics

As I've said, the industry's uptake of MDA will be gradual and uneven. This part of the book looks ahead to some of the technical advances that MDA could bring in the medium and long term. The content is more challenging technically than that of Parts One and Two.

CHAPTER 9

Modeling Transformations with CWM

This chapter explores the Common Warehouse Metamodel's support for transformations. On the surface, CWM's transformation architecture seems to be only about data transformations. However, although it does indeed provide extensive and important support for model driven data transformations, it has more general implications for supporting the ability to define mappings as formal models.

First, I survey the data transformation facilities of this OMG standard and then examine the potential for CWM to grow into something even more significant.

More Than a Database Metamodel

I mentioned earlier that CWM contains more than just a metamodel for relational databases. It also contains metamodels for

- Multidimensional databases
- Record structures
- XML

We'll talk about the significance of the XML metamodel shortly.

Additionally, CWM contains a set of product-specific database metamodels that are extensions of the base relational, multidimensional, and record structure metamodels:

- IBM IMS database definitions
- Unisys DMS II database schemas
- Hyperion Essbase
- Oracle Express

Finally, it contains a set of metamodels for describing rules for processing data in different ways:

- Online Analytical Processing (OLAP) rules
- Data-mining rules
- Data-transformation rules[1]

Data transformation is a significant requirement not only for data warehouses, but also for enterprise application integration (EAI) and business-to-business integration (B2Bi). The required transformations might be from one relational database (RDB) format to another, from one XML format to another, from RDB to XML, XML to RDB, multidimensional to RDB, and so on.

One of the biggest problems in integrating applications within an enterprise is the existence of multiple database schemas for similar data. For example, an EAI system may have to integrate two applications that use roughly similar data about customers but have fairly disparate schemas for the data.

In B2Bi scenarios, when you receive data from a collaboration partner in an agreed-upon common format, you have to translate the data into a format that that your internal systems can use. The agreed-upon format might conform to an international standard, or you and the partner might establish the format via bilateral agreement. Conversely, before you send data to a collaboration partner, you have to convert it to the common format.

The CWM transformation metamodel defines constructs for specifying transformation rules. In accordance with the metamodel, you describe a transformation in terms of a source and target data model, where the source and target models conform to any of the CWM data metamodels. The XML metamodel is considered to be one of the data metamodels. Table 9.1 is a partial list of the kinds of transformations that the metamodel supports.

---

[1]This chapter deals primarily with the transformation metamodel. For a more comprehensive treatment of CWM see [PCTM 2002].

Table 9.1 CWM Transformation Sources and Targets—Partial List

SOURCE DATA MODEL	TARGET DATA MODEL
RDB schema A	RDB schema B
RDB schema	Multidimensional schema
Multidimensional schema	RDB schema
Multidimensional schema A	Multidimensional schema B
RDB schema	XML DTD
XML DTD	RDB schema
XML DTD A	XML DTD B
IMS schema	XML DTD
Record structure	RDB schema
...	...

The transformation metamodel is an M2 model. A set of CWM transformation rules is an M1 model expressed in terms of the CWM transformation metamodel.

The OMG applied XMI's MOF-XML mapping to the CWM transformation metamodel to produce a DTD that constitutes a concrete syntax for representing transformation rules. It also applied the MOF-IDL mapping to produce CORBA IDL for representing transformation rules as CORBA objects. JMI's MOF-Java mapping will be applied to the metamodel as well to generate Java APIs for representing transformation rules as Java objects.

Implementation Strategies

A MOF repository tool generates code for managing transformation rules in the same manner that it does for managing other kinds of metadata. In other words, it reads the metamodel and generates code that:

- Implements the APIs generated from the metamodel and uses them as interfaces to transformation rules in the repository
- Imports and exports XMI containing transformation rules to and from the repository

Figure 9.1 illustrates how the management of CWM transformation rules follows this standard MOF pattern for managing M1 metadata.

In general, a MOF repository tool doesn't know how to actually execute the CWM transformations. To a MOF repository, transformations rules are just another kind of metadata that it manages according to the general pattern. Additional code is required to execute the transformation rules. Such additional code operates on M0 data. In contrast, the metadata management code that a general MOF repository generates operates on M1 metadata.

One strategy for producing the code to execute the transformations is to create a generator that reads a set of M1 transformation rules and generates the transformation code that executes the rules on M0 data. For example, a set of M1 transformation rules might map one purchase order schema onto another one, while the code generated to execute those rules would be applied to transform M0 purchase order records from one format to another. Figure 9.2 exhibits this approach.

Another implementation strategy is to write a generic transformer that reads the M1 transformation rules dynamically at runtime and executes the transformations on the M0 data (see Figure 9.3). A generic transformer is essentially a virtual machine that executes transformation rules. In some scenarios, such generic code is significantly slower than statically generated code.

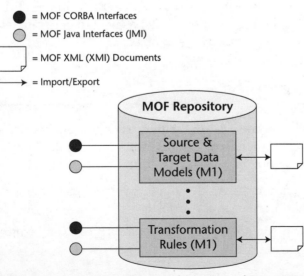

● = MOF CORBA Interfaces

◐ = MOF Java Interfaces (JMI)

▢ = MOF XML (XMI) Documents

◄──► = Import/Export

Figure 9.1 Managing CWM transformation rules as MOF metadata.

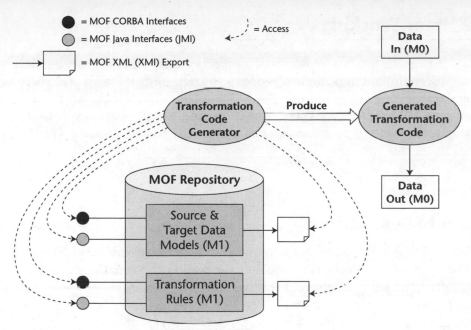

Figure 9.2   Generating transformation code.

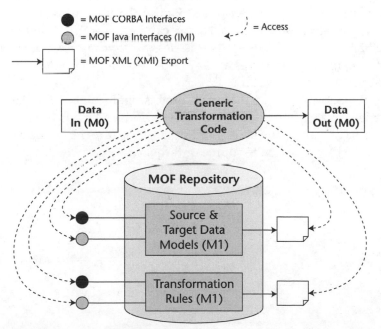

Figure 9.3   Dynamic transformation.

The Inner Workings

The CWM transformation metamodel supports transformation between any two CWM-compliant data models. It does so by defining all the main elements of the data metamodels, including the XML metamodel, as subclasses of a set of general CWM superclasses. The transformation metamodel is expressed in terms of the general superclasses that all the data metamodels share. This section explores this subject in detail.

Common Superclasses

Figure 9.4 is a part of the transformation metamodel that defines *transformation maps*. The transformation metamodel has some additional facilities, but transformation maps are the focus of this discussion.

The figure demonstrates that a CWM TransformationMap is composed of ClassifierMaps that map Classifiers to Classifiers. A ClassifierMap, in turn, is composed of FeatureMaps that map Features to Features, and ClassifierFeatureMaps that map Classifiers to Features or vice versa.

Figures 9.5 through 9.8 illustrate how the main elements of the CWM data metamodels inherit from common superclasses. Figure 9.5 illustrates that a relational Table is a Classifier. Thus, a Table can be the source and/or the target of a ClassifierMap. CWM calls this *classifier equivalence*. Figure 9.5 also shows that a relational Column is a Feature. Thus, a Column can be the source or the target of a FeatureMap.

Similarly, Figure 9.6 shows that in the multidimensional database metamodel Dimension is a Classifier, and DimensionedObject is a Feature. Thus, a Dimension can be the source or target of a ClassifierMap, and a DimensionedObject can be the source or target of a FeatureMap.

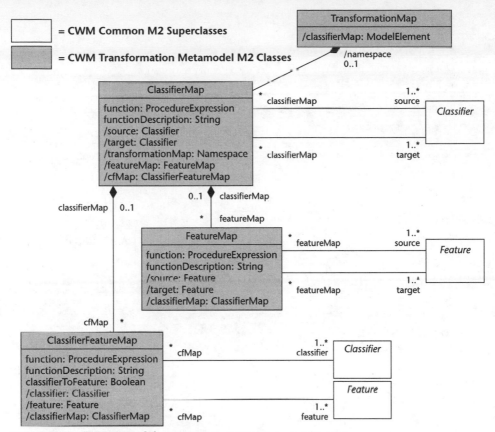

Figure 9.4   Fragment of the CWM transformation metamodel.

Adapted, with permission, from [CWM]

Figures 9.7 and 9.8 show how the record structure and XML metamodels also leverage the common supertypes `Classifier` and `Feature`. This means that records and XML DTDs can also be sources and targets for a CWM transformation map.

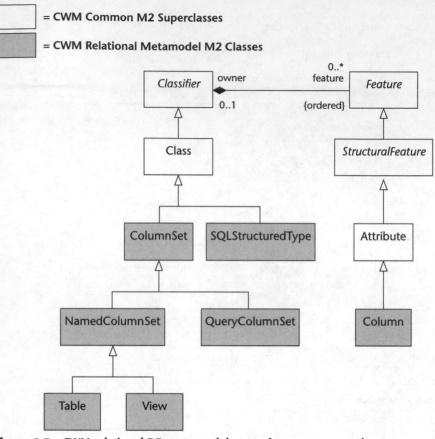

Figure 9.5 CWM relational DB metamodel—use of common superclasses.
Adapted, with permission, from [CWM]

Thus, by defining the primary elements of data metamodels as classifiers and features, and by defining transformations as classifier and feature maps, CWM can support a wide variety of mappings.

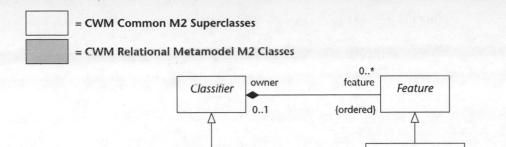

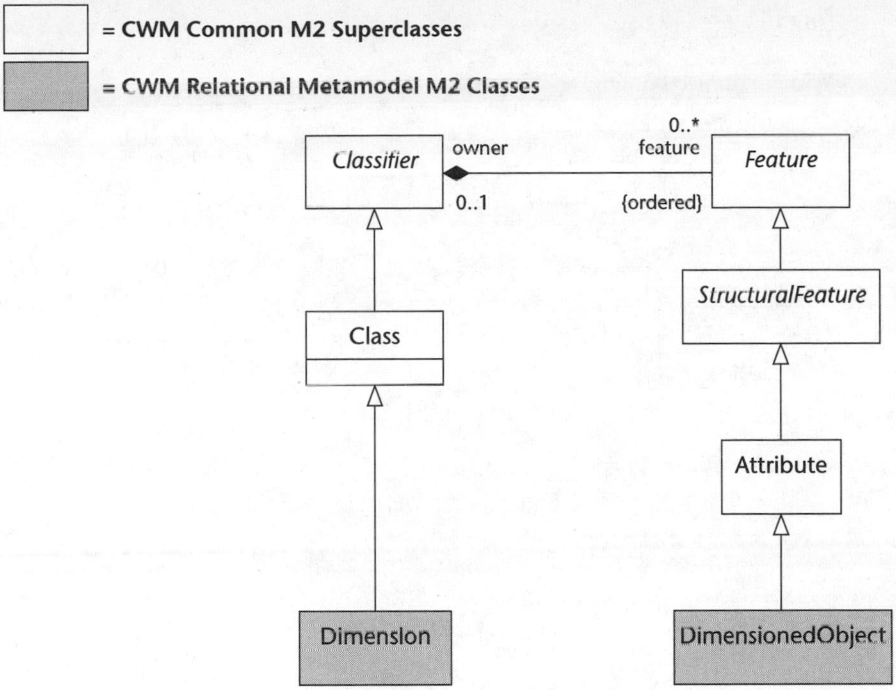

□ = CWM Common M2 Superclasses

� = CWM Relational Metamodel M2 Classes

Figure 9.6   CWM multidimensional DB metamodel—use of common superclasses.
Adapted, with permission, from [CWM]

Mapping Expressions

CWM transformation maps would lack sufficient fidelity were it not for the `ProcedureExpression` that each contains (refer to Figure 9.4 again). These expressions bridge the fidelity gap. CWM does not mandate the language of the expression. Thus, we should look upon CWM transformations as an extensibility framework. Users extend the framework by defining procedural expression languages or reusing ones already defined.

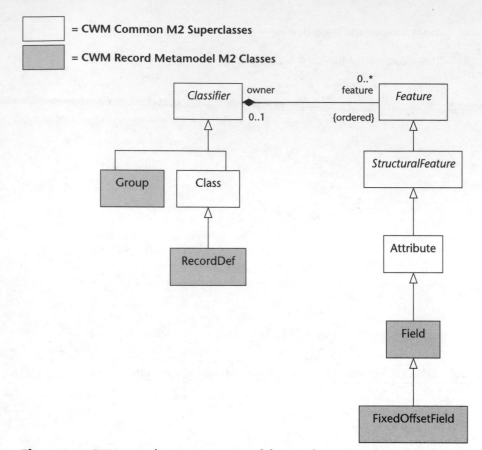

= CWM Common M2 Superclasses

= CWM Record Metamodel M2 Classes

Figure 9.7   CWM record structure metamodel—use of common superclasses.
Adapted, with permission, from [CWM]

To understand the importance of these expressions, consider Figure 9.9, which is the abstract syntax tree for a transformation map named B2BSalesRDBxXML. A company uses this map for exchanging purchase order data with a collaboration partner as part of a B2B sales process. The map defines how to convert relational data in the company's database into an agreed-upon XML format.

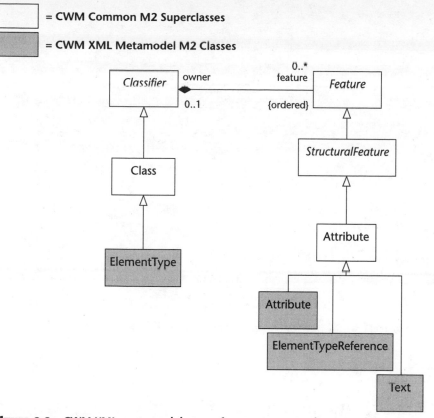

□ = CWM Common M2 Superclasses

▩ = CWM XML Metamodel M2 Classes

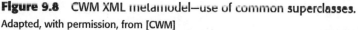

Figure 9.8   CWM XML metamodel—use of common superclasses.
Adapted, with permission, from [CWM]

The figure shows how one of the classifier maps that B2BSalesRDBxXML owns, named PurchaseOrderMap, maps a relational table POItem to an XML DTD element POLineItem. The figure expands the Purchase OrderMap to show how one of the feature maps it owns, named extended PriceMap, maps the pricePerUnit and quantity columns in POItem to the extendedPrice attribute in the XML DTD. Simply associating the two source columns with the target XML attribute, however, is not sufficient to define the transformation. Adding the expression extendedPrice = pricePerUnit * quantity to the feature map makes it computationally complete.

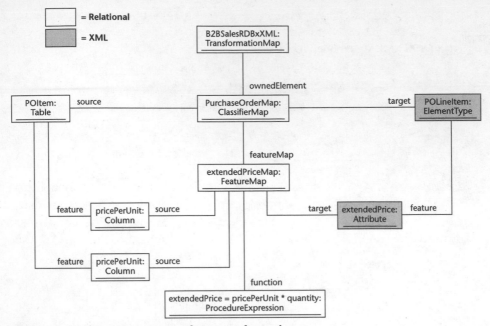

Figure 9.9 Abstract syntax tree for a transformation map.

UML Models as Sources and Targets

At first glance, it might appear that the CWM's Classifier and Feature are in fact the classes from the UML metamodel that bear the same names. If that were the case, then any UML Classifier (such as a Class or DataType) could be the source or target of a ClassifierMap, and any UML Feature, such as an Attribute, could be the source or target of a FeatureMap.

This, however, is not the case. CWM's Classifier and Feature and UML 1.X's Classifier and Feature are not the same. Thus, UML classifiers and features are not CWM classifiers and features and cannot be sources or targets of classifier and feature maps. The CWM architects started out simply reusing Classifier, Feature, and other elements of the UML metamodel, so that the common CWM superclasses actually were UML's Classifier, Feature, and so on. Doing so created problems for implementers, though. For example, if the CWM multidimensional database metamodel's Dimension element descends from UML's Classifier, then it inherits properties that support subclassing, so that one dimension can subclass another. However, dimensions can't be subclassed, so these properties are excess baggage.

Thus, CWM defines its own `Classifier` and `Feature` elements and a number of other elements that are reminiscent of UML counterparts with the same name. The result is a CWM core model of common superclasses that resembles the core of the UML metamodel, but is actually subtly different.

One of the goals of UML 2.0 is to redefine its core so that it separates the concerns of classification and inheritance and a number of other concerns as well. This will make it easier for metamodels to reuse what they need from the UML core without dragging in unneeded baggage. As I've pointed out, one of the weaknesses of the UML 1.X metamodel is that it does not adequately separate concerns.

The plan is for CWM 2.0 and UML 2.0 to share this common core, as illustrated by Figure 9.10. When this alignment of CWM and UML is complete, CWM's relational `Table`, XML `ElementType`, and so on will descend from the common `Classifier` element, and the classifiers that are the sources and targets of a classifier map will all descend from this same element. Then, there will be no problem using a UML classifier, such as a class definition, as the source or target of a classifier map. Similarly, CWM's relational `Column`, XML `Attribute`, and so on will descend from a commonly defined `Feature` element, so there will be no problem using a UML feature, such as an attribute, as the source or target of a feature map.

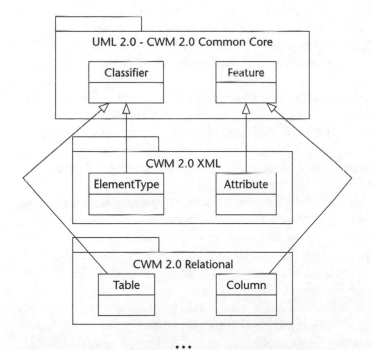

Figure 9.10   Common core for UML 2.0 and CWM 2.0.

There is a caveat worth stating: The architects of the common core will have to be careful to make the set of common superclasses as minimal as possible, lest they start down a slippery slope toward defining one grand metamodel which, as we've seen in Chapter 5, is not practical.

Metamodel-to-Metamodel Mappings

A CWM transformation of the kind we have seen maps an M1 model to another M1 model. In other words, it's a model-to-model mapping, where the models are M1 models. The mapping operates upon M0 instances. Going back to our purchase order example, we might map a purchase order relational schema (M1) to a purchase order XML DTD (M1). We apply that mapping to actual purchase order instances (M0).

Now, consider the fact that the industry needs to define various UML-Java mappings, UML-XML mappings, and so on. A UML-XML mapping is a model-to-model transformation, but it maps an M2 model—the UML metamodel—to another M2 model—the XML metamodel. The mapping applies to M1 instances. It transforms specific M1 UML models to specific M1 XML models, that is, to XML DTDs.

We've seen that a necessary condition for a model to be a source or target of a CWM transformation map is that the model elements being mapped must be classifiers and features. A CWM relational data model can be a source or target, because tables are classifiers and columns are features, and the CWM relational data metamodel subclasses the common superclasses. In Figure 9.9 example, POItem can be the source of a classifier map because it's an instance of Table, which is a classifier.

If we apply this same criterion to a *metamodel* that we wish to use as the source or target of a transformation map, we would say that the metamodel can be a source or target if the metamodel elements being mapped are classifiers and features. For example, suppose we want to define a UML-XML mapping as a transformation map. Doing so would entail, among other things, defining a classifier map in which the UML metamodel element Class is the source and the XML metamodel element ElementType is the target. This would require that Class and ElementType be instances of a classifier. This is analogous to POItem being an instance of Table, which is a classifier, which establishes POItem as a valid source or target for a classifier map.

Now, what is UML Class an instance of? It is an instance of MOF Class. ElementType is also an instance of MOF Class. Just as POItem (M1) is an instance of Table (M2), UML Class and XML ElementType (M2) are instances of MOF Class (M3). Figure 9.11 illustrates this similarity. (This is a case where viewing metalevels as relative is helpful.) Thus, in order for UML Class and XML ElementType to be the source or target in a classifier map, MOF Class, of which they are instances, has to be a classifier. Is it?

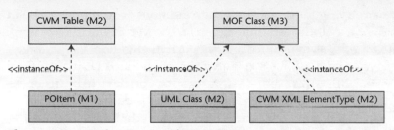

Figure 9.11   M1 instances and M2 instances.

To answer this question, we start by observing that, in "the" MOF model for MOF 1.X, MOF Class descends from MOF Classifier. This could lead us to conclude that MOF Class is a classifier and that our criterion is satisfied. However, just as CWM 1.X's Classifier and UML 1.X's Classifier are subtly different from each other, MOF 1.X's Classifier differs slightly from both CWM's and UML's. I pointed out before that UML 1.X and MOF 1.X are somewhat misaligned, but it's a bit worse than that because there is a three-way misalignment. CWM, UML, and MOF each has a slightly different Classifier element, and each has a slightly different Feature element as well. There are additional, apparently equivalent, elements that are actually out of synch with each other.

The plan to rectify this problem is for MOF 2.0 to share the common core spoken of earlier in the discussion of UML 2.0-CWM 2.0 alignment. Figure 9.12 illustrates that UML, CWM, and MOF will share this same core.

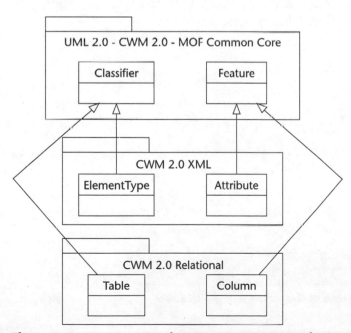

Figure 9.12   Common core for UML 2.0, CWM 2.0, and MOF 2.0.

Let's recap: We are trying to figure out what conditions would have to be in place in order to define a UML-XML mapping as a CWM transformation map, with the UML metamodel as the source and the XML metamodel as the target. More specifically, we want to define a classifier map that maps UML `Class` to XML `ElementType`. UML `Class` and XML `ElementType` have to be instances of something that is a classifier in the sense that classifier is defined for CWM. A common UML-CWM-MOF core that provides a common definition of classifier would satisfy this requirement, as Figure 9.13 demonstrates.

When the alignment is completed, MOF metamodels will be able to be sources and targets of CWM transformations. Thus, CWM transformation maps will be able to describe UML-XML mappings and other metamodel-to-metamodel mappings.

Figure 9.14 illustrates this scenario in general terms. Note the similarity to Figure 9.2. The only difference is that Figure 9.14 is shifted one metalevel upward. The source and target models are at M2 and the instances are at M1, whereas in Figure 9.2 the source and target are at M1 and the instances are at M0. From this standpoint a transformation engine would care only about relative metalevels and the designation of the transformation rules as M1 appears somewhat arbitrary.

In Figure 9.14, the "Generated Transformation Code" is a generator that generates one model from another. Thus, the transformation code generator produces generators, or at least it produces a good portion of them.

Note that we could implement metamodel-to-metamodel transformation dynamically. Then, we would have the scenario represented by Figure 9.15, which looks like Figure 9.3, except for the upward metalevel shift. The "Generic Transformation Code" is a generic generator.

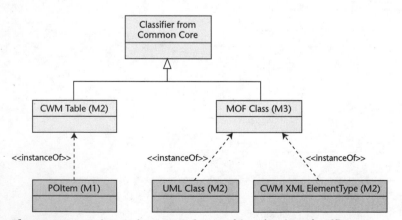

Figure 9.13　Being an instance of something that is a classifier.

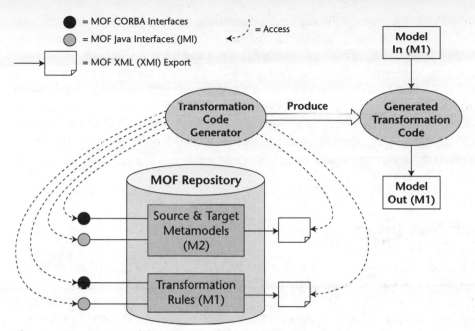

Figure 9.14   Metamodel-to-metamodel transformation.

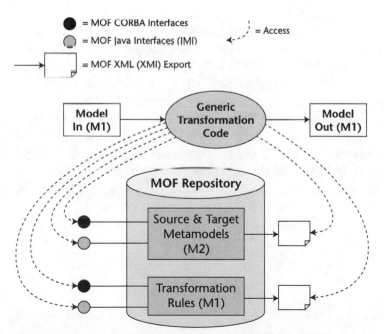

Figure 9.15   Dynamic metamodel-to-metamodel transformation.

The OMG is currently finalizing metamodels for Java, EJB, COBOL, PL/1, C, and C++. These could be sources and targets of transformation maps, as per Figures 9.14 and 9.15. Thus, various UML-Java mappings, UML-COBOL mappings, and so forth could be defined as CWM transformation maps. Since the OMG already has a MOF-compliant CORBA metamodel, even the CORBA language mappings could be expressed as CWM transformations, such as CORBA-C++, CORBA-Java, and so on. This road leads to these mappings being expressed as formal models that can be executed dynamically or processed by a generator that produces generators.

MOF Mappings

We're now ready to examine what it would take to be able to express the MOF technology mappings, such as JMI and XMI, as CWM transformation maps.

Toward this end, let's consider how to define XMI—which is the MOF-XML mapping—as a transformation map. Part of such a map would be a classifier map in which MOF Class, which is an M3 element, is the source and XML ElementType, which is an M2 element, is the target. We've established that, with the projected 2.0 alignment, XML ElementType will be eligible to be the source or target of a classifier map because it is an instance of MOF Class, which is a classifier. However, what about the eligibility of MOF Class?

Here, MOF's self-descriptive nature lends a hand. "The" MOF model for MOF 2.0 will still be self-descriptive; that is, its metamodel will still be itself. Self-description means that MOF Class is an instance of MOF Class, which is a classifier, and in the 2.0 world, classifier will have a common meaning. Since the eligibility criteria for being able to be a source or target in a classifier map is being an instance of something that is a classifier, with 2.0 alignment MOF Class will meet the test (see Figure 9.16). Thus, a classifier map with MOF Class as the source and XML ElementType as the target will be legal. XMI's MOF-XML mapping could be described as a CWM transformation map, as could JMI's MOF-Java mapping and the MOF-CORBA mapping. The XMI 2.0 XML-MOF reverse-engineering mapping could be expressed this way, too.

Thus, CWM transformation maps could describe how to transform a MOF metamodel to a Java model, that is, to a set of Java interfaces. They could describe how a MOF metamodel is transformed to an XML model—that is, to an XML DTD (or Schema). In other words, XMI and JMI could be expressed as formal models. CWM transformation code generators and dynamic transformation engines could be leveraged to implement the models or execute them directly.

Figure 9.17 illustrates such a MOF mapping scenario. The source of the map is MOF, and the target could be an M2 metamodel such as Java. What are the instances that are processed by transformation code that conforms to the map? The map is an M3‡M2 map so, at the instance level, the actual transformation is M2→M1. The source instances to which the map is applied are a set of M2 instances of MOF elements, that is, some MOF metamodel. The target instances are M1 instances of some MOF metamodel. For example, where the M3→M2 map is a MOF-XML map, the source instances would constitute an M2 metamodel such as the CORBA metamodel, and the target instances would constitute M1 instances of the XML metamodel, which together form a DTD (or Schema).

If you think about it, this makes sense—in goes a metamodel, out comes an XML DTD or Schema. That's precisely what we would expect of a MOF-XML mapping. We've seen such mappings before. Now, however, we are seeing how they could be expressed as CWM transformation maps, if the UML-CWM-MOF alignment comes to pass.

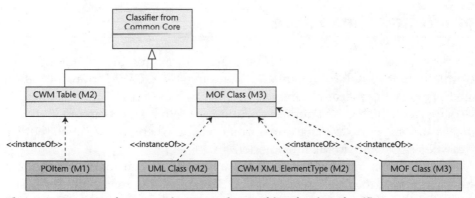

Figure 9.16   MOF class as an instance of something that is a classifier.

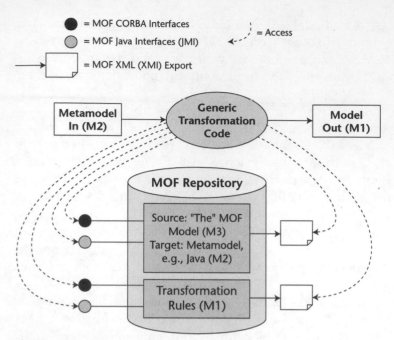

Figure 9.17 MOF-to-metamodel transformation.

Completing the Picture

There are missing pieces to this scenario of expressing metamodel-to-metamodel and MOF-to-metamodel mappings via CWM transformation maps. The missing pieces are the expressions that are part of the transformation maps, for which CWM defines no language. What kind of expression language could support defining transformations between two M2 metamodels or between MOF and an M2 metamodel?

UML Action Semantics points toward an answer, even though it was not actually intended to play this role. Action Semantics statements are expressed in terms of the UML metamodel, so they refer to elements of a UML model. UML and MOF are very close and, as discussed above, are being brought together to share a common set of core elements. Therefore, using Action Semantics statements to refer to elements of MOF metamodels is within reach. And, of course, "the" MOF model is itself expressed in terms of the MOF, so Action Semantics statements could refer to its elements as well. Action Semantics statements can express fine-grained transformation logic.

```
source.namespace->isEmpty () implies
   target.name = source.name and

source.namespace->notEmpty () implies
   target.name = source.namespace.name + "." + source.name
```

Figure 9.18 Sample action statement for a MOF-XML mapping.

Consider a UML-XML mapping that has a classifier map describing how to transform a UML `Class` into an XML `ElementType`. An action expression for the map, using an OCL-like concrete syntax, might look like Figure 9.18. It expresses logic that maps the name of a UML `Class` onto the name of an XML `ElementType`. Refer back to Figure 9.4. Since the context for the expression is a classifier map, the `source` and `target` identifiers in Figure 9.18 traverse the opposite ends of `ClassifierMap`'s associations with `Classifier` in the transformation metamodel.

The concrete syntax of Figure 9.18, which is based on the Action Semantics abstract syntax, knows how to address classifiers, such as the `source` and `target`, and knows how to address the features of a classifier such as `namespace` and `name`. The models being addressed this way are the UML and XML metamodels, which, of course, are MOF models. Thus `source.namespace`, `target.name`, and so on address the properties of a model described in terms of MOF rather than in terms of the UML. This will be legal when UML MOF alignment achieves a common notion of what classifiers and features are.

Alignment will also allow the action language to address "the" MOF model, because addressing its classifiers and features is similar to addressing the classifiers and features of an M2 metamodel. Therefore, expressions in such an action language could be used in transformation maps describing MOF-metamodel mappings such as XMI.

Currently, XMI uses EBNF (Extended Backus Naur Form) to express XMI mapping rules, as shown in Figure 9.19. EBNF could be the language for an expression in a transformation map. However, EBNF is specific to textual syntaxes, whereas a language based on Action Semantics promises to be generic for any M2 metamodel and "the" M3 MOF model.

Note that the EBNF in Figure 9.19 expresses a mapping to XML's concrete syntax, whereas Figure 9.18 expresses a mapping to the XML metamodel's abstract syntax. This is not to criticize the architects of XMI, whose work has been critical for getting MDA off the ground. Remember, we are still early in the evolution of MDA.

```
1. <DTD> ::= <1b:FixedContent>
<1d:XMIAttList>?
<2:PackageDTD>+
1a. <XMIFixedAttribs> ::= "%XMI.element.att;" "%XMI.link.att;"
1b. <FixedDeclarations> ::= //Fixed declarations//
1c. <Namespace> ::= ( //Name of namespace// ":" )?
1d. <XMIAttList> ::= "<!ATTLIST" "XMI" ("xmlns:"
                      //Name of namespace// "CDATA" "#IMPLIED")+">"
```

Figure 9.19 XMI MOF-XML mapping rules expressed in EBNF.
Reused, with permission, from [XMI], p. 4-5.

It's worth repeating that the UML Action Semantics standard specifies only an abstract syntax—that is, a metamodel—for action statements. It doesn't define a concrete syntax. Since Action Semantics is an extension of the UML metamodel, XMI's MOF-XML mapping rules determine the encoding of an action statement in XML. XMI thus provides a concrete syntax that can be used when exchanging action statements among tools. The Action Semantics specification gives tools the freedom to define their own concrete syntaxes, as long as they can encode the rules in a standard concrete syntax such as XMI for exchange with other tools.

An OCL aligned with a common core could also serve as the basis for a transformation language. Currently, the situation of OCL is the opposite of that of Action Semantics. OCL has a concrete syntax but no metamodel, although work on an OCL metamodel is in progress.

Limitations

The approach I've outlined to leveraging UML-CWM-MOF alignment, CWM transformation maps, and UML Action Semantics does not define a universal compiler engine for generating complete implementations of enterprise systems. The kinds of transformation maps we've been examining are declarative. There is no ordering of a transformation map's classifier maps; that is, the transformation map does not specify that one classifier map precedes another. Similarly, there is no ordering of feature maps within a classifier map. The maps simply say that something maps to something else. Even Figure 9.18's expression uses a declarative subset of Action Semantics.

This places some limitations on the kinds of mappings that transformation maps can define. Purely declarative specifications are not sufficient to define any arbitrary compiler. This is the reason that transformation maps can't define the complete logic of a generator that produces system implementations.

However, transformation maps can define the logic of a generator that executes a mapping from one declarative model to another. Such mappings are the only kinds of mappings that standards bodies specify, since it's impractical for such bodies to standardize implementations. For instance, XMI defines how to transform a MOF metamodel to an XML DTD or Schema. JMI defines how to transform a MOF metamodel to Java APIs. MOF metamodels, XML DTDs, XML Schemas, and Java APIs are declarative.

Thus, CWM transformation maps, although mostly limited to mapping declaratives to declaratives, are sufficient for defining standardized mappings, assuming UML-CWM-MOF alignment.

What You Can Do Now

If you are planning to develop software that performs data transformations, take seriously the fact that Oracle, IBM, and some other important vendors are committed to using CWM for this purpose.

If you are planning to develop generators that implement metamodel-to-metamodel or MOF-to-metamodel mappings, don't assume that you have to hand-code each generator as a one-off system. If you have to create a number of generators, it might be more cost-effective to use a transformation specification language, such as CWM, to specify generation rules and to build a generator that produces generators, or to build a generic generator that reads the generation rules dynamically.

If you need to build generators that go beyond transforming declarative models to declarative models, you can still use the principles outlined in this chapter to deal with the part of the generator that transforms the declarative constructs.

Summary

As of this writing, the OMG had just issued an RFP calling for a MOF 2.0 transformation metamodel. It directs responders to consider how to leverage CWM, UML Action Semantics, and OCL. Regardless of how closely the final result resembles what I've outlined here, there are some basic principles to consider:

- The transformation metamodel needs to be aligned with common constructs that are part of a core shared by UML, CWM, and MOF.

- Any expression language used to make transformation models computationally complete should also be aligned with the common core.

CHAPTER 10

Additional Advanced Topics

This chapter delves further into the potential of and obstacles facing the transition to MDA. Some of the discussion is speculative since, as I've taken pains to point out, MDA is still in its early stages. Parts of the material are technically complex, requiring firm grounding on the part of the reader in topics such as distributed computing.

Generating Declarative versus Imperative Code

It's easier for a generator to transform a PIM into declarative APIs and information formats than it is to generate imperative code that implements the declarative code. Let's examine this difference from the standpoint of APIs and information formats.

APIs

Consider the Java APIs generated in Chapter 8. For example, we transformed the class attributes of an enterprise tier component PIM into get and set operation declarations in Java interfaces and classes. There are various ways to do this kind of transformation, but they aren't radically different from each other. Parameterization of the transformation allows for fine-tuning, and the result is likely to produce reasonably optimal APIs.

On the other hand, the number of factors that go into determining the imperative code for the *implementation* of a get and set operation is an order of magnitude larger. The operations could be implemented via JDBC and SQL code that maps directly to a field in a relational database table. There might be a less direct mapping to a table, such as an extended price attribute that maps to the product of two fields—unit price and quantity—in an inventory table. The implementation might call into a packaged application to get and set the values. A get for an attribute representing the current price of a currency option might be implemented by calling across the Internet to a Web service that provides the information. Furthermore, many different caching schemes can be used.

It should be apparent, then, that generating the imperative code that implements the APIs is a bigger challenge than generating good APIs.

Information Formats

Similarly, defining a parameterized mapping for generating declarative information formats from PIMs is well within reach. As we've mentioned, XMI already has come a long way along this road.

In contrast, there are numerous ways to generate the imperative code that serializes information into and out of XML streams conforming to the generated formats. The code is subject to the same kinds of variability that the implementation of get and set operations has to deal with. An element in a DTD or Schema may map directly to a relational table, to something wrapped up inside a packaged application, to something encapsulated by a Web service, and so on. Here again, the higher number of variables makes the task of specifying mappings for implementation generation more ambitious.

The Role of Standards

Because generating declarative code is the easier job, MDA has the potential to provide value at a relatively early date to standards organizations like the OMG. The OMG has always standardized APIs and, lately, XML DTDs. The business case for standard interfaces and formats is based on the potential that such standards hold for creating interoperability among implementations that execute in different technical circumstances.

It thus makes sense for the OMG and other bodies, such as ebXML and the JCP, to standardize parameterized mapping algorithms for generating declarative APIs and XML formats. Domain-specific groups, such as the OMG domain task forces for manufacturing, transportation, and so on, and vertical market standards bodies can specify PIMs and apply the mappings to derive standardized, technology-specific APIs and XML formats.

On the other hand, the OMG has steadfastly avoided specifying implementation because it makes no business sense to do so. The variability of the imperative code for implementing APIs and information formats is the result of the variability of corporate implementation circumstances. It thus should be evident that it makes no practical sense for the OMG to standardize a particular approach to generating imperative implementation code. Imagine trying to standardize the implementation machinery of the get and set operations that we talked about earlier, given the very different ways to realize them.

So, for example, it would be reasonable for the OMG to standardize a UML profile for platform-independent distributed component modeling, and to standardize a parameterized mapping for transforming distributed component PIMs into EJB APIs and deployment descriptors. EJB APIs and deployment descriptors are purely declarative. It would even make sense to standardize the invariants and pre- and post-conditions for the generated APIs. It would not, however, be feasible to standardize a mapping that goes so far as to prescribe a particular implementation of the APIs and descriptors because no implementer could be tied down to one implementation approach.

Green Fields versus Legacy

The more consistent the implementation environment, the greater the percentage of the implementation that generators can produce automatically. The problem we examined earlier with implementing our archetypal get and set operations in a typical enterprise tier component is that there are legacy systems, packaged applications, and so on that have to be accessed in order to get and set attribute values. When this kind of variability is not present, generating implementation code via one parameterized set of transformation rules is easier.

A green field project, that is, one that has no legacy to take into account, is the classic example of a low-variability system. If all structural features in the PIM for an enterprise tier component—that is, all of the attributes and navigable associations—are to be consistently mapped straight through to a database, then a generator can produce all of the persistence mappings and physical data schemas automatically.

Even a green field system where some of the persistence will be through the database and some via Web services is fully tractable if Web service access is via a consistent mechanism. In that case, a transformation parameter on structural features that indicates whether persistence is via the database or a Web service might be sufficient for a parameterized mapping to determine 100 percent of the implementation.

Legacy in the user and workspace tiers can also complicate efforts to achieve full implementation code generation. Legacy interactions cannot be simply swept away because users become accustomed to patterns of interactions and to the look and feel of the GUIs that they use to perform tasks. Green field systems don't have such restrictions and thus are more amenable to full generation of user-oriented implementation code via consistent, parameterized mappings.

Almost all enterprises have legacy systems. However, there are certain kinds of systems within an overall enterprise system that have the characteristics of green fields for which automatic implementation production is tractable. Some of the following sections examine such systems.

Metadata Management Revisited

In Chapter 5, we talked about MOF tools that generate full metadata management implementation code from a metamodel. Such code manages the metadata in a repository, exposes APIs to the metadata, and imports and exports the metadata via information streams such as XML. This section drills deeper into the conditions that have to be satisfied in order to fully automate production of this code.

Metadata Management as a Green Field

Metadata management systems are often in full control of their persistent store because the persistent store is the metadata repository that they manage. When this is the case, they are essentially green field systems, since they can enforce a consistent persistence pattern. When this is not true, then generating all of the implementation code is problematical.

Furthermore, generally MOF tools don't seek to generate metamodel-specific code that interacts with human users. They leave this realm to modeling tools tailored to specific metamodels, such as UML modeling tools for the UML metamodel, data modeling tools for data metamodels, and so forth.

Thus, M2 models—that is, metamodels—are more amenable to full implementation code generation than M1 models of enterprise systems. M1 models describe customers, accounts, and so on, and the persistent store for these in large companies is inconsistent. Legacy user interaction and presentation is also an issue for these kinds of M1 models. M2 models are less subject to these problems.

Implementing Interesting Operations

Metamodels that define interesting operations provide an additional challenge to a generator. Recall that interesting operations are those not implied by the structural features of the metamodel, and thus it's appropriate for them to appear in PIMs.

"The" MOF model defines interesting operations. Consider the definition of AssociationEnd (see Figure 10.1), taken from the MOF specification, which has an operation called otherEnd. The post-condition for the operation, expressed in OCL, defines its semantics completely. A generator that understands OCL can produce the implementation of the operation.

A generator can in fact produce a full implementation of *all* of "the" MOF model's operations from their OCL pre- and post-conditions. This is because an interesting operation in "the" MOF model is essentially a convenience operation that simply collects information already available in the model. At the concrete API level—such as with JMI APIs—a client would have to make several invocations of uninteresting operations in order to gather the information available via one call to the convenience operation. A generator can deduce this sequence of invocations from the OCL, and thus can generate them as the implementation of the operation.

Note that, if an interesting operation must go outside the model to perform some kind of calculation that is a black box as far as the model is concerned, then the post-conditions can't express the full semantics of the operation. Therefore, a generator doesn't have sufficient input from which to produce an implementation. However, none of the standardized metamodels have such operations, and arguably such operations are inappropriate for metamodels.

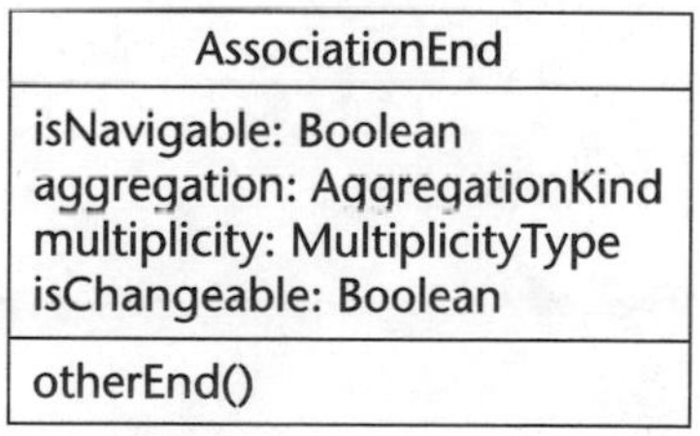

AssociationEnd
isNavigable: Boolean aggregation: AggregationKind multiplicity: MultiplicityType isChangeable: Boolean
otherEnd()

AssociationEnd: :otherEnd post-conditions

--The value is the other AssociationEnd for this Association.

context AssociationEnd: :otherEnd() : AssociationEnd
post: result = self.container.contents -->
    select(c | c.oclIsKindOf(AssociationEnd) and c <> self)

Figure 10.1   The AssociationEnd::otherEnd operation in "the" MOF Model.
Adapted, with permission, from [MOF], pp. 3-49 and 3-105.

Implementing Derived Attributes and Associations

Most OMG metamodels declare no operations, but many declare *derived* attributes or associations. In MOF and UML a derived attribute or association represents information that can be computed from other information in the model. The semantics of such derived properties are defined via OCL expressions. In practice, a derived property and a convenience operation of the sort we see in "the" MOF model are logically equivalent ways of expressing the same semantics.

Figure 10.2 shows a fragment of the UML metamodel's abstract syntax for collaboration modeling. The association between `AssociationRole` and `AssociationEndRole` is derived, as denoted by the / character prefixing the name of the association end `connection`.

The links that populate this association at runtime can be computed from other information in the model. `AssociationRoles` are uses of associations in collaborations. Thus, each `AssociationRole` is linked to an `Association` that the model calls its `base`. `AssociationEndRoles` are uses of `AssociationEnds` in collaborations, and each `AssociationEndRole` has what the model calls its `base` `AssociationEnd`. The connections of an `AssociationRole` are the `AssociationEndRoles` that correspond to the `AssociationEnds` owned by the `AssociationRole`'s base.

Figure 10.3, also taken from the UML metamodel, formally expresses this relationship of the derived association end `connection` to other information in the metamodel.

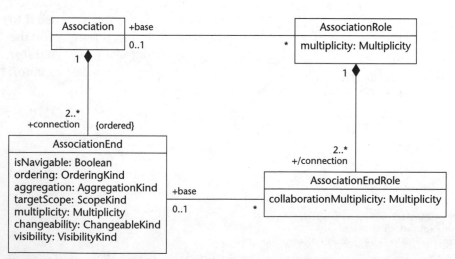

Figure 10.2 Derived associations in the UML metamodel.

Adapted, with permission, from [UML], p. 2-118.

```
--------------------------
--AssociationRole Invariant
--------------------------
--The AssociationEndRoles must conform to the AssociationEnds of the
--base Association.
--
--Note: Sequence{ 1..(self.connection->size) } references the derived
--connection association end as an ordered collection, even though it
--isn't declared as ordered in the model.

context AssociationRole inv:
   Sequence{ 1..(self.connection->size) }->forAll (index |
      self.connection->at(index).base =
      self.base.connection->at(index))
```

Figure 10.3 Semantics of the derived `/connection` association end.
Adapted, with permission, from [UML], p. 2-125.

A derived attribute or navigable association end is a structural feature of the model, from which API production mappings such as JMI generate corresponding uninteresting accessor (but not mutator) operations. As long as the model has a constraint that precisely declares in OCL the relationship of the derived property to the rest of the model, a generator that understands OCL should be there to generate the implementation of the implied uninteresting operations via invocations of other uninteresting operations.

Note that in our example it would be easier for an MDA compiler to generate the implementation of the derived association if the invariant were expressed as an invariant of the derived association itself. The generator could look in the definition of the derived association for its invariants and use it to generate the implementation. Casting the constraint as an invariant for the class `AssociationRole` makes it a little less straightforward for a generator to pick up the fact that it actually defines the semantics of a derived association because the invariant looks like just another class invariant.

Synopsis

A MOF tool can generate complete metadata management implementation code from a metamodel if the following conditions are satisfied:

- The tool is in control of its persistent store.
- If the metamodel has interesting operations, it also has post-conditions that fully define the operations' semantics.
- The metamodel has invariants that fully define the semantics of any derived attributes or associations.

Generating Bridges

One of the important elements of EAI systems are adapters that bridge between different technologies at runtime. It's possible to fully generate implementations of bridges that wrap one API with an equivalent API expressed in another declarative language. CORBA-COM bridges have been generated this way for some years. Most major CORBA implementations have this capability.[1]

This section examines the principles of CORBA-COM bridges, and then shows how MDA builds on these principles to attack the bridging problem more generically.

Mappings—The Essential Knowledge

A CORBA-COM bridge generator reads an interface declaration expressed in CORBA IDL and produces a COM object that acts as a wrapper around CORBA objects that implement the interface. The generator can do this because it understands certain key mappings (see Figure 10.4):

1. The CORBA-COM mapping, which specifies rules for transforming a declaration of a CORBA IDL interface into a declaration of a Microsoft IDL interface.

2. The CORBA-language mapping for the COM wrapper's implementation language. A CORBA-language mapping specifies (among other things) a rule for transforming a declaration of a CORBA IDL interface into a language-specific API that clients use to interact with objects that implement the interface. Regardless of the language in which the CORBA object is implemented, the object can be accessed via language-specific, client-side *stubs* generated for any language for which there is a CORBA-language mapping.

The OMG has standardized both the CORBA-COM and CORBA-language mappings. Let's examine why the CORBA-COM bridge generator has to know them.

A method that implements the bridge's COM interface accepts an invocation by a COM client, translates the input parameters to a form suitable for CORBA, and calls the corresponding method on the CORBA object's interface. When the CORBA object's method returns, the bridge method translates the output parameters and return values to a form suitable for COM and then returns to the COM client.

---

[1]The OMG standards for CORBA-COM Interworking are available in [INTWK], [COM-CORBA], and [AUTO-CORBA].

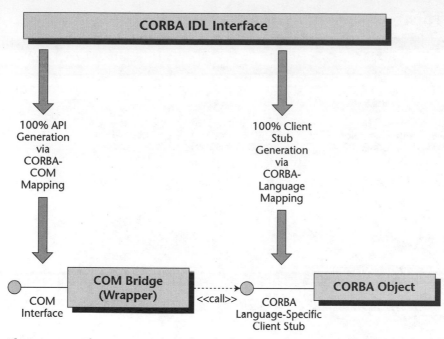

Figure 10.4 The two mappings that the bridge code generator must know.

Thus, in order for the bridge generator to ensure that the wrapper exposes the correct interface to a COM client, it must know the CORBA-COM mapping. In order for the generator to produce the bridge method implementation correctly, it must know the CORBA language mapping for the language in which the bridge is written. If the code for the generated bridge is Java, then the generator must know the CORBA-Java language mapping to correctly generate the invocation on the CORBA object's Java client stub. The CORBA object's method may have been hand-coded or autogenerated.

With knowledge of these mappings, a bridge generator can compile CORBA IDL and generate complete wrapper COM objects (see Figure 10.5). The wrapper object's methods have nothing to do other than translate method invocations from one technology to another. The bridge knows how to generate that code. There is no variability of the sort we have seen in other scenarios. The variability in how operations are implemented is completely encapsulated by the CORBA object. The wrapper interacts only with the CORBA object, not with the complexity behind it. The wrapper's implementation of the corresponding operation need only accept the invocation from the COM client, translate the parameters into CORBA form, and invoke the operation on the CORBA object.

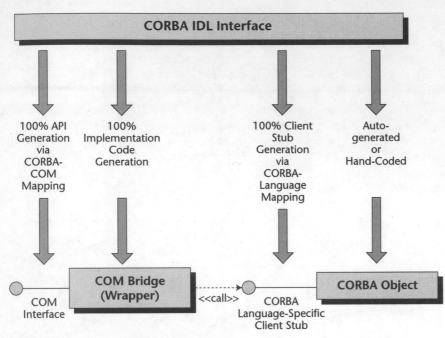

Figure 10.5 CORBA-COM bridge code generation.

Most CORBA products also support the inverse kind of a bridge. A COM-CORBA bridge generator compiles an interface declaration expressed in Microsoft IDL, producing a CORBA object that acts as a wrapper around the COM objects that implement the interface. The two mappings that the compiler must know are the COM-CORBA mapping, which is standardized by the OMG, and the COM language mapping for the language of the wrapper code.

Generalizing the Bridging Problem

CORBA-COM and COM-CORBA bridging have been implemented in shipping products for some time. Such products validate the concept that it's possible to fully generate the code for these kinds of bridges. The same bridging architecture can be employed to support bridges between CORBA and other technologies. In fact, the architecture is basically the same as that used to support full generation of the implementation of client-side stubs that adhere to CORBA-language mappings. However, the architecture isn't used to bridge two arbitrary technologies. It is always used to bridge technology to or from CORBA.

MDA-based bridging addresses the more general objective of building bridges between different technologies and languages. The MDA approach envisions leveraging a series of mappings where MOF or UML is the source and various technologies such as CORBA, Java, COM, WSDL/SOAP, and so on are targets.

Imagine that the M1 API of a Java service was generated from a PIM via a UML-Java mapping, and that we need a bridge that wraps the service as a WSDL/SOAP[2]-based Web service; in other words, we need a Java-WSDL/SOAP bridge. A bridge generator that has access to the PIM fundamentally needs to know two key mappings—the UML-Java mapping and a UML-WSDL/SOAP mapping. With the UML-Java mapping, it can determine the interfaces that the Java service exposes, which are the interfaces that the bridge must call. With the UML-WSDL/SOAP mapping, it can determine the M1 WSDL/SOAP port type that the wrapper must expose to clients. With these mappings, a bridge generator can transform the PIM into XML and 3GL code that implements the bridge (see Figure 10.6).

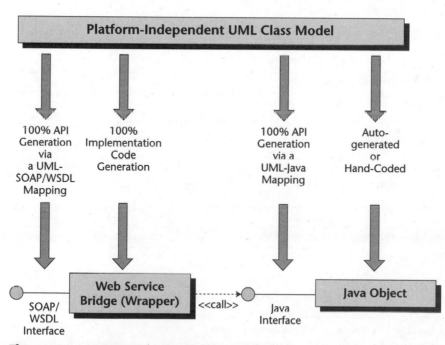

Figure 10.6 An MDA-style Java-Web service bridge.

[2] "WSDL/SOAP" means WSDL with a SOAP binding.

This is how an MDA bridge generator can leverage UML mappings. It's not necessary to design a point-to-point mapping from scratch for each pair of technologies. By pairing any two UML mappings, an MDA bridge generator can produce a bridge between the target technologies of the two mappings (see Figure 10.7). This reduces an $N \times M$ combinatorial explosion to $N \times 1$. For each new technology, a new UML mapping needs to be put in place, but not a whole series of one-off mappings.

Note that this approach of pairing UML mappings applies to building bridges around services that expose M1 APIs. If the service is something like an accounts receivable end-of-month update, then the PIM for it would be an M1 model, and the generated Java API would also be at M1.

On the other hand, if the PIM were a metamodel, then the generated Java interface would be at M2, and the mappings of interest to the bridge generator would be MOF mappings rather than UML mappings; specifically, the bridge would need to know the MOF-Java mapping—that is, JMI—and it would need to know a MOF-WSDL/SOAP mapping.

In our discussion of Human Usable Textual Notation (HUTN) in Chapter 5, we mentioned a prototype HUTN-XMI bridge generator that, given a metamodel, produces XSL stylesheets that transform the XMI representation of a model into a HUTN-based representation. This generator knows two mappings, which, in this case, are MOF mappings rather than UML mappings:

1. The MOF-XML mapping—that is, XMI

2. The MOF-HUTN mapping

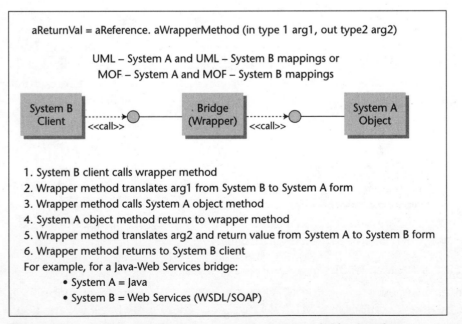

Figure 10.7 contents:

aReturnVal = aReference. aWrapperMethod (in type 1 arg1, out type2 arg2)

UML – System A and UML – System B mappings or
MOF – System A and MOF – System B mappings

System B Client —<<call>>—→ ○ —→ Bridge (Wrapper) —<<call>>—→ ○ —→ System A Object

1. System B client calls wrapper method
2. Wrapper method translates arg1 from System B to System A form
3. Wrapper method calls System A object method
4. System A object method returns to wrapper method
5. Wrapper method translates arg2 and return value from System A to System B form
6. Wrapper method returns to System B client
For example, for a Java-Web Services bridge:
• System A = Java
• System B = Web Services (WSDL/SOAP)

Figure 10.7   A call to a method of a System A–System B bridge interface.

Similarly, a MOF repository tool can use a series of MOF mappings to provide the ability to generate new wrapper interfaces around the repository. A repository tool can implement one kind of API natively, such as JMI, and then generate bridges to support other kinds of clients, such as CORBA or WSDL/SOAP clients.

Of course, bridging may have some performance cost compared with natively implementing the interfaces in the newly required technology, since it introduces a level of indirection. Typically, however, bridge products generate wrappers designed to live in-process with either the client or the object they are wrapping, avoiding an extra network hop. This reduces the relative cost of the indirection in distributed systems.

Special UML profiles that support the setting of parameters in PIMs for bridge generation can be defined to augment the standard UML and MOF mappings. Such parameters could configure bridge code generation and deployment. For instance, a parameter could declare whether the bridge should be co-located with the client, co-located with the server, or reside in its own address space. The potential for having different parameters for each particular pair of technologies reintroduces $N \times M$ explosion to some extent, but in a more tractable form since each pairwise bridge is not reinvented from scratch.

Standards and Bridges

MDA bridge architecture is not new, in that there are products on the market that function somewhat similarly. Such products have a core model that is the source for a series of mappings, which are then paired to produce specific bridges. What defines the MDA approach is the fact that the core models—UML and MOF—are standardized, and the individual mappings from the core models are being standardized. This standardization has the potential to create a market for bridge generators sold by third parties that can be applied to systems for which PIMs have been defined. If the APIs of components in an application have been generated from a PIM via standardized mappings, then an off-the-shelf product can wrap them with automatically generated bridges, whether or not the components' API implementation code was autogenerated or hand-coded.

Thus, automatic bridge generation and an aftermarket of standardized bridge products may be among the earliest benefits of MDA. Such technology does not require solving the hard problems inherent in generating highly variable implementation code for enterprise systems, and thus the technical barriers to entry are less formidable.

Keep in mind that, as mentioned, there will not be one single standard UML mapping for deriving Java APIs, CORBA APIs, and so on from M1 PIMs. For instance, mapping a real-time M1 PIM to Java is different from mapping a UML business component M1 PIM to Java. There will be separate UML profiles for each and separate mappings to Java for each of these profiles. The mappings will share some principles in common, particularly the principles covered in Chapter 7.

Nevertheless, a bridge will need to know which specific mapping to use in each case. To the extent that the mappings themselves are modeled formally—as envisioned in Chapter 9—a bridge generator that knows how to read mapping models doesn't even have to be hard-wired with a knowledge of specific mappings.

Executable Models and Virtual Machines

As we've mentioned, there are circumstances in which virtual machines (VMs) can execute PIMs dynamically without generating 3GL code. The benefit of direct model execution lies in the nature of a dynamic VM environment.

Consider a MOF repository that can load a new metamodel and proceed dynamically to manage the newly defined kind of metadata without the need for static 3GL code generation, compilation, and linkage. Such a repository has an advantage in the 24×7 global environment in which systems increasingly must operate. Additionally, although not all issues of managing model evolution go away, the development process is simplified because it doesn't have to keep the model and generated artifacts in synch with each other.

The disadvantage of direct execution, of course, is the cost of executing at the model's higher level of abstraction. There are two kinds of costs:

Performance.   Performance typically suffers more the farther the executing platform is abstracted from the processor.

Footprint.   The execution platform capable of directly executing a certain kind of model may have a large footprint because it must be able to support all models of that kind. By contrast, a generator can produce streamlined artifacts that bind the facilities needed to support only one specific model.

Examples from Industry

The notion of directly executing models without compilation is not an MDA invention. For example, database systems have executed data models directly for decades. Initially the data models were declarative only, but then they were expanded to include triggers and stored procedures that are executed in many cases without code generation. In effect, then, a database management system is a dynamic virtual machine that executes data models. Another way of saying this is that the database VM is driven by metadata at runtime.

If databases statically generated code for each data model, systems with thousands of columns and millions of rows would become unmanageable. Myriad source files and statically compiled object code files would have to be synchronized, versioned, stored, deployed, taken offline when obsolete, and so forth. Doing this with databases would, of course, be unthinkable today.

GUIs driven by metadata at runtime have existed for some time as well. Metadata-driven data entry utilities for "dumb" terminals appeared in the late 1970s. These utilities were their own little dynamic VMs. They were driven at runtime by declarative models of data entry fields and tables of direct cursor addressing codes for various terminals. More sophisticated metadata-driven GUI tools exist today. The Visual Basic runtime directly executes GUIs constructed via WYSIWYG GUI editors.

Correctness

The results of executing a model can be correct if the model contains sufficient information to specify how to achieve correct results in the context in which it executes. Thus, a data model with its various tuning parameters is sufficiently precise to obtain correct results when executed by a database engine. The database engine knows a lot about the environment in which it operates, and thus the burden on the model is less than it would be if the engine could not make as many assumptions.

A purely declarative, platform-independent M1 class model of a customer business component typically does not contain enough information to specify how to achieve correct results in an enterprise system. What correct results *are* can be can be expressed via invariants and pre/post-conditions. But how to *realize* those results in a specific corporate environment is highly inconsistent.

As we've seen, for example, system variability often makes it impossible to infer from the model how each attribute value is to be accessed and changed. Thus, although we can generate APIs and information formats for different target environments, we cannot generate all the code that implements the APIs and formats. If we cannot generate *all* the code, we certainly cannot execute the model in a virtual machine.

The requirement for the model to contain sufficient information to yield correct results is a necessary pre-condition for full code generation and for direct execution.

Performance

Performance is less of an either-or proposition than correctness, and thus must be judged relative to various factors.

A component may execute unacceptably slowly when invoked iteratively as part of an end-to-end process that involves no user interaction and no traversing of firewalls. On the other hand, that same performance level of the component itself may be acceptable when the component is called once as part of an end-to-end process that involves interacting over the Internet with a browser, because the time it takes the component to execute its logic is a smaller percentage of the overall time it takes for the entire end-to-end process to execute.

Thus, although direct execution often carries performance costs, whether the costs are acceptable depends on the context.

Dynamism at the Lower Level

Another necessary condition for direct execution is that the VM itself executes over a dynamic execution platform. Java byte code executes over the native processor architecture. Native processor architectures are dynamic in that they can execute instructions that they receive dynamically. A database system executes over precompiled 3GL code, which is also machine code that can be handed to a processor dynamically.

Examining a bridge from this perspective, it's feasible for a bridge VM to read a PIM and set up and run CORBA wrapper objects dynamically because such wrappers can be executed over CORBA's Dynamic Skeleton Interface (DSI) and Dynamic Invocation Interface (DII), which provide a dynamic execution platform. The DSI provides a runtime over which a dynamically constructed CORBA object can execute without compilation, and the DII runtime allows a client to bind to the object dynamically without the need for statically generated client-side stubs. The server-side ORB must support DSI, and the client-side ORB must support DII. The DII provides general-purpose operations for invoking any operation on any interface. The client invoking these operations provides metadata describing the operation (and the interface that owns it) and passes in general-purpose data structures containing actual parameter values corresponding to the operation's formal parameters. Figure 10.8 shows a part of the DII that a client uses to package and send a request to an object to which it has not been statically bound.

The feasibility of dynamically deploying and binding to COM wrapper objects is more nuanced because COM traditionally has static *custom* interfaces and dynamic *Automation* interfaces. Custom interfaces are less amenable to dynamic implementation and client-side binding than Automation interfaces. COM provides a dynamic execution platform for Automation objects. Automation interfaces are also known as IDispatch interfaces. It's feasible to construct a bridge VM that reads a PIM, applies a mapping to COM Automation, and dynamically sets up and runs COM Automation wrapper objects, because such wrappers can be dynamically executed on the server side and bound by clients over COM Automation's server- and client-side runtimes. The Automation wrapper object has a logical interface derived from the abstract model. The client *logically* invokes that interface but *physically* uses the general-purpose IDispatch interface in a manner that is functionally similar to the way a CORBA client uses the DII.

It's more problematical to create a bridge VM that dynamically sets up and runs pure C++ wrapper objects (that is, C++ objects that aren't CORBA or COM objects) that expose a C++ based API dynamically derived from a PIM. C++ is a static environment requiring the server object to be compiled and linked. Furthermore, the client of the newly generated API cannot bind to it dynamically. The client's code has to be enhanced, recompiled, and relinked. On the other hand, it's somewhat more feasible with Java because Java Reflection makes it possible for clients to bind to new objects without the clients having to be recompiled. Java Reflection provides a dynamism that C++ does not.

MOF repository tools have a dynamic execution platform over which to execute, namely the MOF reflective APIs. These APIs, which we talked about in Chapter 5, have Java incarnations defined by JMI, and CORBA incarnations defined by the MOF-CORBA mapping. The APIs have general-purpose operations that a client physically uses to access the API logically implied by the metamodel. For example, the JMI reflective APIs make it possible to dynamically set up a Java metaobject and bind to it, that is, to a Java object representing MOF-compliant metadata. Dynamically exposing the metamodel-specific APIs generated from the metamodel and binding to them, on the other hand, is subject to the limitations of the execution platform over which implementations of the interfaces run. For example, metamodel-specific, generated CORBA interfaces can be dynamically implemented and bound only because CORBA has the DSI and DII.

```
native OpaqueValue;
interface Request { // PIDL
    void add_arg (
        in Identifier name, // argument name
        in TypeCode arg_type, // argument datatype
        in OpaqueValue value, // argument value to be added
        in long len, // length/count of argument value
        in Flags arg_flags // argument flags
    );

    void invoke (in Flags invoke_flags // invocation flags);
    void delete ();
    void send (in Flags invoke_flags // invocation flags);
    void get_response () raises (WrongTransaction);
    boolean poll_response();
    Object sendp( );
    void prepare(in Object p);
    void sendc(in Object handler);
}
```

Figure 10.8 Part of the CORBA Dynamic Invocation Interface (DII).
Reused, with permission, from [DII]. pp. 7-4 to 7-5.

Reflection

The CORBA DII, COM Automation, and the MOF Reflective Interfaces, which support dynamic execution in their respective technical environments, all require that the client pass in metadata describing the operation it wishes to invoke.

In one scenario, a client is in possession of this metadata because it's dynamically executing a model. For example, consider a client driven by a model of a workflow or business process that it executes. When it comes to a certain step, the metadata about the step directs the client to invoke an operation on a certain component, mapping data the client has stored to actual parameters for the invocation. The operation's metadata is contained within the metadata for the step, so the client retrieves the metadata and uses it to invoke the operation.

In another scenario, the client comes upon the object not knowing its structure at all. A generic object browser is a good example. A hybrid scenario is one where the client has a reference to the object, has figured out that it needs to call a particular operation on it, but doesn't have the complete metadata for it and doesn't have an access path to the description in a metadata repository. In these scenarios, the client needs to be able to ask the object to provide the full metadata that describes it.

Reflection is the ability of an object to provide the metadata that describes it. Dynamic objects need to support reflection in order to support clients that might need to bind to them dynamically. Reflection is sometimes called *introspection*.

A client accessing a CORBA object via the DII can ask the object to supply a description of its interface via the `get_interface` operation that all CORBA objects support. A client accessing a COM Automation object obtains a description of the object's logical interface via the `GetTypeInfo` operation that all Automation objects support. A Java Reflection client asks a Java object for a description of its methods via the `getDeclaredMethods` operation.

Reflection and Metadata Fragmentation

This summary of the variety of ways to do reflection should make it clear how fragmented metadata management is in the industry (see Table 10.1). CORBA's `get_interface` returns an `InterfaceDef`, whose structure has little in common with the `ITypeInfo` that COM Automation's `GetTypeInfo` returns, which, in turn, is structurally dissimilar to the `Method` that Java Reflection's `getDeclaredMethods` returns.

Table 10.1 Fragmented Metadata Management

	OPERATION THAT CLIENT INVOKES	METADATA THAT THE OPERATION RETURNS
CORBA	get_interface	InterfaceDef
COM	GetTypeInfo	ITypeInfo
Java	getDeclaredMethods	Method

One of the potential long-term benefits of MDA is to provide a consistent approach to reflection. Recall that when an MDA compiler using the MOF technology mappings compiles a metamodel, all of the generated APIs inherit the MOF reflective APIs. The reflective APIs define the refMetaObject operation. A client of an object supporting these APIs calls this operation and gets back a MOF object that has a consistent structure regardless of whether it describes a Java interface, a CORBA interface, a COM interface, or something else. As UML MDA mappings come online, they should support this pattern.

Drawing Conclusions

All of the circumstances we have identified, where generating 100 percent of the implementation from a PIM is possible and where the execution platform over which the model runs is itself dynamic, can technically support direct execution by a virtual machine. This includes metadata management systems, bridges, and so forth.

However, the fact that a model *can* be executed by a virtual machine doesn't mean that it is economically viable to do so. The VM's execution environment must also perform well enough, whatever that means in the circumstances in which it operates. There also must be adequate economic incentive to drive companies to build a virtual machine.

Note that a PIM may contain insufficient information for full implementation in one context, yet sufficient for another. For example, we've seen that we cannot fully generate a complete COM-based implementation from a declarative, platform-independent M1 UML class model for an enterprise application because of the variability of the enterprise environment. However, we have seen how, from the same declarative PIM, we *can* generate all the implementation for a CORBA-COM bridge.

A Middle Way

There are environments in which VMs execute PIMs directly at development time only. Developers use such VMs to test their logic for correctness. They then compile the PIM into production-quality, lower-level artifacts that don't pay the performance price of direct execution at the higher level of abstraction.

A prime example of this approach is the International Telecommunication Union (ITU) Specification and Description Language (SDL). SDL is essentially an action semantics language, although it predates the UML's Action Semantics standard. Developers use SDL VMs for simulation and testing, then run their SDL code through compilers that generate 3GL production code.[3]

From this standpoint, the SDL VM plays the role of a traditional language interpreter. Interpreters have the advantage of interactivity for debugging, but pay a performance price because they execute programs dynamically rather than compiling them to lower-level code. UML-based VMs that play a similar role are now appearing as part of "Forward Engineering Only" MDA tools.[4]

This use of VMs highlights interactivity as a salient characteristic of VM environments. The ability to make a change at some high level of abstraction and have the system respond without a compilation step supports a conversational style of the interaction with the VM.

Raising the Platform Revisited

In Chapter 1, we saw the utility of raising the level of abstraction of execution platforms. As we do so, we close the gap between the development environment—that is, the constructs developers use to specify systems—and the execution platform. 3GLs, 4GLs, SQL, and other technologies that raise the abstraction level of the execution platform were invented to make things easier for programmers. But they make things easier for generators too.

It's easier for a generator to transform a PIM into 3GL code than it is for it to produce machine code. In the latter case, the generator has a much bigger gap to fill. If the kind of model being compiled lends itself to a 4GL-based implementation, then the generator can generate 4GL code, which is easier still. However, this benefit must be traded off against cost. The generated 4GL code is apt to execute more slowly than generated 3GL code, which is compiled to machine code before it executes.

When generating implementation code for a PIM, if the persistent store is a relational database, then the generator can produce SQL code rather than 3GL

---

[3] [MTAL 1998]
[4] [MELLOR 2002]

code that uses low-level, vendor-specific APIs to database engines. SQL raises the level of abstraction for managing persistent stores. This makes the job of the generator easier.

Where the gap between the development language and the execution platform is closed completely, we have a virtual machine, with the potential for interactive conversation at that level of abstraction. In the context of an SQL environment, an abstraction, such as an SQL statement, closes the gap between the development language and the execution platform because both use the same construct. An SQL statement is a construct that a developer can use and one that a database platform can execute directly. However, SQL only closes this gap for a tightly constrained domain. SQL is not relevant to all aspects of software.

Furthermore, SQL narrows but does not close the gap between a platform-independent component modeling language and the platform. A business component PIM is at a higher abstraction level than SQL because it doesn't commit itself to relational database technology.

Over time, the IT industry has steadily lifted the level of abstraction, both of development languages and the execution platform. There is every reason to believe that this trend will continue.

MDA and Systems Engineering

Traditionally, UML has only been used for software engineering. It hasn't typically been used for systems engineering, that is, for designing physical machines. However, there is a move afoot in the manufacturing industry to change that.

Representatives of some major manufacturing companies have formed a Special Interest Group at the OMG and launched activities to move the manufacturing industry to adopt UML as the standard medium for systems engineering. Inevitably, this will require special UML profiles for this domain. An MDA approach to UML for systems engineering could one day bring about a reality where a UML model of a physical system, such as a building, is input to a squad of robots that proceed to construct a good deal, if not all, of the system.

What You Can Do Now

Be alert to identify tightly focused subsets of your overall enterprise system where the potential for automating the development process is particularly high. Focus your transition to MDA on such domains.

Summary

It's an order of magnitude simpler to generate declarative APIs and information formats from a PIM than it is to generate implementations of said APIs and formats.

Solving the easier problem still has significant benefits. It creates the potential for autogenerating technology-to-technology bridges. Also, since standards bodies standardize APIs and information formats rather than implementations, such groups are natural early MDA adopters.

Green field systems are more tractable to implementation generation because they tend to more fully control their persistent store and thus adhere to a consistent, reproducible pattern for accessing the store. On the other hand, inconsistent patterns of access to persistent stores encumbers the typical case involving legacy systems.

Metadata management is a relatively small subset of overall enterprise system functionality and is amenable to full automation via PIMs, because metadata repository tools control their physical store and generally have only modest requirements for supporting interactions with human end users.

Virtual machines that execute models directly make it easier to bring new functionality online in 24×7 environments, but often exact a performance cost. A virtual machine closes the abstraction gap in its context because it is an execution platform that lies at the same abstraction level as the development language. Direct model execution by a virtual machine and dynamic binding by clients is possible when the following criteria are satisfied:

- All of the semantic information required to generate a full implementation is present in the model.

- The virtual machine itself executes over a dynamic platform that supports reflection.

A middle way between static model compilation and dynamic model execution uses virtual machines during development for testing a model's correctness and then submits the model to a generator that produces the runtime implementations. Tools that provide UML virtual machines are standards-based examples of this approach.

A Reality Check

Let's be frank: On many occasions, I've said "MDA could . . ." or "MDA tools should . . ." From the mountaintop of maturity, MDA's growing pains may look relatively unimportant in the arc of history. However, those of us who have to work through this transition cannot sweep problems under the rug just because they won't seem important in the long run.

Generating implementations for enterprise systems from higher-level models is a more difficult problem than generating machine code from third-generation languages. There is more variability in enterprise systems than in CPU instruction sets. Many thorny issues will require hard thinking. Certain constrained subsets of enterprise systems will be amenable to automated production long before others. MDA will go through a protracted period during which it will not be a take it or leave it proposition.

Although the transition to MDA is inevitable, the *length of time* the transition will take is not preordained. We could stumble badly and set MDA back quite a bit by overselling it at this early juncture or, paradoxically, by failing to grasp its potential and properly preparing the groundwork for it. The consequences of a serious setback could be painful for the enterprise software industry. One way to alleviate software production pressure is to cut back on plans for new software initiatives. We're already seeing some of that.

So we have our work cut out for us. Let's get on with it.

Sample Transaction Metamodel

Figure A.1 is a reproduction of the abstract syntax of the simple example metamodel from Chapter 5. This appendix informally describes the semantics of the metamodel classes.

ModelElement

The ancestor of all classes in the metamodel. All classes thus inherit the `name` attribute from `ModelElement`.

Tx

An abstract class representing a transaction definition (specification) rather than a runtime transaction.

ACIDTx

An abstract class representing the definition of a transaction that has full ACID properties. ACID transactions are initiated in the enterprise tier.

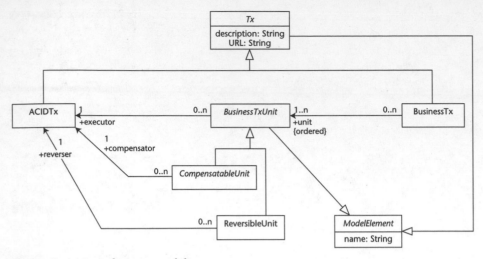

Figure A.1   Sample metamodel.

BusinessTxUnit

A pairing of two `ACIDTx`s:

1. An `executor` `ACIDTx` that executes a unit of work.
2. Either a `reverser` or compensator `ACIDTx` that can undo the work after the executor has been committed.

Reversal differs from compensation in that it results in the change to the persistent store originally executed being no longer visible to the persistent store other than (possibly) in an audit trail. Compensation does not touch the results of the original execution but enters a compensating record into the persistent store.

For example, if an erroneous charge to a customer is reversed, the customer would not see the charge on their invoice. If the charge is merely compensated for, then the erroneous charge would show on the invoice along with another line item that reverses the charge (that is, a credit). Reversal is not always possible, in which case compensation is required.

A `BusinessTxUnit` is a key construct for composing complex business transactions from several ACID transactions. A `BusinessTxUnit` is not fully ACID itself because it isn't visible to the transaction monitors of today.

A `BusinessTxUnit` is an abstract type completely partitioned into two concrete, disjoint subtypes: `ReversableUnit` and `CompensatableUnit`. A `ReversableUnit` includes the specification of an `ACIDTx` that reverses the work of the executor. A `CompensatableUnit` includes the specification of an `ACIDTx` that compensates for the executor's work. Note that the same `ACIDTx` could play the executor role in one `BusinessTxUnit` and the reverser or compensator role in another.

The fact that a `BusinessTxUnit` is abstract and that its subtypes constitute a complete partition reflects the rule that the `ACIDTx` referenced by the `BusinessTxUnit` must be undoable; a `BusinessTxUnit` that does not have a reversal or compensation `ACIDTx` is an oxymoron.

CompensatableUnit

A `BusinessTxUnit` that can compensate for the work committed by its executor `ACIDTx`. (See the definition of `BusinessTxUnit` for an explanation of compensation.)

ReversableUnit

A `BusinessTxUnit` that can reverse the work committed by its executor `ACIDTx`. (See the definition of `BusinessTxUnit` for an explanation of reversal.)

BusinessTx

A transaction whose scope encompasses more than one ACID transaction. Such a transaction isn't fully ACID because it isn't visible to the transaction monitors of today. A `BusinessTx` can sometimes run for many seconds, minutes, or even hours, in which case locking the resources it updates for its full duration, as required for ACID transactions, would be untenable.

A `BusinessTx` is typically initiated in the workspace tier. A `BusinessTx` groups a set of one or more `BusinessTxUnits`, where each `BusinessTxUnit` references an executor `ACIDTx` and a reversing or compensating `ACIDTx`.

Options Trading Concepts

The example in Chapter 8 is a currency options trading system. If you're not familiar with options trading, here are a few basic concepts that will help you understand the example.[1]

Basic Concepts

The basic concepts are organized tutorially rather than alphabetically. If you read them in the order presented, you'll find that the concepts build upon previously defined concepts.

Underlying good   Monetary currency, equity shares, commodities, or anything else for which an open trading market exists.

Call option   The owner of a call option has the right to purchase a specified underlying good at a certain price called the *strike price*. In the case of our examples the good is a foreign currency.

Put option   The owner of a put option has the right to sell a good at a certain price, which is also called the strike price.

Expiration date   An option is a time-limited contract. The contract is null and void once the expiration date has passed.

[1] For an excellent introduction to these concepts, see [KOLB 1997].

Exercise   When the owner of an option elects to do what he has the right to do—that is, to purchase or sell the good—he exercises the option.

In the money   A condition in which the owner of an option would make money if he were to exercise the option, given the current market price of the underlying good.

Market maker   A party that owns or leases a seat on an options exchange and has an obligation to buy and sell options at prices that the party displays on the exchange.

Out of the money   A condition in which the owner of an option would lose money if he were to exercise the option, given the current market price of the underlying good.

At the money   A condition in which the owner of an option would break even if he were to exercise the option, given the current market price of the underlying good.

American option   An option that the owner may exercise at any time before or at the expiration date.

European option   An option that the owner may exercise only on the expiration date.

Examples

If someone owns a call option to purchase 100,000 euros (the underlying good) at a price of 90,000 dollars (the strike price), and the current market exchange rate for 100,000 euros is 95,000 dollars; then the option is 5,000 dollars in the money, because the owner could exercise his right to purchase 100,000 euros for 90,000 dollars and sell them for 95,000 dollars.

On the other hand, if someone owns a put option to sell 100,000 euros at a price of 90,000 dollars, and the current exchange rate is 95,000 dollars; then that option is 5,000 dollars out of the money because were the owner to exercise his right to sell 100,000 euros for 90,000 dollars, he would have to pay 95,000 dollars to buy them back.

Suppose a U.S. company signs a contract to perform a service 6 months hence for a payment of 100,000 euros. The company is exposed to a risk that the exchange rate of the euro relative to the dollar might drop significantly over the course of the 6 months. Imagine that the current exchange rate for 100,000 euros is 90,000 dollars at the time when the service contract is signed. The company might decide to purchase a put option to sell 100,000 euros at a strike price of 90,000 dollars with an expiration date 6 months hence.

If, on the expiration date, the value of 100,000 euros has dropped to 75,000 dollars—that is, the option is 15,000 dollars in the money—the company accepts payment for services of 100,000 euros and exercises its option by selling the 100,000 euros for 90,000 dollars. The option protected the company against the risk. The price of purchasing the option to begin with was much less than the 15,000 dollars it would have lost otherwise.

If, on the other hand, the value of 100,000 euros stands at 110,000 dollars at the end of the 6-month period—that is, the option is 20,000 dollars out of the money—the company lets the option expire without exercising it because the feared exchange rate drop did not materialize, and it would be foolish to sell its 100,000 euros for 90,000 dollars when they are worth 110,000 dollars.

Now, take an opposite scenario: The U.S. company has to *pay* 100,000 euros for a service in 6 months. The risk to the company is that the exchange rate of the euro will *rise* during the period. In that case, the company hedges the risk by purchasing call options giving it the right to purchase 100,000 euros for 90,000 dollars (the strike price) expiring in 6 months.

If, on the expiration date, 100,000 euros are worth 75,000 dollars—that is, the option is 15,000 dollars out of the money—then the company lets the option expire without exercising it because the feared exchange rate rise did not materialize, and it would be foolish to pay 90,000 dollars for the euros when they are only worth 75,000 dollars.

If, on the other hand, the value of 100,000 euros stands at 110,000 dollars at the end of the 6-month period—that is, the option is 20,000 dollars in the money—the company exercises its right to buy 100,000 euros for 90,000 dollars and uses the 100,000 euros to pay for the service. The option protected the company against the exchange rate increase, which did, in fact, materialize.

References

Books

[ACM 2001] D. Alur, J. Crupi, and D. Malks, *Core J2EE Patterns: Best Practices and Design Strategies,* Sun Microsystems Press, 2001.

[CONN 2000] J. Conallen, *Building Web Applications with UML*, Addison Wesley, 2000.

[COOP 1999] A. Cooper, *The Inmates Are Running the Asylum*, SAMS, April 1999.

[CUMMINS 2002] F. Cummins, *Enterprise Integration: An Architecture for Enterprise Application and Systems Integration*, John Wiley & Sons, 2002.

[DIJK 1976] E. Dijkstra, *A Discipline of Programming*, Prentice Hall, 1976.

[DSZWIL 1999] D. D'Souza and Alan Cameron Wills, *Objects, Components, and Frameworks with UML: The Catalysis Approach*, Addison Wesley, 1999.

[FOW 1997] M. Fowler with K. Scott, *UML Distilled: Applying the Standard Object Modeling Language*, Addison-Wesley, 1997.

[GDB 2002] T. Grose, G. Doney, and S. Brodsky, *Mastering XMI: Java Programming with XMI, XML, and UML*, John Wiley & Sons, 2002.

[GHJV 1995] E. Gamma, R. Helm, R. Johnson, and J. Vlissides, *Design Patterns, Elements of Reusable Object-Oriented Software*, Addison-Wesley, 1995.

[GM 1995] M. Guttman and J. Matthews, *The Object Technology Revolution*, John Wiley & Sons, 1995.

[GR 1993] J. Grey and A. Reuter, *Transaction Processing: Concepts and Techniques*, Morgan Kaufmann, 1993.

[HRG 2000] P. Harmon, M. Rosen, and M. Guttman, *Developing E-Business Systems and Architectures: A Manager's Guide*, Kaufmann, 2000.

[HS 2000] P. Herzum and O. Sims, *Business Component Factory: A Comprehensive Overview of Component Based Development for the Enterprise*, John Wiley and Sons, 2000.

[HUBE 2002] R. Hubert, *Convergent Architecture: Building Model-Driven J2EE Systems with UML*, John Wiley & Sons, 2002.

[JBR 1999] I. Jacobson, G. Booch, and J. Rumbaugh, *The Unified Software Development Process*, Addison Wesley, 1999.

[KILOV 1999] H. Kilov, *Business Specifications: The Key to Successful Software Engineering*, Prentice Hall, 1999.

[KOLB 1997] R. Kolb, *The Options Primer*, Blackwell Publishers, 1997.

[KR 1994] H. Kilov, and J. Ross, *Information Modeling*, Prentice-Hall, 1994.

[MELLOR 2002] S. Mellor and M. Balcer, *Executable UML: A Foundation for Model-Driven Architectures*, Addison-Wesley, 2002.

[MEYER 1997] B. Meyer, *Object-Oriented Software Construction*, Second Edition, Prentice-Hall, 1997.

[PCTM 2002] J. Poole, D. Chang, D. Tolbert, and D. Mellor, *Common Warehouse Metamodel: An Introduction to the Standard for Data Warehouse Integration*, John Wiley & Sons, 2002.

[WK 1998] J. Warmer and A. Kleppe, *The Object Constraint Language: Precise Modeling with UML*, Addison Wesley, 1998.

Articles and Presentations

[CLARK 2001] Material circulated on ebXML email discussion lists in June, 2001, by Jim Clark of I.C.O.T. (who now is with Microsoft).

[COOK 2000] S. Cook. *The UML Family: Profiles, Prefaces and Packages*. Proceedings of UML2000, edited by A. Evans, S. Kent, and B. Selic, 2000, Springer-Verlag LNCS.

[CW 1999] T. Hoffman, "Study: 85% of IT Departments Fail to Meet Biz Needs," *Computer World*, October 11, 1999.

[FRAN 2000] D. Frankel, *UML Profiles and Model-Centric Architecture*, Java Report, June 2000, Volume 5, Number 6, pp. 110–118.

[HENN 2002] M. Henning, *Computing Fallacies or: What is the World Coming To*, presentation to OMG Plenary, OMG document omg/01-07-02.

[INFW 2001] "Web Services" by Tom Sullivan, *Info World*, vol. 23, issue 11, March 12, 2001.

[MTAL 1998] S. Mellor, S. Tokey, R. Arthaud, and P. LeBlanc. *Software-Platform-Independent, Precise Action Specifications for UML*, OMG document ad/98-08-03.

Standards and Specifications

[ACTION] UML Action Semantics Revised Final Submission. OMG document ad/01-08-04.

[AUTO-CORBA] CORBA 2.6, Chapter 19 "Mapping OLE Automation and CORBA," OMG document formal/01-12-57.

[BPSS] ebXML Business Process Specification Schema Version 1.01, www.ebxml.org/specs/index.htm#technical_specifications.

[CCM] CORBA Component Model, OMG document orbos/99-07-02.

[COM-CORBA] CORBA 2.6, Chapter 18 "Mapping COM and CORBA," OMG document formal/01-12-56.

[CWM] Common Warehouse Metamodel Specification Version 1.1, Part 1, OMG document ptc/01-09-03 and Part 2, OMG document ptc/01-09-04.

[DII] CORBA 2.6, Chapter 7, "Dynamic Invocation Interface," CORBA Specification. OMG formal/01-12-45.

[GRM] ISO/IEC JTC1/SC21, Information Technology, Open Systems Interconnection - Management Information Services - Structure of Management Information - Part 7: General Relationship Model, 1995, ISO/IEC 10165-7.

[HUTN] Human-Usable Textual Notation Initial Submission, OMG document ad/02-03-02.

[INTWK] CORBA 2.6, Chapter 17 "Interworking Architecture," OMG document formal/01-12-55.

[JCOL] Java Collections Framework Overview, http://java.sun.com/products/jdk/1.2/docs/guide/collections/overview.html.

[JSR26] Java Specification Request 26, Java Community Process, http://jcp.org/jsr/detail/26.jsp.

[JSR40] Java Specification Request 40, Java Community Process, http://jcp.org/jsr/detail/40.jsp.

[JVO] Java Blueprints Value Object Pattern, http://java.sun.com/ blueprints/patterns/j2ee_patterns/value_object/index.html.

[MOF] Meta Object Facility Specification Version 1.4, OMG document formal/02-04-03.

[RMODP] ISO/IEC, Reference Model of Open Distributed Processing, Parts 1-4, ISO/IEC 10746-1, 10746-2,: 10746-3, and 10746-4,1996.

[U2 DIAG] UML 2.0 Diagram Interchange Work In Progress, OMG, http:// www.omg.org/techprocess/meetings/schedule/UML_2.0_ Diagram_Interchange_RFP.html.

[U2 DSTC] UML 2.0 Superstructure Initial Submission, DSTC Pty Ltd., OMG document ad/01-10-08.

[U2 INFRA] UML 2.0 Infrastructure Work In Progress, OMG, http://www. omg.org/techprocess/meetings/schedule/UML_2.0_Infrastructure_ RFP.html.

[U2 OCL] UML 2.0 OCL Work In Progress, OMG, http://www.omg.org/ techprocess/meetings/schedule/UML_2.0_OCL_RFP.html.

[U2 SUPER] UML 2.0 Superstructure Work In Progress, OMG, http://www. omg.org/techprocess/meetings/schedule/UML_2.0_ Superstructure_ RFP.html.

[UML] UML Specification Version 1.4, OMG document formal/01-09-67.

[UML4CORBA] UML Profile for CORBA, Version 1.1, OMG document ptc/01-01-06.

[UML4EAI] UML for EAI: UML Profile and Interchange Models for Enterprise Application Integration Final Submission, OMG document ad/01-09-17.

[UML4EDOC] UML Profile for EDOC Final Submission, OMG document ad/01-08-19.

[UMM] UN/CEFACT Modeling Methodology (UMM), http://www. ebtwg.org/projects/documentation/bioreference/.

[W3C DOM] Document Object Model. W3C, http://www.w3.org/DOM/.

[W3C RDF] Resource Description Framework. W3C, http://www.w3.org/ RDF/.

[W3C SW] Semantic Web. W3C, http://www.w3.org/2001/sw/.

[XMI] XML Metadata Interchange Specification (XMI) Version 1.2, OMG document formal/02-01-01.

[XMI SCHEMA] XMI Production for XML Schema Specification, OMG document ptc/01-12-03.

Glossary

Abstract syntax   The essential structure of a language, independent of techniques for encoding the language in concrete technologies

Abstract syntax tree   A parsed representation of a model or expression

Abstraction   The suppression of irrelevant detail[1]

ACID   Atomic, Consistent, Isolated, and Durable

Business model   A model that describes aspects of a business, irrespective of whether those aspects are or should be automated

Business system domain   A domain of control managed by a business unit, within which that unit can maintain a consistent, recoverable representation of state[2]

Computational model   A logical model of a system that makes at least some technical design assumptions

[1] [RMODP]
[2] [CUMMINS 2002]

Computation-independent　Free of technical design assumptions

CWM　Common Warehouse Metamodel

Declarative specification　Specification by setting property values

Full round-trip engineering　Round-trip engineering with iterative reverse engineering

Generator　A tool that takes one or more development artifacts as input and generates one or more as output

Heavyweight extension　An extension of UML defined via MOF

Imperative specification　Specification via procedural instructions

Introspection　Reflection

JCP　Java Community Process

JMI　Java Metadata Interface

Lightweight extension　An extension of UML defined via UML's profiling mechanisms

Logical model　A model that describes the logic of a system

Metamodel　A model of the constructs that make up a language

Model　An abstraction of a system

Modeling framework　A module containing specialized languages, generators, and other supporting tools that plugs into an MDA development environment

MOF　Meta Object Facility

Partial round-trip engineering　Round-trip engineering without iterative reverse engineering

Physical model　A model that describes physical artifacts and resources used during development and at runtime

PIM   Platform-independent model

Platform   A specified technology or set of technologies

Platform-independent   Independent of some specified platform or platforms

Platform-specific   Specific to some specified platform

PSM   Platform-specific model

Reflection   The ability of an object to provide the metadata that describes it

Requirements model   A logical model of the system that ideally makes no technical design assumptions

Round-trip engineering   Ongoing synchronization of modifications to code and models at different levels of abstraction during iterative development

Semantics   The meaning implied by a construct in a specification, as opposed to the syntax of the construct

System model   A model that describes aspects of a computer system that automates aspects of the business

Virtual metamodel   A formal model of a UML profile

WYSIWYG   What You See Is What You Get

XMI   XML Metadata Interchange

Index

MDA Metalevels

METALEVEL	DESCRIPTION	ELEMENTS
M3	MOF, i.e., the set of constructs used to define metamodels	MOF Class, MOF Attribute, MOF Association, etc.
M2	Metamodels, consisting of instances of MOF constructs	UML Class, UML Association, UML Attribute, UML State, UML Activity, etc. CWM Table, CWM Column, etc.
M1	Models, consisting of instances of M2 metamodel constructs	Class "Customer", Class "Account" Table "Employee", Table "Vendor", etc.
M0	Objects and data, i.e., instances of M1 model constructs	Customer Jane Smith, Customer Joe Jones, Account 2989, Account 2344, Employee A3949, Vendor 78988, etc.